HOW TO READ LIKE A WRITER

HOW TO READ LIKE A WRITER

10 LESSONS TO ELEVATE YOUR READING AND WRITING PRACTICE

Erin M. Pushman

BLOOMSBURY ACADEMIC

LONDON • NEW YORK • OXFORD • NEW DELHI • SYDNEY

BLOOMSBURY ACADEMIC
Bloomsbury Publishing Plc
50 Bedford Square, London, WC1B 3DP, UK
1385 Broadway, New York, NY 10018, USA
29 Earlsfort Terrace, Dublin 2, Ireland

BLOOMSBURY, BLOOMSBURY ACADEMIC and the Diana logo are trademarks of
Bloomsbury Publishing Plc

First published in Great Britain 2022

For legal purposes the Acknowledgments on p. xi constitute an extension
of this copyright page.

Cover design by Rebecca Heselton
Page from an antique book © duncan1890/ iStock

A catalogue record for this book is available from the British Library.

Library of Congress Cataloging-in-Publication Data
Names: Pushman, Erin, author.
Title: How to read like a writer : 10 lessons to elevate your reading and
writing practice / Erin M. Pushman.
Description: London ; New York : Bloomsbury Academic, 2022. |
Includes bibliographical references and index.
Identifiers: LCCN 2021037283 (print) | LCCN 2021037284 (ebook) |
ISBN 9781350119413 (hardback) | ISBN 9781350119406 (paperback) |
ISBN 9781350119437 (ebook) | ISBN 9781350119420 (epub)
Subjects: LCSH: Reading. | Authorship.
Classification: LCC PN83 .P87 2022 (print) | LCC PN83 (ebook) | DDC 808.02–dc23
LC record available at https://lccn.loc.gov/2021037283
LC ebook record available at https://lccn.loc.gov/2021037284

ISBN: HB: 978-1-3501-1941-3
         PB: 978-1-3501-1940-6
         ePDF: 978-1-3501-1943-7
         eBook: 978-1-3501-1942-0

Typeset by Integra Software Solutions Pvt. Ltd.
Printed and bound in Great Britain

To find out more about our authors and books visit www.bloomsbury.com
and sign up for our newsletters.

For my mother, Cindy, whose early reading to me made all the difference.

CONTENTS

Contents

ILLUSTRATIONS

ACKNOWLEDGMENTS

I am grateful to Vivian Bikulege for her careful reading of early chapters; to Vivian (again), Jo Wiley, Ann Marie Chilton, and (in memoriam) Anne O. Jay for the fast-walking discussions about literature and writing; to Beth Johnson for her assurance it was okay to step away from other projects in order to write this one; to my family—Chris, Lucille, Nicholas, and Wade Aldred—for understanding I needed time to write and revise; to Sarah Stephens and Ernestine Aldred for helping make that time; to Limestone University for the sabbatical that supported my work on this book; and, at Bloomsbury, to David Avital for the original inspiration and Lucy Brown for the follow-through.

PROLOGUE: (OR BRIEF INTRODUCTION)

Yes, I promise, this introduction is brief. Give me a few pages of your time, so you can see that changing the way you read will change the way you write too. Being a writer means you have to be a reader. Readers are as crucial a part of the literary community as writers. If you are reading this book, chances are that you are both.

Reading Closely and Reading Critically—the Way Writers Do

Writers read—but not only for pleasure. Writers read critically, and writers read closely. In fact, good writers read all the time. Noble Prize-winning authors read as much as they can, so do some of the most prolific popular writers of our time. J. K. Rowling urges new writers to read. So does Stephen King. One of the most crucial steps to becoming a writer—besides, of course, writing—is to read and to read the way writers do. Once you elevate your reading skills, you will elevate your writing too.

Let's take a closer look at what it means to read closely and critically. Writers read words the way mechanics study engines or botanists dissect leaves. Writers read a text to figure out the way the text works. Writers read to identify genre and form; to study plot and delineate structure; to recognize a central conflict, image, or theme; to learn about characters and their development; to study point of view; to explore setting; and to interpret language and voice. Writers read to learn what writing does and what writing has the potential to do. Writers read to learn from other writers. Writers read to elevate their craft.

Think about one of your favorite pieces of writing, or, better yet, pull it down from your bookshelf or up on your screen. Now think about this series of questions:

- What kind of a piece of writing is this text? Is it a poem? A short story? A novel? A memoir? An essay? Something else?

- Why does this piece of writing work in the form of a short story, instead of a novel? A poem instead of a story? A memoir instead of a fiction?

- Who is the main character inside this piece of writing? What does he or she want, and how does the writer convey both to the reader?

- What phrases or images do you remember from the piece of writing and why?

We could on with these questions, but we won't—because this is a brief introduction. The point is that creative writers make a myriad of decisions about each creative piece they write, and thinking about those decisions and how they work inside a text will make you a better reader and a better writer.

Lessons in Reading the Way Writers Do

Throughout this book, we will work through a series of brief lessons in reading the way writers do. Each lesson will explore one kind of decision writers make. The lessons will address the questions above, as well as other important aspects of creative writing. You will be able to apply the lessons to the readings you are assigned for class, the creative manuscripts your classmates or writing group members bring for workshops, the reading you do on your own, and to your own creative work.

Before this introduction ends, let me tell you a bit about the material you can explore with each lesson.

Sample Readings and Questions

To ground this book in the practical experience of reading the way writers read, you will find contemporary creative writing both inside the lessons and in the Readings section. As you read through each lesson, you will see that these readings are discussed as practical examples of the topics addressed in the lesson. To work through the specific choices writers make, you will find reading like a writer discussion questions at the end of each lesson.

Reading to Generate Material

Here is one more secret good writers know: Reading can help you generate new material. Reading a good piece of creative writing closely and critically can inspire you to write new ideas or to revise work you have already started. To help you apply what you have learned from reading these pages to the pages you will create as a writer yourself, each lesson will offer writing prompts geared toward generating new material and revising a manuscript-in-progress.

Getting Started: Strategies for Reading the Way Writers Do

Before we move on to Lesson 1, you might be wondering how, exactly, writers work to figure all of this stuff out while they read. While each writer has a unique strategy, writers have figured out a way to read creative work so they can learn from it. For most writers, those ways involve some writing of their own. I will not prescribe a strategy for each reader to follow. Instead I will offer suggestions to help you get started. These strategies work for many writers, including the one writing this book. Try different strategies. Mix, match, and adapt them, until you find one that works for you.

- Read asking yourself the questions noted above. At the end of each page, chapter, or section, answer the questions.
- Read creative writing slowly. Slow down even more when you realize you are reading a passage of particularly good writing. Read slowly enough to "hear" the words inside your head.

- Read and read again. After you finish a piece of creative writing, go back and reread passages you think are the most important in terms of the message conveyed or the way the words are written. When you are reading short stories, essays, or poems, read each one over again in its entirety.

- Read with a pen or pencil. Make notes in a reading-like-a-writer log. Or turn the page into a log itself and make notes in the margins.

- Read with a highlighter. Highlight places that teach you something about writing.

- Read with your notes application or email open on your phone or computer. Write yourself notes, or email yourself insights you have about the craft of writing as you read.

- Read with an eye to finding your favorite places in a creative piece. Then figure out why those places are your favorites. Determine what the writer is doing that makes those places stand out for you.

- Each time you read, try to figure out how the text is working as a poem, story, essay, or other piece of creative writing.

- Consider a craft element you are working on in your own writing (plot, character development, structure, etc.). Read to figure out how the writer has worked that element. (How did the writer develop plot and character or structure the piece on the page?)

- Keep a wow or ah-ha! list. Note specific sections in creative texts where the writer wows you with what is accomplished on the page or where you realize the writer has managed something tricky.

- Keep an I-want-to-try-that list where you note interesting approaches or risks writers have taken that you would like to try in your own way.

- Find a section in a creative piece that strikes you as a masterful piece of writing. Reread it to figure out why it is masterful. Note your findings.

- Dissect a piece of writing by pulling out and studying the elements in each of the lessons in this book. Create your own diagram to illustrate your dissection.

LESSON 1
READING GENRE

The Concept of Genre

Let's talk definitions. When writers write, they write inside a genre, or type of writing. Paying attention to genre will help you think about why a writer picks a particular genre to tell a particular story or communicate a particular idea. This may seem like a lot of particulars, but writers are particular people. When writers read—as when they write—they pay attention to genre.

Consider this sentence:

When I was six years old, I killed my sister with a gun I did not know how to shoot.

Well, that sentence would make a compelling first line, wouldn't it? The first line of what, though? A story? A memoir? A poem? Why does it matter? Because truth and fiction matter to us in different ways.

We read fiction differently than we read nonfiction, and we read those differently than we read poetry. Genre influences how we read a text. Paying attention to how genre influences the way we read is a fundamental beginning to reading the way writers do.

In creative writing, the prose genres are fiction and creative nonfiction. To keep things interesting (we are creative writers, after all) creative nonfiction is also sometimes called literary nonfiction. To begin considering the way genre influences our reading, we will think about the prose genres first.

Let's read that opening sentence again, twice.

Read the sentence as the first line of a **novel**, a work of fiction.

When I was six years old, I killed my sister with a gun I did not know how to shoot.

Reading this sentence as the first line in a work of fiction, what are we thinking about? As readers reading for pleasure, we are probably wondering what the dickens happened and feeling eager to read the next sentence in hopes of figuring it out. Reading this first line of a novel as writers, we might also consider these thoughts:

- Introduction to the narrator (the I who killed the sister)
- Establishment of conflict (the gun, the killing of the sister, the not knowing how to shoot)
- Use of language (simple, uncomplicated words worked into a sentence with an interesting structure—a sentence that begins with a preposition, when, and ends with a verb)

Reading fiction, we care about the characters and the events as they unfold. Think about your favorite novel or short story, and tell me you don't care—I dare you. But we also know the characters and the events are not real.

Now read the sentence again. This time, read the sentence as the first line of a **memoir,** a work of creative nonfiction.

When I was six years old, I killed my sister with a gun I did not know how to shoot.

Reading this sentence as a work of creative nonfiction, the stakes are different. We are still wondering what happened and wanting to read on to find out. But we also read the line knowing that this really did happen; somewhere, a real six-year-old killed his or her sister. Reading this first line of a memoir as writers, we might also consider these thoughts:

- Introducing the narrator as a character, even though this is also the real person who killed his or her sister as a child and has now written a book about it
- Being honest while establishing the conflict (the sister really did die; the narrator really was six)
- Use of language (simple, uncomplicated words worked into a sentence with an interesting structure—a sentence that begins with a preposition, when, and ends with a verb)

When we read creative nonfiction, we read in part because we want to learn about what really happened and we care about how it matters in the world or in the lives of the people involved.

Now read the sentence one more time, this time as the first line of a **poem.**

When I was six years old, I killed my sister with a gun I did not know how to shoot.

That sentence doesn't look much like poetry does it? No, it doesn't. Let's think about why. A complete sentence written out in a straight line reads like prose, right? Right. As a general rule, a complete sentence written out in a straight line *is* prose. Of course, in creative writing, there are always exceptions to the general rules. One of them is prose poetry, which we will get to in Lesson 2. If we did read the entire sentence as one line of poetry, we would think about why the language is organized into a complete and measured sentence and why the line is so long.

Thinking of the sentence as a poem, though, we might expect the content to look something like this:

Six years old
with a gun
I didn't know
how
to shoot
I killed
my sister.

Reading these lines as poetry, we read the words quite differently—almost entirely differently—than we read the words as prose. Readers come to poetry for language and rhythm as much as for the meaning of the words themselves. Reading these words as lines of poetry, we might also consider the following:

- Using the right words to convey a feeling, experience, or narrative
- Evoking rhythm and sound
- Shaping of the poem into lines and stanzas (notice how many words come before line breaks and how that shapes the overall poem: 3,3,3; 1; 2,2,2)

The stakes in poetry are different. As readers, we care how the poem moves us, how the language feels.

We do not usually keep reading poetry to find out what happens next (except in narrative poetry). We keep reading to reach a feeling or insight. And we keep reading to fall into the language and rhythm of the poem. We keep reading to see the world through the lens of the poet. Language, rhythm, image, and feeling are part of the stakes of poetry.

Now let's come back to the idea of truth. Does poetry have to tell the truth? The truth discussion in poetry is both complicated and simple. Poetry often tells the truth, but it does not have to. Many writers agree that the more honest a poet is in the writing, the more meaningful the poem. But some poetry does invent stories, characters, or events. *The Rhyme of the Ancient Mariner* is a classic example.

While many contemporary poets do choose to write the literal truth that stems from their own experiences, there are contemporary poets who write about experiences they have not had themselves. Poets are free to invent characters or events that reflect certain truths about life or human nature. This is called poetic truth. Look again at my example of the sister and the gun. Although I did not shoot my sister—or anyone else—when I was six, these tragedies do happen. The lines of poetry reflect this type of tragedy and provide some language by which to contemplate it.

Creative writing genres always live up to more than their dictionary definitions. Just like people, genres are more than the words we use to define them. But we are writers, and dealing in words is what we do. To bring us all onto the same page (pun intended), here are some words organized into baseline definitions of genre.

Fiction

When we think of fiction, we think novels and short stories. We probably also think that fiction doesn't really need a definition. I mean, fiction is fiction, right? Right. Fiction is a narrative form of writing. Fiction tells a story to the reader, using a plot and characters that the writer invents. When we read fiction, we read knowing we are reading something imagined by the writer and delivered to us on the page.

But, you may be thinking, so many great fiction writers write stories inspired by their own lives or based on actual events. (You are wise to be thinking along these lines. Thinking about fiction this way means you are thinking the way writers think.) Much fiction is inspired by real life, including real history or personal experience. An example of this in our Readings section is Sophie Yanow's graphic novel *The Contradictions*, a fictionalized version of her own experiences during a study-abroad stint in Europe. Some fiction is also well researched to make it realistic and detailed. Historical fiction (one of this reader's favorite fiction subgenres) is often researched to make the narrative as historically accurate as possible.

The difference is that while certain events or characters in a piece of fiction may resemble those in real life/real history, a piece of fiction is not bound to the truth. In other words, however much a writer's life or real events may have inspired a piece of fiction, the writer is still free to make things up.

Fiction holds many subgenres; examples include horror, mystery, science fiction, women's fiction, historical fiction, dystopian fiction, and on. As a writer, you should know that fiction is often broken into two main categories: genre fiction and literary fiction. "Genre fiction" (also referred to as commercial or popular fiction) is a term writers and publishers use to refer to all popular subgenres of fiction, including those mentioned above. Sometimes, those popular genres have subgenres of their own: vampire fiction and zombie fiction are only two examples. Often, readers pick up genre fiction to be entertained and to escape from their own reality for a while.

The lines between literary and genre fiction are blurry. The lines are also drawn more by the publishing industry than by writers. For these reasons, it's probably better not to worry too much about the distinction now, when you are exploring yourself as a writer and figuring out what it means to read like one. For the sake of definition, though, literary fiction is fiction that is not confined by popular subgenre categories. Readers often pick up literary fiction to experience writing as an art form and to engage in a story that will make them think. Literary fiction is often considered to be "serious" fiction because it tends to explore the reality we live in, often offering us new ways to consider the world we thought we knew. Literary fiction is usually more character-driven than plot-driven, which means what happens to the characters and how they react pushes the story forward more than big events in the plot.

Remember those blurry lines, though. Many excellent genre fiction novels do the same things we have just discussed as being part of literary fiction. (Chances are, you are ticking examples in your head, even as you read this sentence.) The fiction in the Readings section of this book is literary fiction. As you read these selections, consider the ways these stories are different from genre fiction you have read recently.

Creative Nonfiction

As I mentioned earlier, creative nonfiction is sometimes also referred to as literary nonfiction. This genre is also sometimes called the fourth genre, particularly in the United States. Each of these terms works to communicate the fact that this genre is different from plain nonfiction. It is the creative/literary part that places this genre among those of creative writing. In this book, we are going to use the term "creative nonfiction" because that is the term most widely used. We will also use the term "essay" to refer to shorter, stand-alone pieces of creative nonfiction. Literary essays are the creative nonfiction equivalent of short stories in that they are a short (as in not book-length) form of creative writing.

Creative nonfiction is fundamentally different from the other kind of nonfiction because like other genres, creative nonfiction is written as a form of art. A newspaper article reporting the facts is nonfiction but not creative nonfiction. A textbook is nonfiction but not creative nonfiction. Writers of creative nonfiction write creatively; they use language in an artistic or literary way. They write to tell a true story or to explore an idea in a compelling way that will engage and entertain readers. Much, but not all, creative nonfiction is narrative in that it includes plots, characters, and other aspects of narrative writing. Some creative nonfiction is also poetic in its lyrical approach to language and content.

Creative nonfiction is fundamentally different from other genres of creative writing because writers of creative nonfiction do make sure they are presenting real facts. Another way to say this is that creative nonfiction deals in factual content but presents that content in more than a just-the-facts sort of a way. Writers of creative nonfiction enter into a truth contract with the reader. However compellingly written the plot, however poetic the language, however creative the presentation of ideas, creative nonfiction maintains veracity. In other words, creative nonfiction sticks to the truth.

But, you may be thinking, some creative nonfiction writers change the names of people or obscure their identities, or leave out parts of what happened in real life. Yes, sometimes creative nonfiction writers do all of that, but only when doing so has no bearing on the sustenance of the content and does not alter the veracity.

Now, to keep the truth contract (this is a nonfiction book) I want to remind you that, for the purposes of discussion, I made up that earlier sentence about shooting my sister. I did not kill my sister when I was six years old. In fact, I do not have a sister. However real tragic accidents like this may be, the accident has not happened to me. Writing a piece of prose about this happening to me would be a work of fiction.

Like fiction, creative nonfiction can be both short and long. Shorter forms are often called essays and sometimes include their own subgenres, like lyric essay, but also include the same subgenres as book-length creative nonfiction. Book-length forms are usually referred to by their subgenre. Subgenres include narrative nonfiction, memoir, literary journalism, and place-based narrative, nature/environmental nonfiction, etc.

Poetry

Like all writing, poetry conveys meaning through language. More than other genres, though, poetry relies on rhythm, sound, and the structure of lines to create feeling or image. Poetry generally uses language much more sparsely than prose. When we read poetry, we read the words that are on the page, and we make connections among them. In poetry, we read every word more carefully than we read every word in most prose works. Because sound and rhythm help create meaning in poetry, we also pay attention to the way the words and syllables sound when read aloud or inside the reader's head. Because poets also employ line breaks and stanza breaks to help create meaning, we pay special attention to breaks when we read poetry, too.

As noted earlier, the truth in poetry is a poetic truth—an element of the poem that captures a larger truth about human experience. The literal truth is often but not always present in a poem. As smart readers of poetry look for meaning in sound and language, they also read looking for the poetic truth. The exception to this is confessional poetry, which is typically associated with specific American poets who rose to literary fame in the 1950s and 1960s and who published poems that illuminated some of the dark struggles of their lives.

Most readers and writers categorize poetry into five main subgenres: epic, lyric, narrative, satirical, and prose poem. As you have guessed from its name, narrative poetry tells a story. So does epic poetry, but here the speaker or main character is involved in a struggle of epic proportions—think *Beowulf.* Prose poetry is written out in paragraph form, like prose. Lyric poetry conveys the state of mind, emotions, or ideas of the poet or the persona in which the poet is writing. Lyric poems are also short-ish. While there is no specific length requirement, lyric poems will not fill pages and pages the way epic or narrative poetry can.

Within these subgenres are further forms or ways of exploring poetry, and careful readers (and writers) will also notice that one poem may draw on a poetic genre other than its home. Look at the gun poem I've provided as an example. This is a lyric poem, but it does contain some narrative elements, however sparse. If you are reading this page and thinking that most contemporary poetry is lyric in nature, you are correct. Reading through current issues of literary magazines, you will probably also notice that some contemporary poets are turning to prose poem as well.

Drama and Other Genres

But wait, aren't there other genres of creative writing? Yes, there are. Movies and stage plays (screenwriting and playwriting, respectively) make up their own genres. They are not prose, and they are not poetry. Though they can—and often do—hold elements of both. Screenplays and stage plays are written—and read—quite differently from the other genres. Smart readers, however, will recognize some similar elements and similar language used to describe them (dialogue and scene, anyone?). It also happens that sometimes the same story is told in more than one genre. This is what happens with some best-selling books. The entire *Harry Potter* series is a well-known example. Those works of fiction were adapted into screenplays. Cheryl Strayed's memoir *Wild* was also adapted to a screenplay. When books become movies, the screenwriters do make changes to parts of the narrative. When nonfiction, like a memoir, becomes a screenplay, it is important to note that the screenplay may vary from the truth.

In this book, we are going to focus on the genres many students study in creative writing and literature classes: fiction, creative nonfiction, and poetry. When you turn the pages to Lesson 2, we'll look at how to read works that blur the lines among those categories.

Reading Inside Genre

Earlier in this chapter, we discussed paying attention to how genre influences the way writers read. The next step is thinking intentionally about how the writing is working inside that genre. In other words, how is the writer working the craft to make a publishable piece of fiction, creative nonfiction, or poetry? A related question is why did the writer choose the particular genre to present the particular idea?

These questions are connected because writers work inside (or intentionally blur the lines among) the conventions of genre. Fiction entertains or provokes the reader with a story. Creative nonfiction tells the reader about actual happenings in compelling and entertaining ways. Poetry explains a feeling or idea the writer cannot explain in any other way.

Sit with me now to reflect on three selections from the Readings section and consider why their genres matter. Look at the following text from Zadie Smith's "The Embassy of Cambodia," Chang-rae Lee's "Sea Urchin," and Mary Oliver's "Lead."

Chang-rae Lee's "Sea Urchin"

July, 1980. I'm about to turn fifteen and our family is in Seoul, the first time since we left, twelve years earlier. I don't know if it's different. My parents can't really say. They just repeat the equivalent of "How in the world?" whenever we venture into another part of the city, or meet one of their old friends. "Look at that—how in the world?" "This hot spell, yes, yes—how in the world?" My younger sister is very quiet in the astounding heat. We all are. It's the first time I notice how I stink. You can't help smelling like everything else. And in the heat everything smells of ferment and rot and rankness. In my grandfather's old neighborhood, where the two- and three-room houses stand barely head-high, the smell is staggering. "What's that?" I ask. My cousin says, "Shit."
"Shit? What shit?"
"Yours," he says, laughing. "Mine."
On the wide streets near the city center, there are student demonstrations; my cousin says they're a response to a massacre of citizens by the military down south in Kwangju. After the riot troops clear the avenues, the air is laden with tear gas—"spicy," in the idiom. Whenever we're in a taxi, moving through there, I open the window and stick out my tongue, trying to taste the poison, the human repellent. My mother wonders what's wrong with me.

Zadie Smith's "Embassy of Cambodia"

0 – 1

Who would expect the Embassy of Cambodia? Nobody. Nobody could have expected it, or be expecting it. It's a surprise, to us all. The Embassy of Cambodia!
Next door to the embassy is a health center. On the other side, a row of private residences, most of them belonging to wealthy Arabs (or so we, the people of Willesden, contend). They have Corinthian pillars on either side of their front doors, and—it's widely believed—swimming pools out back. The embassy, by contrast, is not very grand. It is only a four- or five-bedroom North London suburban villa, built at some point in the thirties, surrounded by a red brick wall, about eight feet high. And back and forth, cresting this wall horizontally, flies a shuttlecock. They are playing badminton in the Embassy of Cambodia. Pock, smash. Pock, smash.
The only real sign that the embassy is an embassy at all is the little brass plaque on the door (which reads, "*the embassy of cambodia*") and the national flag of Cambodia (we assume that's what it is—what else could it be?) flying from the red tiled roof. Some say, "Oh, but it has a high wall around it, and this is what signifies that it is not a private residence, like the other houses on the street but, rather, an embassy." The people who say so are foolish. Many of the private houses have high walls, quite as high as the Embassy of Cambodia's—but they are not embassies.

Mary Oliver's "Lead"

Lead

Here is a story
to break your heart.
Are you willing?
This winter
the loons came to our harbor
and died, one by one,
of nothing we could see.
A friend told me
of one on the shore
that lifted its head and opened
the elegant beak and cried out
in the long, sweet savoring of its life
which, if you have heard it,
you know is a sacred thing,
and for which, if you have not heard it,
you had better hurry to where
they still sing.
And, believe me, tell no one
just where that is.
The next morning
this loon, speckled
and iridescent and with a plan
to fly home
to some hidden lake,
was dead on the shore.
I tell you this
to break your heart,
by which I mean only
that it break open and never close again
to the rest of the world.

Let's start big by dividing these readings into poetry, "Lead," and prose, "The Embassy of Cambodia," and "Sea Urchin." Look at the text. One looks like a poem. On the page, it has the feel of poetry because of its line breaks and white space. The others look like prose because of their paragraph form. (We will talk in Lesson 2 about the times when poetry looks like prose, and prose feels like poetry, but for now let's read according to the genre definitions we've discussed here, in Lesson 1.)

In "Lead" Oliver tackles a large and difficult topic: the destruction of nature and our willingness to recognize the sadness of it. She does this in seven sentences structured into thirty brief lines. Reading "Lead," as in all poetry, we read into the lines on the page, and we read into the white space around them to make associations among the words, lines, and phrases, which are relatively few, compared to prose. Reading poetry as writers, we make the associations, and we study the poem to see how the poet has written in such a way as to make these associations possible.

Let's begin by noticing that in this poem, Oliver fashions her sparse words into complete sentences, which adds to the poem's complexity. Here is this linguistic completeness in the face of natural destruction. Alone, each sentence in this poem creates one image or emotion. Look, for example, at the first three sentences: If we read each sentence on its own, we have no more than this: A warning, a question, an image. But reading the sentences together and as the beginning to the entire poem, we make associations among them. The image portrayed in this poem is going to hurt us—if we agree let it.

In discussing this poem, I am being careful not to excerpt lines and place them into these paragraphs. This is making the discussion a little tricky, but consider the reason: Oliver believed poems should not be dismantled. That is an important lesson to remember in reading poetry because reading each line and each word affects the reading of each other line and word. Reading "Lead" as a whole, we see Oliver has provided a devastating lens through which to view the destruction of the environment. Only by making associations among the sentences do we see the destruction in the form of these beautiful, dying birds. They are keening for life, and by the end of the poem, a careful reader is keening, too. After reading these lines, how can we not accept Oliver's invitation? For the invitation is part of the emotional context of the poem. Reading the lines, do you see how the invitation is a gentle one, but urgent in its gentleness? This is how Oliver articulates so much in these thirty lines. Even as the poem asks questions, it also offers a vivid and central image of the loons. See them! Hear them! The poem gives them to us, down to the appearance of their feathers and the sound of their death song.

Now let's come back to poetic truth, truth, and fiction. As a reader, it's my inclination to literally believe Oliver in "Lead." By literally, I mean I want to believe she is telling the actual truth. During her life, Oliver was well known for writing about her experiences with the natural world. As a reading writer, I have to acknowledge that I do not know. What I do know is that birds dying because of environmental pollutants has been a documented problem since Rachel Carson published *Silent Spring* in 1962 and that Oliver's poem has given me a beautiful and honest way of understanding my own feelings about the loss of birds and the larger problem of what is happening to our environment.

Move, now, to the prose pieces, "Sea Urchin" and "The Embassy of Cambodia." Writers need to be specific, so let's get specific with this discussion. Both "Sea Urchin" and "The Embassy of Cambodia" are narrative prose, which means the writers are filling the paragraphs with story. Both of these stories seem realistic, but only one of them is true. While we might recognize Lee as a novelist, "Sea Urchin" is published as an essay, or stand-alone piece of creative nonfiction. We know we are reading about Lee's real life (as opposed to a short story written in a first-person point of view) because this piece is published as a true story. Like much well-written, narrative creative nonfiction, Lee's essay-length memoir reads like a short story. Why? The essay is interesting. The essay holds our attention. These are important but sweeping statements we often make about narrative prose. Reading like writers, though, we need to unpack those statements. In essence, that is what we will be doing each time we discuss a piece of narrative prose in one of the lessons. We cannot cover everything here, but let's look further into some of the basics.

Notice Lee's use of the narrative elements; two of those being character and plot development. The narrator is the main character, and, as such, he is a fully developed person on the page. We get his vital stats: He is fifteen; his family is visiting Seoul after moving away. We also get to know about particular ways he is behaving: He can't stop staring at the girls. We come to know his inner landscape: he hopes for "the scantest touch" of one of the girls he sees everywhere. We see the way he interacts with other characters and what those characters think or say about him: "My mother is telling my father he's crazy, that I'll get sick from food poisoning, but he nods to the woman, and she picks up a half and cuts out the soft flesh." We will discuss more of Lee's character development in Lesson 6. For now notice these details as the kind that are crucial to a coming-of-age story.

As Lee develops the narrator, he also develops the plot. Notice how plot does not have to mean life-altering disasters. As readers, we are willing to become enthralled in a plot about a teenage boy wanting to stake a sensory claim on the world he finds himself in as he grows up, even during a trip back to the city of his birth. Tasting the sea urchin, vomiting it up, and realizing he needs to go back to eat it again: this is the stuff of a coming-of-age plot.

We also know we are reading only about this one, coming-of-age experience of tasting the sea urchin for the first time. While creative nonfiction is written about true events, creative nonfiction does not have to include every event that happened, only those that need to be told in the particular narrative the writer is crafting. This is to say that we don't know what else happened during Lee's trip, who else he met, or what else he ate. For this essay, it doesn't matter. To write this narrative as creative nonfiction, Lee does not have to give us details about his entire journey. The eating of the sea urchin and his coming of age, that is the focus of this narrative. If Lee included every detail of his trip, the narrative would lose its focus, and Lee would probably lose his reader's attention. As writers of creative nonfiction shape real experiences into essays or books, they decide which details and information must be part of the plot or the characters developing on the page. While Lee's family journey back so Seoul in 1980 must have included experiences and people beyond those we encounter in this essay, those experiences and people (what and whomever they were) are extraneous to the true story Lee is telling in these pages.

As in all creative nonfiction, the story is not about everything that happens in one life, it is about specific happenings. Because of the way Lee has used narrative elements to craft this true experience into an essay, we read the piece riveted to the words.

Reading Zadie Smith's "The Embassy of Cambodia," we also find ourselves riveted to the word as we move back and forth across the page and down through the paragraphs in each section. As this story is a work of prose, Smith guides her reader through the text using paragraphs, a hallmark of prose, to transition from one thought to another. When the changes are big enough, Smith ends one section and begins a new one. For example when time has moved forward or when the plot and characters are developing in a new way, the section changes.

While we know Zadie Smith has also published books of essays, "The Embassy of Cambodia" is a fictional narrative. We know that because it was published first as a long short story in *The New Yorker*, then as a short novel. Fatou's struggles feel real and urgent because they include hardships and horrors that are happening to real people right now. While human trafficking and modern-day slavery are real and serious problems, the narrative Smith writes here is fictional, and its characters are fictional too.

But wait, there is an Embassy of Cambodia in London. It has an address in Willesden Green. It has a website! And *Metro* is a real news source—and it runs articles like the one Fatou reads in the *Metro* she finds on the floor.

Good fiction often includes elements of reality. Some good fiction is based on reality. Other good fiction includes inspiration from real life in plot or setting. When you think about it, even fiction set in worlds quite removed from the realities here on planet Earth still usually uses some recognizable element of reality, even in small things like the way characters experience emotion or eat their meals.

Zadie Smith's story uses a lot of realities, and many of them are difficult. Smith's story is also a work of literary fiction. Literary fiction often tackles difficult realities, be they large or small. "The Embassy of Cambodia" deals with the current, systemic, and global problem, a large difficult reality. It's all too easy to discuss human trafficking in the terms I did above. Those terms, true as they are, do not evoke emotion or provide a sense of what it feels like to be a victim of human trafficking. Much more difficult is thinking about human trafficking in personal terms. With the creation of Fatou (the main character) and the house and neighborhood in which she lives and struggles (the setting), Smith gives the reader a way to experience human trafficking through the eyes of a victim.

Because the story is fictional, Smith has the freedom to create details, even as she writes about a real problem. These created details of Fatou's life make her a believable character while allowing the reader to see her experiences. Look at the crucial character details in section 0–7, as Fatou reads the newspaper she found on the floor. "It was not the first time that Fatou had wondered if she herself was a slave." Here we see Fatou's inner landscape and realize she has asked herself this fearful question for some time. As we continue reading through Fatou's thoughts, we cringe because as she convinces herself she is not a slave, the uneasy comparisons she makes between herself and the girl in the news story confirm for the reader that Fatou is living the life of a modern-day slave. We also read the details of her history—the trajectory of her journey from Ivory Coast to Italy, the father who began the journey with her, her job in the hotel. We understand enough in this passage to understand how Fatou has gotten where she is.

Fatou's circumstances are realistic. So are those of the girl in the news story to which Fatou compares herself. Readers familiar with human trafficking will find both believable. Readers less familiar with the crisis will grain some understanding of it through the character details written in this story.

At the same time, notice how Smith plants small, memorable character details that stick. She attends church with Andrew "just off the Kilburn High Road." She eats cake "always paid for" by Andrew. She swims in "a sturdy black bra and a pair of plain black cotton knickers." These details bring Fatou into focus. They make Fatou more than a victim of human trafficking. They make her Fatou.

As a reading writer, you see how crafting a fiction around the realities of human trafficking raises the stakes and makes the story both urgent and relevant. When reality enters fiction, skillful writers like Zadie Smith shape the inclusion of reality to serve the narrative. In other words, Smith includes insights into human trafficking and other realities as she develops the narrative elements.

Writers of each genre approach their writing as a craft in much the same way musicians or artists approach their creative work as a craft. Writers spend time working the words into something someone else wants to experience. So reading writers (including you and me) approach our reading by thinking about the craft. As we move through the rest of this book, we will look at the key elements of craft and explore how those elements work inside each genre.

Lesson 1 Discussion Questions and Writing Prompts

Discussion Questions: Focus on Genre

1. Consider Karen Donley-Hayes's "What You Learn in College" (found in Lesson 3, page 39); Beth Uznis Johnson's "Negative Results" (found in Lesson 3, page 41), and Alan Michael Parker's "Sixteen Ways Old People Terrify the Young" (found in Lesson 2, page 31). Creative nonfiction, fiction, and poetry are represented by these readings. First, note any similar qualities among each reading. Next highlight the differences that make each an example of its genre.

2. Read Chang-rae Lee's "Sea Urchin" (found in the Readings section); Zadie Smith's "The Embassy of Cambodia" (found in the Readings section); and Mary Oliver's "Lead" (found on page 12). Consider the concerns you have as you read each piece. What is at stake? What are you gaining from reading the piece (are you learning, are you entertained, are you considering an emotion or experience in a new way)? As a reader, how do your concerns and your benefits change as you read the pieces in different genres?

3. Select one piece of creative writing from the Readings section. Identify the genre. Then read the piece as a reader reading inside genre. Why you think the writer chose to craft the piece in this genre? What special considerations do you think the writer had to embrace? What special challenges did the writer have to face?

Writing Prompts: Focus on Genre

New Material Prompt

Pull out a writing idea you've been toying with. Explore the idea by writing the first few sentences or lines three different ways. In no particular order, write the idea as the first three sentences of a short story, the first three sentences of an essay, and the first three lines of a poem. After you write, think about the possibilities for writing this idea in each genre. Pick the one that seems most compelling to you and keep writing!

Revision Prompt

Remember the ways genre influences a reader's approach to a text. With that in mind, find a draft of a story, essay, or poem you have already written. Reread your work, then genre-hop. Explore the same idea by writing about it in a different genre. As you write, consider what you can change in terms of language, veracity, and substance now that you are writing inside a different genre.

LESSON 2
HYBRIDS AND MULTI-GENRE WORK

Reading beyond Genre Lines

Now let's talk undefinable. Writing is complicated—in a good way. One of the most exciting things about creative writing right now is that more and more writers are working between and among genres more and more often. In other words, writers are mixing it up. If you have read a graphic novel or memoir, you are wondering where those fit into the genre paradigm. Sometimes creative writing does not fit neatly into one genre. In Lesson 1, we discussed the concept that writers write inside a genre. To complicate the genre concept (writers are complicated people, after all) let's make one revision: Writers write inside a genre some of the time.

The rest of the time, writers are bending, blurring, mashing up, and experimenting with genre boundary lines. If genre means one type of writing, hybrid or multi-genre work means using more than one type of writing. Remember the poetic subgenres we discussed in Lesson 1? One of those is prose poetry. While prose poetry belongs to the genre of poetry, it is also one example of hybridizing between creative writing genres. (A complicated concept, but there you have it.) Hybrid work can also reach beyond creative writing or any writing at all to mesh with other artistic forms. Graphic novels, for example, blend fiction with visual art.

Coloring outside the lines (as it were) is fun for writers. Before we go any further, I want to pause to explain why writers of any genre should take time to read genre-bending work. In a time when just about everything has been done before, hybrid writing can offer a new trip over otherwise-familiar terrain. Reading this kind of work shows new, emerging, and even not-so-new writers the kinds of possibilities that exist.

Beyond exploring possibilities, it's important for us to remember that as readers, we are part of the literary community—quite an essential part! As members of the literary community (just as members of any other community) it is important for us to wiggle outside of our comfort zones from time to time. Most readers and writers find ourselves feeling at home inside of particular genres. Reading hybrid work helps us step outside our literary homes. To grow as writers (and as people) we need to broaden our vision of the categories we've learned to place ourselves into. In the simplest terms, reading work that breaks genre constraints helps us remember that we don't always have to write inside those constraints. All readers and writers need to remember this—the one writing this book, included.

Naming and Identifying Hybrid/Multi-genre Work

Now let's come back to words. So far, we have been using many terms to describe this kind of line-blurring work. That's because there are many terms floating around out there. Some writers refer to blurring the genre lines as "multi-genre," or "cross-genre." Some call this kind of writing "hybrid." Some refer to this work simply as, "experimental." While "multi-genre," "cross-genre," "hybrid," and "experimental" are the most common terms, some writers and editors use more unique terms. For example, the American literary journal *Arts & Letters* refers to genre-breaking work as "unclassifiable," and hosts an annual contest of the same name. The point is that new writers have more chances than ever before to read outside of genre lines, but everyone is still using different words and phrases to name this sort of work. As you read around in literary journals, in books, and on the web, train your eyes to notice work that plays with genre boundaries, and pay attention to the words writers, editors, and other members of the literary community are using to label and discuss such work.

Now, to keep this lesson simple (or as simple as it can be) we are going to stick with the terms "hybrid" and "multi-genre," which we will use as synonyms. While we are talking terms, you may still be wondering how exactly to identify a hybrid work.

When you are reading along, and you realize the poem, story, or essay you are reading is not behaving strictly according to its genre definition, you are reading a hybrid piece of writing. Some hybrids announce themselves, like prose poem and graphic essay, the examples I mentioned earlier. Some hybrids, especially those that are more experimental or taking on forms just now emerging, are more subtle or difficult to classify. You may, for example, find yourself reading an essay that reads like an outline or a poem that looks like a top-ten list. Or you may realize you are reading a prose piece that uses image but is not exactly a graphic essay or short story. Or you may find yourself reading something you simply cannot fit into any type of genre definition. When this happens, you know you are reading multi-genre work, and reading multi-genre work requires some special considerations.

Throughout this lesson, we will discuss the hybrids that are included in our Readings section and throughout the other lessons. Most of the hybrids also belong to one of the four genres covered in Lesson 1. The hybrids included in the Readings section are as follows: "Cuttings" by Vivian I. Bikulege, "Sixteen Ways Old People Terrify the Young" by Alan Michael Parker, "Jerry's Crab Shack: One Star" by Gwen E Kirby, "Hestur: A Photo Essay" by Randi Ward, "Grace" by Joy Harjo, "Cartography" by Poornima Laxmeshwar, *The Contradictions* by Sophie Yanow, and the two tweeted micro essays by Chris Galvin Nguyen. This is a long-ish list, but when you begin reading the way writers read, you begin noticing how many creative works pull from more than one genre. Sometimes, in fact, a hybrid can do such a good job being a hybrid that it can be impossible to tell which genre the piece belongs to, at least from reading alone. "Cartography," by Poornima Laxmeshwar is one of those. Is "Cartography" a work of micro fiction or essay, of prose poetry? We will take a closer look at Laxmeshwar's piece and its use of multi-genre elements later in this chapter. For now, know that all the works I listed above fall under or in-between two categories we will use to break down our discussion of hybrid, or multi-genre, work a little further: established hybrids and emerging hybrids.

Established Hybrids

This is the term I like to use to discuss hybrids that are easily recognizable, announce themselves with their own labels, and are relatively established in the literary community. These are hybrids we have come to expect. Established hybrids include graphic narratives or other graphic prose, photo essays, lyric essay, prose poetry, and choreopoem.

Graphic Narratives and Other Graphic Prose

As its name suggests, graphic narratives combine graphics and text. Typically, the same person is doing the writing and the illustrating/drawing/painting/otherwise-image-creating. In other words, most graphic narratives are often (but not always) illustrated by their own authors. In traditional graphic prose the words themselves are also hand-drawn by the writers, rather than typed using a predesigned font and appear with the images—in the same frame, as it were. In more recent explorations of this hybrid form, though, writers sometimes include typed text among the drawn images and words. (You can find examples online, for free, on *Mutha Magazine*.)

Graphic narratives can be fiction (graphic novels or stories) or creative nonfiction (graphic memoirs or graphic essays). While most of the graphic prose available right now is narrative in nature, there are pieces of graphic prose out there that do not take a narrative form.

Whether narrative or otherwise, graphic prose is gaining popularity. Type "graphic novel" or "graphic memoir" into Amazon, and you'll see novels and memoirs on all topics. You'll also see graphic adaptations of books we have come to think of as classics, like Anne Frank's diary and stories of Edgar Allan Poe. You'll see graphic takes on topics you've never seen anyone tackle with graphics before, like female shame, human trafficking, and race in America. Like all creative writing, graphic prose can go to some difficult places. If you'd like to explore the ones I've noted here, check out Erin Williams's book *Commute: An Illustrated Memoir of Female Shame,* Vannak Annan Prum's *The Dead Eye and the Deep Blue Sea: A Graphic Memoir of Modern Slavery*, and Mira Jacob's *Good Talk: A Memoir in Conversations*, or Jacob's graphic work on *Buzzfeed*.

Now, because well-informed readers are good readers, I want to discuss the terminology. Graphic novel and graphic memoir are becoming often-used, if not quite standard, terms in the literary community. But writers and editors use other terms too. If you look at the titles in your Amazon search again, you will notice words in the subtitles like "illustrated" and "comic." The reason some writers and editors shy away from these terms is the presumed association with newspaper comics and children's books, but these terms can still be used to describe serious graphic prose written for mature readers. So when looking for a good graphic prose read, don't pass over works with subtitles containing these other terms.

Literary Photo Essay

Photo essay has its roots in photojournalism and can be traced back to *Life* magazine, the first news periodical to employ photographs instead of illustrated images. Photojournalism, while compelling, is part of reportage, not creative writing. In recent years, however, a new type of photo essay has sprung into the literary world. Photo essays designed to do something other than straight reportage are appearing in literary magazines, on websites, and elsewhere.

Like graphic prose, photo essays combine image and text. Unlike graphic prose, the text is typed, not drawn by hand. The photos appearing in literary photo essay are taken by the writers, or, on rare occasions, by a photographer/writer team. While there may not be a standard format (thank goodness) for photo essays, there are two common structures. The first includes a text introduction in paragraph form, followed by photographs with brief captions that identify the subject matter of the photos as well as providing a touch of additional information or insight. The second intersperses paragraphs of text with photographic images.

Special Considerations When Reading Graphic Prose and Photo Essay

As avid readers of social media, most of us are already accustomed to reading image alongside text. Reading graphic and photographic prose, however, requires a special way of reading image. In graphic narrative and photo essay, text and image work together to tell the story. Unlike many other forms of writing that employ image (marketing reports, for example), the images in creative graphic prose do not repeat what the words say. Our Readings section incudes "Hestur: A Photo Essay" by Randi Ward and an excerpt from *The Contradictions*, Sophie Yanow's graphic novel.

Reading graphic prose and photo essay means reading text and image together, recognizing they work together in delicious and complementary ways. Instead of repeating each other, image and text each add a layer of meaning to the other. When you read "Hestur: A Photo Essay" and *The Contradictions*, you will see that neither the image nor the words show the whole story on their own. We read one with the other: image and text; text and image. It's almost the way we *read* individual fragments of glass in a mosaic. Looking at each piece of glass, we see its beauty and appreciate what it has to tell us, but we can't see the entire picture unless we read each piece as part of the whole.

When creative writers read graphic prose and photo essay, we read looking to see how the text and the images *talk* to each other, how they interact. Another smart way to read graphic and photographic work is to think critically about what the writer does and does not have to say in words, given what the writer is able to make you understand with images.

Special Terminology in Graphic Narrative

Reading graphic narratives like a writer also means knowing some of the terms of the genre. Here are the most important **graphic narrative terms.**

Panel: Each individual frame containing an image. Each panel typically offers one unit of action. Often, panels contain text too. Occasionally, panels will contain only text. The spatial arrangement of panels on a page is the way the writer organizes the story. Writers vary the size and arrangement of panels according to how much action they want to provide on one page.

Border/Frame: Lines or borders drawn around panels.

Gutter: The space between panels. The gutters serve as transitions between panels.

Tier: One row of panels, moving across the page.

Captions: Narrative lines or blocks of text that are usually somewhat separated from the image in a panel. Captions can contain any element of the narrative not explained in the images.

Speech/Thought Balloons: Aka bubbles, these enclose a character's dialogue or thoughts (internal dialogue).

Sound Effects: Onomatopoeia text illustrating sounds and often drawn in special effects lettering.

Figures: Drawings of the characters, human or otherwise.

Let's get acquainted with these terms by studying the following page from Sophie Yanow's *The Contradictions*.

In this page of *The Contradictions*, there are six panels, arranged in two tiers. The first three panels are framed. The last three panels are **open panels**, meaning they are not enclosed on all sides or not enclosed at all. The last image **bleeds** off the page, meaning the page stops before the image is finished. On this page, we get a series of actions we read together to see what Sophie is doing. Yanow uses **captions** to narrate the exposition—how Sophie ended up in Paris. The other text is Sophie's dialogue in a **speech bubble** and **sound effects**. On this page, the **panels** are dominated by the figure of Sophie entering a museum while the **captions** focus on her past. In terms of narrative time, the images, dialogue, and sound effects work in the narrative present. The captions work in the narrative past. On this page, Yanow uses image (with the accompanying sound effects and speech bubbles) to keep the narrative moving through what is happening for Sophie right now, in the narrative present. Yanow uses the captions to explain what happened to Sophie before the story started, back in the narrative past.

To think more about the ways image and text work together, let's read the next page of *The Contradictions* closely, using the terminology of graphic narrative.

MY PARENTS WERE ADVENTUROUS LEFTIES WHO HAD RAISED ME ON THEIR STORIES OF TRAVEL AND LATE 60s POLITICAL UNREST.

I'D ALWAYS BEEN TOO NERVOUS FOR RISKY BEHAVIOR —WITH THE EXCEPTION OF SOME THOROUGHLY RESEARCHED DRUG USE— AND TOO WISHY-WASHY TO STICK IT TO THE MAN.

HERE I WAS, AGE TWENTY, AND SO FAR I FELT I HAD FEW STORIES WORTH TELLING.

BUT NOW I WAS ABROAD. IF SOMETHING WAS GOING TO CHANGE, SURELY THIS WAS THE PLACE FOR IT.

First, try looking at the panels without reading the captions or sound effects. What would you guess this page is about? (A girl wishing for a bike?) Now read the captions and sound effects without thinking of the images. Here you have her backstory—her age, her reflection on her parents' adventurous past and on her own less adventurous life. Now read the captions *with* the images. Here we have the whole, well, picture, a picture that includes this young woman's yearning for something to happen and the longing for a bike.

Another part of the relationship between text and image in graphic narrative is the placement of text and image. Most panels on this page include captions. One panel that does not have a caption does include the words "sketch sketch" as a sound effect. When a panel has no caption or no text at all, we read it differently. We read only the image. The image has a different weight on the page because it is not counterbalanced with words. The image of Sophie gazing at the bike advertisement has the weight here. Notice how we see the seat, the wheel, Sophie's breath. Foreshadowing anyone? Something is going to happen; it is going to involve a bike, and it is going to take Sophie somewhere she has not been before.

Savvy graphic prose readers also recognize intention in the hand-drawn text of graphic prose. We don't just read the words; we look at the way the words are drawn. Here are some important questions: Are the words illustrated in all capital letters or using traditional capital and small letters? Are they drawn in black or in another color? Do the letters appear pointy and jagged or round and smooth?

Here are some answers: All capital letters. All in black. Pretty pointy but not jagged. All of this elicits an emotional response or reflects an important element of the story. Answering each of these questions as we read graphic prose will help us understand how the writer/graphic artist constructed the piece. In graphic prose, the hand-drawn text is another important part of the mosaic. In *The Contradictions*, the black text works with the black-and-white pallet used throughout the narrative. The shape of the letters is part of Yanow's style, but the style of the letters also fits with the narrative, which is poignant and gritty.

One more part of your job as a reader is to consider how the colors work in the narrative. In *The Contradictions*, the colors are the opposite of each other, not exactly a contradiction, but close. Also, in black and white, we don't focus on the literal colorfulness of European-study-abroad environment. Instead, we are left to focus on the main character, Sophie, and what happens to her as she makes one choice after another.

Most of what we discussed above also applies to reading literary photo essay. Like reading graphic prose, we read looking for interaction between image and text. Both the photographs and the words are pieces of a whole. We read photo essay knowing the approach the writer takes in the essay will be inherently different than it would be if the writer were using words alone, just as a mosaic artist approaches the subject differently when creating a picture from individual shards rather than an image on a solid canvas.

While photography has its own lexicon of specific vocabulary, literary photo essay does not. In a different book we might discuss the technicalities of the photographs themselves, but when we read literary photo essay as writers, we only need terms we already know:

Photograph: The photos themselves.
Layout: The way the photographs are arranged the page or screen.

Captions: Text appearing beneath the photographs to provide context, give additional information, or move the narrative to a place it cannot reach with the photos alone.
Paragraphs: Paragraphs of text.

The overall organization of a photo essay and the use of captions and paragraphs are up to the photo essayist. The writer of a photo essay may decide to write a textual introduction in paragraph form, as Randi Ward does in "Hestur: A Photo Essay" in our Readings section. Or a writer may weave paragraphs of text among the photos. A photo essayist may include captions or not include them.

Look at this excerpt from Randy Ward's "Hestur: A Photo Essay," which includes the textual introduction and the first photograph and caption.

Anxious to disembark, I went about gathering my luggage into a manageable pile on the rumbling car deck of Teistin. The ferry's hydraulics made a shrill yelp when the hull opened and the ramp began to lower, jouncingly, toward Hestur's deserted quay. The final crash of the heavy ramp striking rain-soaked concrete made me flinch, and then it hit me: I was the only person going ashore that afternoon. The rest of the passengers were waiting for the ferry to resume its course across Skopunarfjørð to the more populated island of Sandur.

Hestur, which literally means "Horse," is one of 18 storm-swept islands situated north-northwest of Scotland, approximately halfway between Iceland and Norway, in the North Atlantic Ocean. As a self-governing territory of the Danish Kingdom, the have their distinct language, culture, parliament, and flag. The capital city of Tórshavn, along with the surrounding villages incorporated into its municipality, is home to nearly 20,000 of the archipelago's 52,000 inhabitants. Hestur's 20 residents joined Tórshavn's municipality in 2005, but the population of the village itself continues to decrease. Those who remain, most of whom are at or well-beyond retirement age, divide their days between farming/fishing and part-time jobs in the public sector providing services that keep the island habitable.

Though many people have labeled Hestur a "dying village," I witnessed firsthand the traditions and various acts of kindness and reserved devotion that sustain the community's infrastructure and morale. These touching deeds seem even more remarkable in the face of the subtle tensions between families or individuals, resentments that have simmered for generations and occasionally threaten to disturb the village's delicate balance.

It was rather inevitable that I too would become subject to the roiling social currents of the village of Hestur. As a newcomer to the island, its youngest resident, an independently employed, single female and a foreigner to boot, my life was ripe for interpretation; it wasn't long before my daily routines and social interactions came under all kinds of scrutiny. Yet it was this complex configuration of intense proximity and solitude that made my time in Hestur, where I spent my last 6 months in the Faroe Islands, exquisitely vivid. I experienced an incredible spectrum of life and humanity and often participated in it to near-overwhelming extremes. Whether I was assisting at the sheepfold, raking freshly mown hay, enjoying a colorful conversation with Hjørleiv, teaching Jørmund how to use email, or borrowing Ebbe's clothesline for an afternoon, perhaps my most tender act of solidarity was simply turning on my kitchen light of an evening so people could see I was still there.

The Faroe Island's maritime climate at 62°00'N means that consecutive days of dry weather are relatively rare. Precipitation falls an average of 260 days per year. This makes it difficult, and labor intensive, for farmers to dry enough hay for their livestock's supplemental winter fodder. Some farmers use trestles to take advantage of stiff ocean winds for drying the grass they've mown.

In "Hestur," as in all literary photo essay, the text occupies a separate space on the page. Like the text and drawings in Sophie Yanow's graphic narrative, neither the text nor the photographs in Randi Ward's essay would make complete sense, one without the other. Unlike Yanow's work, though, the words stay outside the frame of the images in Ward's essay.

When writers read literary photo essay, we examine the format the essay uses, paying attention to the arrangement of the text and the photographs as they fill the page or screen. What do we encounter first on the page, a photograph or words? Are there paragraphs of text followed or preceded by a series of photographic images, or do the photos intermingle with the text? Does the writer pair the photographs with traditional captions or something else? When we answer these questions, we can figure out how these choices make the photo essay work. Ward's tender introduction tells us about her arrival and provides a poignant introduction to this place believed to be a "dying village." Like traditional photo captions, Ward's captions tell us what we are seeing—but they also do something else. They give us more facts about the place, facts that deepen our understanding of this place, providing information and adding to the poignancy of the piece.

Just as writers read essays considering how the author has arranged textual paragraphs, when writers read photo essays, we consider how the writer/photographer has arranged the photographs. In Ward's photo essay, for example, the images vary between stark landscapes and people with wrinkled faces. As readers, we are meant to understand more about this place because of the arrangement of the photos. Pay attention to which photos appear in the beginning, middle, and end. Notice which photos are grouped together. Considering the way the writer/photographer has put the photo essay together is an important part of reading photo essay like a writer.

Readers also read color when we read image. In "Hestur: A Photo Essay," we see the images in stark black and white—the same palate used to print words on a page. Seeing the stark, black-and-white images of this place affects the way we read the essay. Imagine the different interpretation you might have if you read the images in color.

We will think more about the relationship between text and image in graphic and photographic narrative as we move through other lessons in this book. For now, it is time to move to other hybrid forms.

Lyric Essay

Back in Lesson 1, I mentioned lyric essay as a subgenre of creative nonfiction, and so it is. Writers have to be flexible sometimes—at least in as much as we work in the fluidity of words. Talking about lyric essay gives us an opportunity to consider the idea that some creative writing forms can be considered hybrids by their very nature, even as they are also firmly part of one genre.

Published under the genre of creative nonfiction for decades, lyric essay has roots in both essay and poetry. Lyric essay gets its name from the poetic, or lyric, quality of the writing mixed with the literal truth of essay. Borrowing their name from lyric poems, lyric essays stay grounded in fact but leave poetic space among the ideas, which are often linked as they are in lyric poetry, through association and emotion. Simply put, in lyric essay, we read with an eye to the lyricism. Reading lyric essay, we consider how the lyricism we traditionally associate with poetry gives the essayist a way to communicate the ideas differently than they could be communicated in a different form of creative nonfiction.

Vivian Bikulege's "Cuttings" is a lyric essay. As is sometimes the case for lyric essays, "Cuttings" falls into more than one literary category. It is also a segmented essay and a hybrid essay.

---

1 Bits

A.

There is a snapshot in the archives of the *New York Daily News* of Leiby Kletzky waiting on the street for Levi Aron to pay his dental bill. The Brooklyn boy got lost walking home from camp and the moment was captured by a surveillance camera on July 11, 2011. Leiby waited seven minutes before getting into Aron's 1990 Honda Accord trusting that the next stop would be home.

B.

I walk my beagle Toby on a path beside the Coosaw River. A tidal creek splits from the river cutting into the marsh forest. We play a running game to the top of a sandy ridge in the South Carolina Lowcountry. As I wait for my chubby canine friend, I catch sight of a white heron wading on stilt legs in the pluff mud, quiet and focused.

In the above excerpt from "Cuttings," we can see the linking of seemingly divergent ideas into one piece. We move from one image—a boy "getting into Aron's 1990 Honda Accord"—to another a woman playing with her dog and "a white heron wading on stilt legs in the pluff mud." As readers, we are left to dwell in the lyric language and to make associations between these ideas.

Prose Poetry

Aptly named, prose poetry tells us the hybrid is happening between—well—prose and poetry. In prose poetry, the reader finds a poem written in paragraph form. In prose poem, we will find poetic language, association, and emotion, but when we read the poem, it will not have the line breaks and white space we associate with poetry.

To begin our prose poetry discussion, look at Joy Harjo's "Grace."

I think of Wind and her wild ways the year we had nothing to lose
and lost it anyway in the cursed country of the fox. We still talk
about that winter, how the cold froze imaginary buffalo on the stuffed
horizon of snowbanks. The haunting voices of the starved and mutilated
broke fences, crashed our thermostat dreams, and we couldn't stand it
one more time. So once again we lost a winter in stubborn memory, walked
through cheap apartment walls, skated through fields of ghosts into
a town that never wanted us, in the epic search for grace.

Like Coyote, like Rabbit, we could not contain our terror and clowned
our way through a season of false midnights. We had to swallow
that town with laughter, so it would go down easy as honey. And one
morning as the sun struggled to break ice, and our dreams had found us
with coffee and pancakes in a truck stop along Highway 80,
we found grace.

I could say grace was a woman with time on her hands, or a white
buffalo escaped from memory. But in that dingy light it was a promise
of balance. We once again understood the talk of animals, and spring
was lean and hungry with the hope of children and corn.

I would like to say, with grace, we picked ourselves up and walked
into the spring thaw. We didn't; the next season was worse. You went
home to Leech Lake to work with the tribe and I went south. And, Wind,
I am still crazy. I know there is something larger than the memory
of a dispossessed people. We have seen it.

(For Wind and Jim Welch)

Here Harjo explores the collective memory of "displaced people," alongside the speaker's memory of the prejudice she and her friends lived through as Native Americans who, "skated through fields of ghosts into a town that never wanted us." Since first writing "Grace," Harjo has written and discussed the poem in ways that tell us the poem is about her own life as a graduate student. We know the poem holds literal truth, and the truth is a hard one. While the poem is composed in complete sentences and paragraphs, readers still need to make inferences among the words, phrases, images that bring so much troubling history and lived experience together into one poem. The paragraph form belies the complexity and emotion of people who have suffered both the prejudice and the history displacement. To see all of this in the poem, we have to make inferences between the paragraphs—or stanzas—as well and the ongoing "epic search for grace."

Another hybrid by nature, prose poetry shares many qualities with lyric essay. Many writers and readers associate prose poetry with creative nonfiction because, like "Grace," many prose poems do hold literal truth. Just as in other forms of poetry, however, prose poetry is bound only to tell the poetic truth, so it is better to associate prose poetry with prose in general instead of a specific prose genre.

Distinguishing a prose poem from a lyric essay or a lyrically written piece of fiction can be a tricky business, especially if the prose poem is long-ish or the lyric essay or story is short. Because of the paragraph form, one quality prose poetry and lyric prose share is resemblance. (What a lovely discovery it is to find a work that seems to hover between identities.)

When you find a prose poem, lyric essay, or short story like this, first appreciate it for its literary aesthetic, chameleon and otherwise, then pay attention to how the writer classified it for publication. If it is published as a prose poem, read it as a poem (which holds poetic truth) and notice the way the prose form makes the poem work. If it is an essay, read it recognizing the literal truth and examining its lyric qualities.

Either way, writers reading these hybrids will explore both the prose and the poetic qualities and notice how each influences the work. When reading Poornima Laxmeshwar's "Cartography" for example, it is important to read with this question in mind: Why does Laxmeshwar place this poem into the prose form? Writing a poem into paragraphs makes the essence of the poem different than it would be if it appeared in the traditional line breaks of poetry. Another way to think of this is that in prose poetry, we read with an eye trained on the prose aspect. We can try this now with the "Cartography" excerpt below.

She was excited about Amsterdam. The infamous Red-light district, the coffee shops, she was already preparing her to-do list while he wanted Venice—a boatman singing, the flowing romance and her.

They slept with their own set of dreams and the map led them to places where they wanted to go.

The anniversary arrived and departed like a birdsong. The map supine on the study table next to the books appeared like a heart with spread arteries. It gained thin layers of dust, became an unfulfilled promise.

In "Cartography," we stay folded into the paragraphs of the poem. The reader cannot break out of the paragraphs any more than the "he" and "she" of the poem can break out of their map-dreams and into a real trip. In prose poem, the neat appearance of the paragraphs can heighten the emotional tensions of the poem by holding the reader inside the paragraph.

Prose poem also placing the emotion and imagery of the poem inside the tidiness of paragraph form. In "Cartography," the paragraphs reflect the anniversary that comes and goes without much fuss, other than the map and the eventual letting go of the idea of an anniversary trip. Notice the poignant language in the poem, though, the "spread arteries," the "unfulfilled promise." These people are hurt, even if the hurt is calm and tidy, like a paragraph.

One interesting side note on "Cartography": We are discussing the work as a prose poem because Laxmeshwar wrote it as a prose poem. But remember what I noted about how much the genre lines can blur in hybrid work. "Cartography" was originally published as a piece of micro fiction. Do you see why? As much as "Cartography" is a prose poem, it is also a narrative poem. Laxmeshwar is telling a story here, and by virtue of its prose form, it lends itself to being read—and published—as a micro fiction. Earlier in this chapter, I cited "Cartography" as an example of a hybrid work that does such a good job of being a hybrid that its genre is impossible to name by reading alone. After reading "Cartography" as a writer, as we have done here, we can identify all the genre elements involved—narrative, poetry, prose. But the only ways we can identify the piece as a prose poem is because (well, forgive me) I say so. I can say so with confidence because I asked Laxmeshwar herself, and she said she originally wrote the piece as a prose poem. You are probably already thinking the reason we can also identify "Cartography" as micro fiction and rule out micro essay is because that is how the piece was originally published. Sometimes identifying hybrid work comes down to looking at the decisions made by writers or editors.

Choreopoem

Ntozake Shange (one of those writers who seem to inhabit hybrid space almost as a literary home) was the first writer to use the word "choreopoem." She invented the word to describe her groundbreaking work *For Colored Girls Who Have Considered Suicide When the Rainbow is Enuf*. In 1975, this work might simply have been called a play, but that would not have been an accurate description.

On the page, choreopoem reads (and looks) like poetry. On the stage, choreopoem uses dance-like movement and elements of song. Shange gave this kind of work a new name, and the name stuck. Since then, many other writers, working alone or collaboratively, have written choreopoems. (Social Media Hint: Type "choreopoem" into YouTube to see a sampling of choreopoems from emerging writers, established writers, and writing students. You will be able to find productions of Shange's work there too.)

While choreopoem is part of the playwriting genre, it is also part of poetry. Since many writers and readers of poetry believe that poetry is meant to be read aloud, choreopoem fits not uneasily into that genre too. Like all poetry, when we read a choreopoem, we will expect a poetic truth that may or may not contain literal truth. Reading choreopoem, though, we also read looking for the additional layers we see when we read a play, like stage direction, dialogue, and character descriptions, and we will expect the words to be spoken by characters, as in other dramatic productions.

As with any performance piece, we also read choreopoem remembering that it is intended for the stage. Read choreopoems imagining how they would look, sound, and feel on stage. Imaging the additional layers that a director and audience would bring to the piece. After all, that's what writers are doing as they draft choreopoems.

Emerging Hybrids: Borrowed Forms (in General) and List Forms (Specifically)

Two hybrid types seem to be in the process of establishing themselves in the literary world: any creative writing that borrows the form of something else and creative writing borrowing the list form. Both are becoming widely enough used that we might consider them to be emerging. In both cases, the writer uses a form, or mode, of writing that has not been part of creative writing, historically. Another way to think of this is creative writing disguised as something else.

List Essays and Poems

Creative writing in list form is (of course) one way creative writing is borrowing the form of something else: a list. Writers are using this particular kind of borrowing enough right now for us to think of the list form as its own emerging hybrid. We might consider the list form to be a specific subgenre, if you will, of borrowed forms. It is important to know that the list form can be structured in many different ways, from a numbered list with brief entries (see Alan Michael Parker's list poem in Lesson 2, page 31) to lists written in paragraph form. (For easy access to a variety of list structures browse through *Brevity Magazine* online.)

Until recently, lists have been nothing more than lists. People make to-do lists, grocery lists, pros and cons lists, packing lists, and on. Former late-night television host David Letterman popularized the comedic top-ten list.

Why does anyone make a list? Why does anyone read a list? A list is a brief, succinct way to put down (in writing) or pick up (in reading) a series of related ideas. How those ideas are related depends on the type of list. Often the list's title, or label, tells us how to understand the relationship, as is the case with comedic top-ten lists.

When we read list literature, we are reading a series of connected ideas just as in any other kind of a list, but we are reading the list as literature, which means we want to be entertained and we want to find the language esthetically pleasing. The titles of list literature are as important as the rest of the piece. In any list piece, titles are the key, telling us how to read the essay or poem. In fact, browsing through titles of list literature can be an important reading as a writer activity—an activity most of us can do from our smartphones. Try, for example, visiting *Brevity Magazine*'s website and looking through the list essay titles. List forms can hybridize with any genre, but list pieces seem to show up most in creative nonfiction and poetry. Closely reading list hybrids in any genre will help us understand how to write list pieces in the genre of our choosing.

When creative writers use the list form to create an essay or poem, they are asking us to read literature the way we would read a list. Thinking of the category, we will make associations among the items on the list. List pieces always tell us the type of list, or category, we will be reading and usually give a hint about the associations we should be considering as we read the list.

Look at Alan Michael Parker's poem, "Sixteen Ways Old People Terrify the Young." From the title, we readers have a sense of the category, old people, and the association, the ways young people are afraid of them.

Sixteen Ways Old People Terrify the Young

1. They have sex with each other.

2. They drive around.

3. They pretend they're thinking. They pretend they're not thinking about dying.

4. The vigor of diving through the waves (through time) or the splash of the body sprinting toward love. What's a sea, if not for swimming.

5. And what about those old people who walk—I don't know— like seventy-nine miles every morning on the beach? Skin cancer! Yo! They're going to die.

6. "Vex not his ghost: O, let him pass! he hates him

    That would upon the rack of this tough world

    Stretch him out longer" (*Lear*, 5.3.315-17).

7. It's a lie: they were never young.

8. Holidays were invented by old people to dress up and pretend they're all presents for young people.

9. The arc of Story graphed upon the axes of Love and Death.

10. They actually invented the computer.

11. Oh, and they wrote the poems.

12. Their whacked-out sense of sound. No guitars or headphones, no cars or guns; just TV commercials on MUTE, telephones, cats, and the sky.

13. It's like grout or glue or maybe gum. Whatever holds those bones together.

14. They like to die.

15. They like to die in big buildings surrounded by other people. Although occasionally, one of them will take off—to die in the woods or at the beach, some place far away—which accounts for the better old people movies.

16. Or they just die, one on the beach, just like today. With only three people there in the winter to see. A body.

When a list piece is numbered, we need to think about why the numbers are there. Will the numbered entries build to a sort of crescendo, the way a top-ten list does? When you read Parker's poem, notice how it builds as the numbers grow higher. Read how the sixteenth entry is a climax, a finale.

Numbered or unnumbered, though, list literature brings readers a chance to read the piece in two different ways. A list is fundamentally not a creative work. When a list is applied to a poem or essay, it shatters a rule. This kind of shattering makes us reinvent the way we read. One reason hybrid work is compelling: hybrid work makes us read in ways other than we normally do.

Look again at Parker's poem. The way I've discussed it above sounds funny, and parts of the poem are funny, but this is not a humor poem. This poem deals with the frightening concepts of aging and death and how those of us who do not count ourselves among the elderly are perplexed and afraid of all those coming days may hold. Also, in this poem, Parker has applied a numbered list to this concept. Now we are reading about our own perceptions of aging, death, and dying, crafted in the poignant language of poetry, and this all comes to us in a numbered list. A list that brings us to and he brings the poem to the poignant moment of one person dying on a beach. Suddenly, we feel the literary ground shaking beneath our feet.

We don't expect people to die in a list. List literature is full of images and topics we don't expect in a list. That's what makes list literature work—and makes list literature compelling. When we read list literature as writers, part of what we need to do is figure out why putting this content into the form of a list makes the ground shake.

Borrowed Forms: Creative Writing Disguised as Something Else

Speaking of shaking the literary ground, another way writers are hybridizing work is by making a creative piece look and act like a different kind of writing altogether. Essentially, this works the same way list literature works, but instead of playing with the list form, the writer plays with something else—another form of writing not originally intended to be creative. Before we move on, I want to clarify that disguised creative writing can be found in any genre, but sometimes it goes by other terms. "Hermit crab" is one term some writers use to describe borrowed forms. Two creative nonfiction writers, Brenda Miller and Suzanne Paola, coined the term in a book about writing creative nonfiction, so "hermit crab" is a term most often applied to essays, though it can work for any genre. "Found" is one more term sometimes used to describe borrowed forms.

Whatever terms we use to name them, when we read borrowed form hybrids, we need to pay attention to what the borrowed form means for the piece. What happens, for example, when we read what looks like a Yelp review, but turns out to be a short story? As a reader, we will apply what we know about Yelp reviews, and that will give this story an angle we haven't seen before and don't expect. When we read a creative piece pretending to be something else, we read through a different lens. When we read these works as writers, we pay attention to how the writer builds the lens and how the lens changes the reader's investment in the piece.

Look at Gwen E. Kirby's short story, "Jerry's Crab Shack: One Star" and Vivian I. Bikulege's essay "Cuttings." Both of these pieces play around with other forms. "Jerry's Crab Shack: One Star" tells us its form in its title. "Cuttings" takes the form of an academic outline, though it is in fact a lyric essay. Like the other hybrid works we've discussed, both of these pieces are members of their genres (fiction and creative nonfiction, respectively), but they are both also multi-genre works by virtue of their assuming the disguises of other kinds of writing.

We've all read online reviews. Online reviews are a form of social media. Anyone who has access to the internet can post—and anyone does. Sometimes those reviews get a little uncomfortable. (If you don't believe me, read Rachael Herron's Diva Cup review on Amazon or Twitter.) Sometimes the weirdness is good—as in the case of Rachel Herron's Diva Cup review. Sometimes the weirdness is just weird. This is the concept underlying Kirby's short story told as a Yelp review.

Study this excerpt from Kirby's story, "Jerry's Crab Shack: One Star."

"Jerry's Crab Shack: One Star"

Gary F.

Baltimore, MD

Yelp member since July 14, 2015

Review: Jerry's Crab Shack

Review posted: July 15, 2015, 2:08am

1/5 stars

After perusing the restaurant's website and reading the positive reviews on Yelp, my wife and I went to Jerry's Crab Shack this evening. We did not have a good experience. It was not "a home run," as another reviewer suggested. I don't know where these reviewers usually go to dinner, and I won't post the speculations I typed and then deleted because they were unflattering and, dare I say, so accurate as to be hurtful and it is not my intention to be hurtful. I simply want to correct the record.

I'm going to review Jerry's Crab Shack in a methodical, fair-minded way so that other people who use this site, people like my wife and I who are new to Baltimore and rely on this site to make informed dinner plans, can know what they are getting into and make their own decisions. If you are going to take the time to do something, as my dear wife says, take the time to do it right or don't bother with it and let her do it like she does everything else (ha ha).

This is a story of a relationship unraveling, and during the unraveling, two romantically involved characters have a nasty scene in a restaurant, or, rather, they decide not to create a scene but have a nasty time. This may be a story that has been done before—as they say. But it has not been done as a Yelp review. The Yelp review makes this story. The mock review gives the story a form—the review—and a frame: in order to work in the review form, the entire story has to be told only in the context of what happens in the restaurant being reviewed.

Bikulege's essay, "Cuttings," works a little differently. Read the excerpt again.

1 Bits

A.

There is a snapshot in the archives of the *New York Daily News* of Leiby Kletzky waiting on the street for Levi Aron to pay his dental bill. The Brooklyn boy got lost walking home from camp and the moment was captured by a surveillance camera on July 11, 2011. Leiby waited seven minutes before getting into Aron's 1990 Honda Accord trusting that the next stop would be home.

B.

I walk my beagle Toby on a path beside the Coosaw River. A tidal creek splits from the river cutting into the marsh forest. We play a running game to the top of a sandy ridge in the South Carolina Lowcountry. As I wait for my chubby canine friend, I catch sight of a white heron wading on stilt legs in the pluff mud, quiet and focused.

"Cuttings" borrows from the structure and shape of an academic outline with its use of the numbering and lettering convention: 1. A. B. C. D., 2. A. B. C. D. ... Reading "Cuttings," we read knowing we will get a story we have to piece together the way we piece together information from an outline. (Notice how the title picks this up, as well as playing with a more horrific idea.) A careful reading of "Cuttings" means being cognizant of the way outlines work while we read the brief numbered and lettered sections, which all add up to something whole.

"Cuttings," though, does not read like an outline, the way Kirby's story reads like a Yelp review. For that reason, "Cuttings" does not fit squarely into the category of creative writing pretending to be something else.

Unlabeled Multi-genre Work

Some multi-genre works do not announce themselves. These are the kinds of hybrid creative writing pieces the reader—and the writer, for that matter—cannot label as one of the established or emerging hybrids we have discussed here. "Cuttings" falls somewhere between a piece of writing pretending to be something else and an unlabeled hybrid. "Cuttings" plays with the conventions of outline, but it doesn't mimic outline. Instead, Bikulege hybridizes essay with outline to give the reader a way to make sense of the fragments she has pieced together here.

To find other unlabeled multi-genre creative writing, read around in literary magazines, literary blogs, and author's pages. You might, for example, Google Monica Ong, click on her gallery, and read/look through many hybrid works that layer writing and image. Or you might visit Ben Cartwright's webpage and click on his piece *Looney*, to see the way he uses colored columns of text.

When you do come across a piece of creative writing that defies labeling, read and look at it carefully to figure out what the piece is doing. In each case, the writer is using hybrid to create meaning, as Bikulege does in "Cuttings." In other words, the writer is telling you something that cannot be told without this mixing or layering of genre. Reading this kind of multi-genre work requires the reader to read the words along with the way the words appear. If the words appear in columns, in a diagram, or as part of an image, read thinking about how their appearance influences the piece.

Reading Hybrid and Multi-genre Work: The Big Picture

You may have guessed by now that it would be impossible, inside this lesson, to discuss every type of hybrid work a reader can find. Even if we could, writers are publishing new kinds of hybrid work every day. Creative writing hybrid pieces can be found in chapbooks, books, and individual pieces and can be published in print and online. There are even publications that are embracing the hybrid concept for the publication itself. Two examples are the *A3 Review*, a British literary magazine that folds out like a map, and *Hoot,* a mini literary magazine published each month on a post card. (Check out their aesthetics—and their submissions guidelines—online.) While these magazines are not dedicated solely to publishing hybrid work, the map and postcard forms in which they appear bring these publications into the hybrid realm and change the ways readers approach their content.

Whichever form of hybrid work you read, the most important part of reading these works with the eyes of a writer is to figure out what the genre-bending brings to the work.

Lesson 2 Discussion Questions and Writing Prompts

Discussion Questions: Focus on Hybrid

1. Both Poornima Laxmeshwar's "Cartography" (found in Lesson 3, page 42) and Sophie Yanow's *The Contradictions* (found in the Readings section) are hybrids in more than one way. Explain why this is true. Make sure to identify the different genres or forms the writers of each work pull from to create these pieces.

2. Read Gwen E. Kirby's "Jerry's Crab Shack: One Star" (found in the Readings Section); Joy Harjo's "Grace" (found in Lesson 2, page 27); and Randi Ward's "Hestur: A Photo Essay" (found in the Readings section). As you read, pay attention to the way your reading must change to approach these hybrid works. How do you read them differently than you would read other short stories, essays, or poems? What specific elements of the work are you looking for?

3. Select three pieces from among the works we have identified in this lesson as being hybrid or multi-genre works (for example, Alan Michael Parker's "Sixteen Ways Old People Terrify the Young," found in Lesson 2, page 31; Chris Galvin Nguyen's tweeted micro essays, found in Lesson 3, page 46; and Vivian I. Bikulege's "Cuttings," found in the Readings section). Explain how each writer uses hybrid forms to tackle the subject matter in a compelling way. Consider why the writers decided to break traditional genre boundaries. List at least three examples detailing what the genre-bending brings to the work.

Writing Prompts: Focus on Hybrid/Multi-genre.

New Material Prompt

As you can see from the genre-bending readings in this book, hybrid, or multi-genre, work constitutes a wide range of creative writing. Using one of the readings as inspiration, draft your own hybrid piece. If you are also gifted with the ability to take photographs or draw illustrations, use those gifts in your hybrid work. If you prefer to stick to works, try mashing up more than one kind of writing to draft an idea in a form you have not tried before.

Revision Prompt

Sometimes our best revisions are radical. Take a piece of writing you have been working on and revise it to push the genre boundary lines. As plan your revision, remember that genre-bending will both bring a new element to the work and change the way readers will encounter it.

LESSON 3
SHORT FORMS AND DIGITAL MEDIA

Spoiler Alert: This will be a short chapter. As we will discuss in this lesson, short forms are important. So, too, are creative pieces appearing on digital media, including Twitter—the shortest digital platform.

Length and Short Forms

One size does not fit all—even within one genre. While short-short stories have been published since the 1800s, contemporary readers should notice the increasing popularity of short and micro forms of prose. Until recently, creative writing using a compressed number of words generally belonged to the realm of poetry. While some forms of poetry, like haiku, are often associated with the concept of "short" in poetry, shorter poems have been around since the dawn of literacy. In other words, short forms of poetry have been a thing since people started being able to read and write. After the advent of prose, poetry began to be associated with a relatively few number of words.

In the last few decades, though, short-form prose has found more outlets. As it is continuing to gain popularity in the literary world, contemporary short-form prose will be our focus in this lesson. Both fiction and creative nonfiction writers are publishing short-form work in print and online.

In short-form creative prose, the underlying concept is to write a story or essay that feels complete but uses a tight economy of words. How many words? Few. How few? That depends. Size matters in short-form writing, and there are two kinds of short: the short and the very short. Prose work called, "short," or "flash," generally means stories or essays written around or under the 1,000-word mark. Prose work termed "micro" generally means essays or stories that come in under 300 words, sometimes far under. Think anything from six-word stories to work that can fit on less than one page, or work counted by characters instead of words.

Like multi-genre work, though, short-form work goes by a variety of literary names. The term "short-short" probably dates back to the 1930s, when the idea of shorter-than-short stories took root. While "short" and "flash" are two of the most common names used to label short-form prose, other terms are out there, including "brief" and "sudden." Some writers (this writer included) think "sudden" implies that a piece might be publishable without revision, which is almost never true. Note, though, that publishers may use a variety of terms for short and micro forms and that the terms will sometimes overlap. Where one editor might call a 300-word story a "micro," another editor may place the same story in the "flash" category.

In terms of word count, a reader (or writer) of short-form prose also needs to know the exact word or character counts that qualify as short-form work are ultimately left up to the editors who call for submissions. Often, the specific word-count limit is defined by the publication in which short-form prose is published. *Brevity*, an online, short-form creative nonfiction magazine, publishes essays of 750 words or fewer. *Hoot* (the post card magazine) and *The A3 Review* (the map magazine) both publish creative writing of 150 words or fewer.

Some editors and publishers have also coined their own terms for short and micro forms—and given their specific word or character count guidelines to go with them. For example, *Tin House Online* publishes "Flash Friday," which is fiction in 1,500 words or fewer. Meanwhile, the literary magazine *Creative Nonfiction* publishes "Tiny Truths," micro essays that are not only Twitter-length creative nonfiction pieces but have also actually been tweeted (more on this and other digital media platforms below).

Notice how much of our discussion has revolved around defining short and micro forms and considering where and how they are published. Part of reading like a writer is reading with these concepts in mind. To read flash fiction like a writer, you have to know what flash fiction is. To read a micro essay on Twitter, you have to understand what makes the micro essay work. It helps to consider why both of these and other shorts are publishable—and where.

Here is another way to think about reading short-form work. Read short prose to figure out how the writer works a complete story or essay into as few words as possible. When you read short prose, read it in part the way you read haiku. If you read haiku to understand how the poet uses those three lines of five, seven, and five syllables to depict a certain moment, read short prose to unearth the ways the writer crafts an entire story or essay within an extreme economy of words.

Careful readers of short fiction and creative nonfiction will notice most of this work is steeped in sensory detail and uses language carefully, the way poems do. In flash fiction, read looking for nuanced character details and a plot complete with a beginning, middle, and end. In short essay, look for tightly written details that accumulate throughout the essay and moments of reflection that propel the essay beyond the immediate narrative time of the piece or make a connection to a larger idea. If a short essay narrative in nature, look for plot and character arc, too. But wouldn't we read all creative prose looking for these elements? Yes, we would. The difference is reading to see how the writer frames all of this with so few words.

Look at Karen Donley-Hayes's "What You Learn in College" (found on the next page) and Beth Uznis Johnson's "Negative Results" (found on page 41). As a smart reader of short-form prose, you may already be sizing up these narratives and calculating words. At 808 words, "What You Learn in College" clocks in as short (or flash) nonfiction. "Negative Results," at 380 words, belongs in the flash fiction category, but can also work as a micro fiction, depending on who is counting. Both pieces are as tightly written as prose can be. Notice how no information gets repeated. Any repetition in these pieces is intentional and serves an aesthetic and structural purpose. "The bottle spins," in "What You Learn in College," makes it clear that time is passing while also adding a poetic quality to the language. The word "lie" becomes an undercurrent running through "Negative Results," directing our attention to the theme Johnson explores in this narrative.

Now, closely read Karen Donley-Hayes's "What You Learn in College."

"What You Learn in College"

You learn that although you loathe the taste of beer, you love intoxication, and it is possible to quickly drink through the loathing. You love the daring of your intoxicated self, the way you're not stymied by your own naiveté. You feel brave and worldly when you join your new college friends in a bawdy exchange thick with sexual innuendo and brag. You laugh along with them, these people who welcomed your sober self before ever meeting your intoxicated self. You laugh when they close the door against dorm-mates attracted to the banter, and you sit right down on the floor in a circle with them to play strip-spin-the-bottle.

You learn you are having fun, and you revel in your bravery and the way you're unperturbed by the first round or two of the game, during which you peel off your sweatshirt and toss it over your shoulder.

The bottle spins.

You learn you are perhaps not so intrepid as your beer-bravado led you to believe. A few more spins, the last of the beer-foam winging away from the lip of the bottle, and this strip-spin-the-bottle game is requiring more stripping than you expected. (What did you expect?). By the time the game spins you out of your shoes, socks, and finally your t-shirt, you have realized you are not really drunk at all anymore.

You learn you are still naive when Ed says, "Nice headlights, Karen," and you are reasonably certain he is not talking about your eyes. You laugh along with everyone else, but you don't look at Ed, or at any of your other friends. You keep smiling, keep acting intoxicated, realizing you passed your comfort level with the game one spin ago, when you lost your t-shirt. You want to leave. You want to bolt into the cold dark of the night, but you don't.

The bottle spins.

You learn you couldn't leave even if you had the nerve, because the disgruntled wanna-be-party-goers in the hallway have pennied the door, tiny rounds of copper wedging door against frame. You watch Ed, in his briefs, try to yank the door open then shrug and return to the circle of strippers. No one is leaving.

The bottle spins.

You learn that if, immediately after your turn, you laugh, comment about your head swimming, and climb onto Ed's bed, you can credibly feign a drunken blackout. You hope this will keep you from losing more clothing or anything else. You lie frozen on Ed's bed, the only escape you can think of, fake slumber through the hubbub, the clink of the bottle, the giggles and wolf-calls, the throbbing of your heart.

The bottle spins.

You listen to glass scraping against linoleum, the sound melding with the smell of stale beer and sweat and not-quite-clean laundry, the smell of slept-on sheets. You keep your eyes closed. Your friends continue the game to complete nudity (although you do not open your eyes to verify). They try to wake you for your turns, but you do not move, leave your body in the slack of boozy slumber. You resist the intense impulse to cover your semi-nakedness. You stay in character.

The bottle stops spinning.

You learn that while your crush on Ed is in part what got you into this room and thus onto his bed, it is not enough to keep you here after the party breaks up and the participants redress, unjam the pennied door, and disperse. You sit up at the first sufficiently loud noise, feign bleary-eyed surprise—"Where'd everyone go?" "Where's my shirt?!"—put on your clothes, and, with appropriate stumbling and giggling, wobble out the door.

You learn how relieved and grateful you are to be walking alone in the frosty black night. To be out of that room and away from your drunk, laughing, happy, naked friends. To leave behind what could have happened, how your life might have shifted, to have escaped unchanged. And yet. A pulsing disappointment follows you, a regret born of rejected possibilities. Almost a sentient thing. You could turn and consider it, even reach out to it, ask where it's been and where it goes. But darkness and naiveté are easy and known, cool against your face, so you keep walking and do not turn to ponder.

You learn this is the last time you will make this walk across campus from Ed's room to yours. And with this learning, that almost-sentient regret breaches like some black-backed sea creature glittering in the night. You do not see it behind you any more than you saw your friends' nakedness. But just the same, you sense it as it slides away into the deep, beyond your sight. But the regret isn't gone. It will never be gone, and you don't need to learn that. You already know it.

Notice how Donley-Hayes steeps the reader in sensory details without using many of the verbs often written to explain experiencing the senses—that is, the narrator does not "hear" the progress of the strip poker game; instead she describes "faking slumber through the hubbub, the clink of the bottle, the giggles and wolf calls … " This passage exemplifies both the economy of words and the grounding in sensory details that are hallmarks of short essays.

Notice, too, how most of the essay is framed in one scene: inside the dorm room while the bottle spins and spins and stops spinning. While the essay tackles more than the game itself, framing it in the scene of the game gives Donley-Hayes a way to keep the writing brief.

Because "What You Learn in College" is a narrative essay, readers should also pay attention to the character development and plot here too. The conflict builds as the game escalates and the narrator reacts to what is happening in the locked dorm room. In this short essay, though, the conflict and character detail are all delivered to the reader in sensory description of the scene and in reflection on learning in a, well, nonacademic way. "You learn you are having fun, and you revel in your bravery and the way you're unperturbed by the first round or two of the game, during which you peel off your sweatshirt and toss it over your shoulder."

Donley-Hayes also tackles reflection and application to a larger understanding that are crucial to personal essay and memoir in general and to short essay specifically. In the last two paragraphs (almost a quarter of the words, for those counting), the narrator first leaves the scene of the game then leaves the immediacy of that night altogether. In the leaving, she conveys the larger idea, and it is still steeped in sensory language: "And with this learning, that almost-sentient regret breaches like some black-backed sea creature glittering in the night. You do not see it behind you any more than you saw your friends' nakedness. But just the same, you sense it as it slides away into the deep, beyond your sight."

"Negative Results" works in a stream of conscious narrative, as the main character waits for then receives STD test results. Closely read this excerpt from "Negative Results."

"Negative Results"

You tell yourself, people lie. You've been sleeping with a pathological liar for a couple years, you should know. You aren't invested, the lies amuse you mostly, but they're still habitual falsehoods to questions with real answers. You'd like to think he wouldn't lie about things like sexually transmitted disease, but who knows to what extent liars will go? I'm clean, he likes to say, of course I'm clean.

What if, by chance, that's a lie? Who knows what liars actually believe?

And this new man, he doesn't seem like much of a liar, but that could be his cover for the lies. This man could sleep with anyone he wants, he's very good at it and knows exactly what he's doing. It's almost sad to think he's well behaved. Not really, but you have a husband and three children, a life that's mostly good. The baby is out of diapers and your team won the bowling league. You're spontaneous though and painfully alone and imagine how life could be different, for better or worse. You slept with a new man who may or may not be a liar.

Plus there's that other man who's serial.

Sure, the first test was negative—you did get tested—but who knows how many women he's slept with since then?

So now, you've got yourself to worry about, one person who lies, one who probably doesn't but might. He's worried. All this leads to the need for confirmation, you have no choice as you owe it to yourself, the man who probably doesn't lie, and even the man who does. The test is ten-fold and includes the window period. You hear the word negative. You see it on the page. Ten times. You're relieved, of course, but now that you know it's negative (you knew it would be), you're relieved because it means the liar is somewhat truthful, he wasn't that bad, even though you're done sleeping with him. You hate him for putting you through it even though you knew going in. Risks are risks, but being stupid is entirely different and, now that you know the new man is actually truthful, it makes you like him even more.

What if, by chance, he'll make it all better?

You want to crawl inside his skin and live there for a while.

Notice how Johnson works the elements of plot and character development in this very short form. This narrative has a beginning, middle, and end: The narrator worries about disease, the narrator waits, the results come back. Notice the complexities, too, and the way Johnson writes character development and plot together. The narrator's entire life is on the line: " ... but you have a husband and three children, a life that's mostly good. The baby is out of diapers and your team won the bowling league. You're spontaneous though and painfully alone and imagine how life could be different, for better or worse." Through brief and poignant strokes of character development and plot, Johnson drafts an entire story in this small space. It's not just that she's waiting for test results and worrying about lies, she is also cheating on her "mostly good" life. In this way, the undercurrent of the lies becomes part of the beginning, middle, and end—the very plot—of this micro fiction. Notice these brief flashes of detail that explain just enough about the narrator's life to make sure that in this very short story, there is more on the line than one woman's test results.

Because "Cartography" was published as micro fiction, let's pause here to read the piece, looking to see how this prose poem can also be read under the micro fiction lens.

"Cartography"

Their eighth anniversary was on its way, just like a cheesy pizza. Just that it came every year on 26th Feb even if they didn't want it. This year they spoke about unexplored Europe.

She was excited about Amsterdam. The infamous Red light district, the coffee shops, she was already preparing her to-do list while he wanted Venice—a boatman singing, the flowing romance and her.

They slept with their own set of dreams and the map led them to places where they wanted to go.

The anniversary arrived and departed like a birdsong. The map supine on the study table next to the books appeared like a heart with spread arteries. It gained thin layers of dust, became an unfulfilled promise.

A map knows not to lie.

Here, too, vivid details prick the senses: "a cheesy pizza," "a birdsong," "the map supine." Character details work to both describe the separate, incompatible dreams of the couple and create conflict. The brief narrative ends with "dust," "unfulfilled promise," and the final sentence: "A map knows not to lie." Taken alone, the final sentence is compelling because of the personification. We never think of a map having the capacity to lie and knowing not to. Taken as the end of a well-crafted micro narrative (or a narrative prose poem) about an unwanted anniversary, the sentence is devastating.

Reading these and other stunning passages in short prose will show you how to be a better writer because you can see what a writer can accomplish with such economies of words. Studying the carefully chosen words and tightly written sentences drafted by great writers of short prose will strengthen your own writing practice—in short-form prose and beyond.

Digital Media Platforms for Creative Writing

As the field of creative writing broadens and technology expands, writers are finding digital platforms for publishing their work. We often want a shorter read online, so short-form work lends itself well to online platforms. Many online magazines and literary websites exclusively publish short-form stories and essays. A few known for publishing excellent writing include *Brevity, NANO Fiction, Smokelong Quarterly,* and *Hobart.* Writers who plan to publish short-form work would do well to read around in these digital publications, which are free and accessible to anyone who can get online.

Reading online requires an additional layer of reading skills, in that reading like a writer online means also paying attention to *how* we read online. Think about it. What is one of the most basic parts of reading online? Scrolling. When you read online, think about why the words keep you scrolling.

Let's pause here to acknowledge that writers are also publishing longer pieces online. Many online literary magazines are set up to publish the way book publishers publish e-books. The idea here is that when we read these types of publications online, we are reading them in pretty much the same way we would read in print, but we are reading on a screen. This is an environmentally responsible and convenient way to read. But it is different, at its essence, than reading creative work written specifically for digital and social media platforms. It is this intended-for-digital-media work we are focusing on in this lesson.

Reading and writing are social interactions. While this is true in print, it does not feel so. In much digital media and all social media, the social interaction is much more tangible. Reading literature on digital and social media means you recognize the interaction. Reading digital literature like a writer means realizing that writers and publishers are leveraging that social interaction aspect. Here is an example: Notice how many online literary magazines, *Brevity* included, are set up to look and feel like blogs, complete with space for readers to leave comments. When you read creative writing on social or other digital media, it's worth taking time to scroll through some of the comments too, at least enough to see what it is about the piece that has engaged readers to the point of writing a response.

Also true is the fact that digital and social media make creative writing more accessible to readers. Most readers do not have the resources to subscribe to dozens of literary journals. But every reader with access to the internet can read creative work published online. Readers can also read work published via digital and social media at times and in places that don't lend themselves to reading work published in print. As writers, it's important for us to notice how other writers and editors are using social media to get work out into the world and to think about how we might do the same.

Let's look at two examples of creative work that exist in the world via digital and social media. The first example is Beth Uznis Johnson's "Negative Results," which we discussed above. Johnson's piece was published on *The Rumpus*, in a collection of brief works written by writers who read *The Rumpus*. Johnson's piece was considered for publication because she was reader of this online outlet for pop culture and creative writing. *The Rumpus* has a large following and impressive readership. By engaging in this particular creative online media as a reader, Johnson was also to engage as a writer and tap into that readership.

Writers are also leveraging digital and social media platforms by establishing their own blogs or contributing to already-established blogs. Here, I'll offer up a post from my own blog, *The Face of Bravery*, as an example. "They Point at Her Face and Whisper" is a blog post, but it is also a piece creative nonfiction. As you read the following excerpt, notice the literary devices that keep this piece in the creative realm. Among them are those we will discuss later in this book: narrative arc, plot, character development, dialogue, scene, and literary use of language.

They Point at Her Face and Whisper

Erin Pushman Living with a Facial Tumor October 16, 2018 4 Minutes

Lucille stood in her room, surrounded by a pile of discarded uniform options, her frustration welling into tears.

"I have to wear a skirt," she said, kicking a pair of uniform shorts across the wood floor.

"But you love shorts," I said, trying to hand her a comfy looking pair. This was only the second week of school, early September in North Carolina, where we are still broiling in summer heat.

"No," she said batting my hand away.

By now, I was frustrated too. The minutes were ticking down toward eight o'clock, and she still had to eat breakfast, brush her teeth, and find her shoes. Generally, we aren't a family known for punctuality. But we make an effort to get the kids to school on time. Anyway, I thought, good parents probably don't let their kids get tardy marks during the second week of second grade.

"Lucille," I countered, my voice rising in my own frustration. "We just bought you all these new shorts to wear to school." And here they were all in the prescribed khaki and navy, piled up on the floor. Lucille attends a public school with a uniform policy, and buying enough pairs of uniform shorts to get through these last weeks of heat had been an end-of-summer-break priority.

"I need a skirt," Lucille insisted, her enlarged chin jutting out, reminding me to be gentle.

"Why?"

"They say I look like a boy."

So there it was. And here we were.

"Tell me about it," I said, cupping her face in my hand, holding the bone that holds the tumor.

It hadn't happened in second grade yet, but hearing people's comments about her face was nothing new. Well-intentioned, ill-intentioned, or innocent, the comments came. A chiropractor asked if Lucille had Lion's disease and suggested we watch the movie <u>Mask</u>. Two smirking kids at the pool had pointed to Lucille's face, called her "bigmouth," and asked what she had swallowed. A tiny child in a public restroom simply asked "What happened to your face?" And on. So, too, many, many people, who know and love us have said, "She's still pretty."

Still. Right.

Lucille has a tumor, specifically a <u>central giant cell granuloma</u>. It is lodged in the middle of her lower jawbone. It is rare. It is aggressive. It is benign. It is not cancer, but it behaves like a cancer in many ways.

What does it look like? Lucille's surgeon and her oncologist measure in centimeters and speak of facial disfigurement. I think the tumor looks like a ripe apple, wrapped in skin, right at the place where, a year ago, Lucille had a normal chin.

At its essence, the post works almost as an essay. But there are some key differences. The first is almost too obvious to note, but as reading writers, we need to note it anyway. The post engages social media by including tags, clickable links, and buttons that allow a reader to like, share, and follow—as blogs should. It also contains a comments section, and it is searchable via internet search engines. What else does the blog post include that an essay does not? Images. In this blog post, as in most literary blogs, the writer has incorporated images to add interest for the reader. The editors of many literary journals set up like blogs do the same thing: pair image with text to make the on-screen package more compelling for the reader. Unlike photo essay or graphic narrative, though, the images are not a crucial part of the narrative. As a reader, you may not be drawn as much to what you see on the screen without the images, but reading the piece without the photographs would not change the way you understand what you are reading in the words.

When we read literary blogs, we also want to notice how the writing is different—in style, in breadth, in the framing of ideas—than creative writing published in other forms. Writing this blog allows me to explore my experience as the mother of a child battling a rare and disfiguring disease. The exploration happens in posts that frame one particular aspect of my daughter's fight against the tumor. The writing in each individual post is narrower and less complex than writing I tend to produce for essays. A reader can click on the post, read it, and like/comment/follow without spending a lot of time analyzing complex characters or narrative arcs. I also write these posts more quickly and with less revision, compared to my writing for essays or book chapters. Writers can also publish blog posts the moment we are finished revising them. All this changes the way writing works on blogs, and as readers, we need to pay attention to those changes.

It's also true that writing blog posts sometimes leads to other publishing opportunities. For example, *Mutha Magazine* picked up *The Face of Bravery* blog and decided to run a series of some of my posts as essays. *Mutha* is one of those online literary magazines that is formatted like a blog. In fact, it uses a blog platform to publish content. So here too, the lines get pretty blurry.

While *Mutha Magazine* looks like a blog, it is nevertheless a literary magazine, so as a writer, I had to meet the needs of a different and wider readership when my blog post became an essay. In other words, I made small but significant revisions to my original posts before they went live as stand-alone essays on *Mutha*. (The essay version is included in the Readings section.) My revision includes explanations to replace the clickable links, moves a little further into character development, incorporates carefully placed exposition for readers who are not familiar with the blog, and works the language a little more. Savvy readers (and writers) should read literary blogs noting what the blog platform includes as well as the subtle but significant differences in creative writing on blogs.

Reading literature on a specific type of social media also means that as you read, you also have to be cognizant of how that medium works and how the writer has made the prose work within the form of the media itself. Take the *Tiny Truths* re-tweeted by *Creative Nonfiction*, for example. These micro essays work within Twitter's particular form of media, which is to say, 280 characters or fewer. Writers who submit to *Tiny Truths* do so via Twitter, and while *Creative Nonfiction* publishes a small selection in the print magazine, they re-tweet worthy micro essays daily.

Study these two micro essays tweeted by Chris Galvin Nguyen, using the hashtag #cnftweet. Both were re-tweeted and later published in print in *Creative Nonfiction*. The first box shows both Chris Galvin Nguyen's tweet and *Creative Nonfiction's* (*CNF's*) re-tweet. The second shows only Chris Galvin Nguyen's original tweet.

Tweet by @ChrisGNguyen

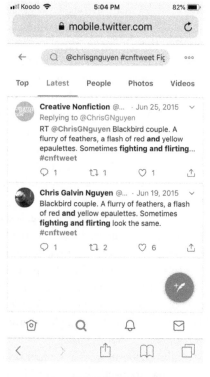

Re-tweeted by @cnfonline

Tweeted by @ChrisGNguyen

Pay attention to the Twitter-sized word—well, character—economy. Even with the economy though, one is clearly longer. Do you know why? Look at the date. The first was tweeted in 2015 when Twitter limited posts to 140 characters. I point this out to demonstrate the way Galvin Nguyen is able to write creatively within the Twitter platform.

Consider the reasons a Twitter audience *and* literary magazine editors would find these tweeted essays compelling. Like other short and micro forms of creative writing, both of these tweeted essays are steeped in specific details. From the "flurry" and "flash" of the blackbirds' feathers in the first tweet to the dialogue of the parent suffering from dementia in the second tweet, readers get a tiny but vivid snapshot of real life. The tweets both also have a beginning, a middle, and an end, albeit in micro-scale. The blackbird micro essay begins with the action of the birds and ends with Galvin Nguyen realizing what the birds are up to. The dementia essay begins with the problem of caring for a parent suffering from the disease, moves to trying to decipher the parent's words, and resolves with Galvin Nguyen recognizing beauty within the dementia language.

Another way to think about reading social media literature as a writer is to consider what the online journal *Nanoism* is doing with its micro fiction. While *Nanoism* doesn't publish via

Twitter, they borrow the form of Twitter—stories written in very few characters. So isn't that interesting? To read—or write—*Nanoism* stories, you have to apply what you know as a Twitter-savvy reader.

Reading like a writer on social and digital media means thinking in three ways: like a writer, like a reader, like a smart social media user. If that isn't critical thinking, I don't know what is. When you think about the way a piece of writing works on several levels (e.g., what makes this a publishable story, and a compelling tweet, and an enjoyable few seconds of reading), you are thinking like a writer.

Lesson 3 Discussion Questions and Writing Prompts

Discussion Questions: Focus on Short-Form Writing and Digital Media

1. Read Beth Uznis Johnson's "Negative Results" (found in Lesson 3, page 41) and Poornima Laxmeshwar's "Cartography" (found in Lesson 3, page 42), both of which were published as micro fiction. Explain how each writer creates nuanced character details and conflict in this short form. Provide examples from the text.

2. Read Karen Donley-Hayes's "What You Learn in College" (found in Lesson 3, page 39) thinking about how this essay works as a short—an essay that comes in under 1,000 words. Why do you think this narrative lends itself well to the short form? What choices do you think the author made in order to present a complete-feeling version of this experience in so few words?

3. Reread Chris Galvin Nguyen's tweeted micro essays (found in Lesson 3, page 46). Or, better yet, find them or another micro essay or story re-tweeted or otherwise published by a literary editor (e.g., *Tiny Truths* re-tweeted by *Creative Nonfiction*). Explain all the ways you read this micro prose differently on Twitter than you would on the page. Reflect on what reading on this media teaches you as a writer.

Writing Prompts: Focus on Short-Form Writing and Digital Media

Generative Prompt

Option 1: Write a short or micro story or essay that you can imagine submitting (someday, when it's revised and ready) to one of the publications discussed in this lesson.

Option 2: Write a *Tiny Truth* or a Twitter-length micro story. Revise it. (Really, revise it. One of my students whose Tiny Truth was selected for a re-tweet by *Creative Nonfiction* told me he write more than five drafts of his micro essay before he tweeted it to the journal.) When it is ready, submit your essay to *Creative Nonfiction's Tiny Truths* via the Twitter hashtag you can find online or your story to *Nanoism* via their online submission guidelines.

Revision Prompt

Select two paragraphs from a work-in-progress. Using the tight writing from the readings discussed in this lesson for inspiration and example, cut as many words as you can from those paragraphs. Remember to remove any repeated information. Then rewrite the sentences as needed to steep them in sensory detail.

LESSON 4
PLOT, NARRATIVE ARC, CONFLICT, AND CENTRAL THEME, CONCEPT, IMAGE, SENSE, OR EMOTION

In the first three lessons, you have already encountered some of these words writers use to talk about what drives a piece of writing. It's impossible to talk about genre, hybrid, and form without also mentioning plot, narrative arc, and central theme and image because these are crucial to every piece of creative writing.

Reading writers know that genre and form influence the type of central concept that drives a piece of writing. In poetry, we read to find an abiding image; in fiction and much creative nonfiction, we read to uncover the plot. In other creative nonfiction, readers look for a central theme. Another important aspect of reading as a writer is studying the concepts that hold the work together, the tensions that drive the work forward, and the images, emotions, or themes that abide throughout the work.

That was a long list. The reason for the list is this: Reading writers have to remember that not all creative writing is narrative in nature. Narrative couldn't exist without plot, narrative arc, and conflict. At the same time, non-narrative creative work uses central theme, concept, emotion, or a combination thereof to hold the work together.

Regardless of the type of creative writing we are reading—fiction, poetry, creative nonfiction, or hybrid; narrative or non-narrative; short or long; book-length or stand-alone; online or in-print—we need to remember that certain forces hold a piece of writing together. This lesson will discuss reading to explore those forces.

Narrative Forces

Let us begin with narrative, and let us not forget that narrative includes fiction, narrative creative nonfiction, narrative poetry, and hybrids that are narrative in nature. Beginning here means we begin with plot and narrative arc. While it's easy to think of plot and narrative arc only in terms of fiction, it is important to remember that plot and narrative arc are important craft elements of narrative creative nonfiction and narrative poetry, too.

Plot

I feel a bit silly writing out a definition of plot because we probably all already know what plot is. To make things official, though, plot is the series of events that happen in a narrative and continue to happen as one event triggers responses from the characters, which, in turn, trigger more events.

When we read for plot, we read to study the way the writer constructs the plot. All narrative writers do this, including narrative nonfiction writers. In fiction, the writer invents the events and works them into a plot with a complete narrative arc. In creative nonfiction, the writer arranges the telling of true events into a compelling plot and recognizable narrative arc.

Narrative Arc

The narrative arc (also called the story arc) is the term many writers and literary scholars use to discuss the way the plot unfolds on the page. In traditional parlance, the narrative arc has five parts.

- Exposition (or Stasis): The setup for the story. Here the writer introduces all the important elements—main characters, setting, and the conflict that will shape the plot.

- Rising Action: The writer drives the story forward. Characters act in ways that stir the conflict. Events occur that change characters' lives or stand in the way of characters getting what they want.

- Climax: The writer brings the narrative to a crux. Something must happen, and it does. Characters make revelations. The plot comes to a boiling point. The characters and their situations cannot go on as they have; the moment of change arrives.

- Falling Action: The now-what? time in a narrative. The writer pushes the characters and plot on through the actions everyone must take and the events that will occur after the climax.

- Resolution (or Denouement): The end. Here the writer puts the final pieces into place, tying up loose ends and giving the reader a sense of closure.

One helpful technique in reading for plot and narrative arc is to draw out the plot as it unfolds on the narrative arc. Draw a long arc with the five points listed above, like this:

Narrative Arc

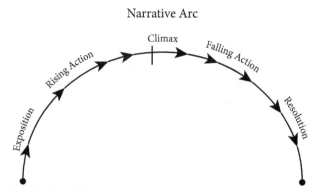

Figure 1 Narrative Arc Drawing.

Next, note what happens for each of the points in a narrative you are reading, like this:

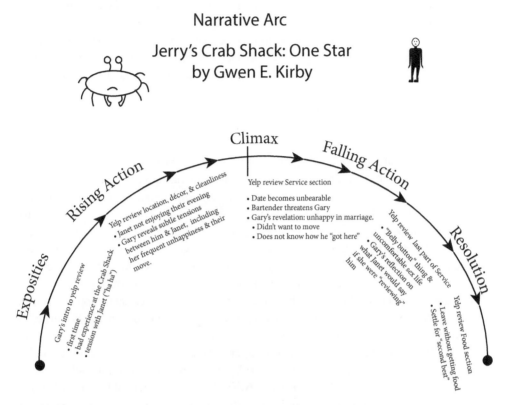

Figure 2 Drawing of the Narrative Arc for "Jerry's Crab Shack: One Star".

I drew this arc for Gwen E. Kirby's "Jerry's Crab Shack: One Star" in the Readings section. I don't draw very well, but you can see the important points on the narrative arc are here. Exposition: Gary's intro to his Yelp review—he just got on Yelp, he is unhappy with Jerry's Crab Shack, there is a tension there between him and his wife ("ha, ha"). Rising Action: the location, décor, and cleanliness sections of the Yelp review. Janet is not enjoying the restaurant Gary has selected, and Gary reveals the subtle tensions between them, including Janet's frequent unhappiness and their recent move. Climax: most of the service paragraphs of the Yelp review. Their date at Jerry's Crab Shack becomes unbearable. The bartender threatens Gary. Gary reveals how unhappy the marriage has become—he did not want to move; he doesn't know how he "got here." Falling Action: the end of the service section of the Yelp review. Gary explains the whole, uncomfortable "belly button" thing—their sex life is miserable. He imagines what Janet would say if she were reviewing him and reveals a key problem in their marriage. Resolution: the food section of the Yelp review. They leave before their food arrives. Gary decides they will settle for what they've got.

Other techniques for studying plot and narrative arc include highlighting or marking up each point as you read. Some reading writers do this as a matter of habit, assigning a color to each point and marking up the points in the designated colors for each text they read. A solid strategy that works for print and digital reading is to make notes about the narrative points. These notes can be color-coded too. Some reading writers even keep ongoing logs in which they make notes about plot and narrative arc for every narrative they read. Remember, a log doesn't have to mean on paper. Most of us can keep a log by opening a notes application in our phones or sending ourselves an email.

Whatever strategy you choose—one of these or one you invent for yourself—you want to pay careful attention to plot and narrative arc because studying how other writers create them will teach you how to create your own. You will also want to look for plot and narrative arc in all narrative genres.

Conflict

As a building block of plot, conflict begins when the narrative begins, or, as some writers may put it, conflict begins the narrative. Conflict also drives the narrative forward, and when the conflict ends, so does the story. Crafting conflict sounds simple but is not. Good narrative writers work and rework conflict, until they get it to a point where opposing forces are equal to each other—no one wants to read a narrative whose ending can be guessed from the start because one force is clearly poised to win over the other. Good narrative writers also keep working on conflict until it builds throughout the story, never going static, reaching the climax, then continuing—each character doing what he or she must—until the conclusion.

Reading for conflict, we also look for two kinds of conflict: internal (what is happening inside the character's own mind) and external (what happens to or with the character). The narratives included in this book are ripe with both kinds of conflict. Look, for example, at "Jerry's Crab Shack: One Star" (found in the Readings section) and "What You Learn in College" (found in Lesson 3, page 39). Within the first two paragraphs of each narrative, careful readers will see the conflicts characters have within themselves (what they should or should not do, what they wish were different in their own lives) and the conflicts in which they take part (where they go and what they've been through).

As a writer, you already know how difficult it can be to keep notching up the conflict. As a reading writer, read to see examples of how writers make conflict happen and continue to happen inside one narrative.

Reading for Plot, Narrative Arc, and Conflict

We've already drawn the narrative arc for "Jerry's Crab Shack: One Star." As we discuss the story now, we have to remember that while we are discussing a work of hybrid fiction, the concepts we discuss can be applied across narrative genres. This short story reminds us that plots do not have to revolve around large-scale mayhem or catastrophe. In this plot, no one finds his or her life in danger; indeed no big life events happen. But life is happening all the same. The relationship between the two main characters is unraveling in small ways, like relations sometimes do. The subtle plot includes revelations that show us how the characters came to be at this point in their relationship. No one has cheated or divulged a relationship-changing secret. Instead, the revelations show a different kind of unhappiness: Janet wanted to move. Gary, her husband, did not.

Study this excerpt from the "Service" section of "Jerry's Crab Shack: One Star" to see the ways the conflict is subtle and brilliantly worked.

Food took forty-five minutes. Or I should say: after forty-five minutes, things at the table had become tense. We were both tired and hungry. Moving is a lot of work. There have been more than a few nights spent eating leftover pizza on the floor because the new table we ordered online is stuck in a warehouse in St. Louis and even when my wife called the company and used her most terrifying voice they told her that we would have to wait, that they were working on it. We had both been looking forward to this dinner.

Are they sending someone out to catch the crabs first, Janet said, and I knew she was about to stand up and ask where our food was. So I got up first, to avoid making a scene. I hate drama in restaurants. I hate it a lot. I may have snapped at Janet before going over to the bar, but that was kind of on her, since she knows how much I hate when people bother waitresses who are just doing their jobs.

(You know, Janet has a lot of good qualities. I want to say that right now. This is not a review of my wife.)

If this were a review of my wife, I might review her based on:

1. Supportiveness
2. Empathy
3. Stability
4. Sense of humor
5. Physical appearance
6. Tolerance for me

Janet is supportive. When I wanted to go to graduate school for a masters in musicology, she said I should do it, and then she paid for it even though we weren't married yet. (Janet is a lawyer.) I think supporting her then–long term boyfriend's masters in musicology also speaks to her empathy, because when you tell people you are a musicologist they mostly look at you like you are insane or made your job up. She did not do that. She loves that I love music and that I work for Smithsonian Folkways, which is my dream job, and so what if I now live an hour-and-a-half commute away from that dream job and can't go out with coworkers after work because she wants to own a house, which we can't afford to do in DC, and have children.

Obviously, I want those things too.

Janet is very stable. You could call her a boulder. A flat-bottomed boulder. Not that she has a flat bottom. (Rating her on attractiveness I give her a 10++.) What I mean is, you couldn't roll her down a hill or something because she isn't that type of boulder. When she says she is going to do something, she does it. If she had said we were going to a nice restaurant, we would have shown up at Jerry's to discover a bodega with white linen and locally sourced cocktail bitters. Sometimes I think she simply wills things and people into line with the force of her mind.

She also has a wonderful sense of humor. When we walked into Jerry's Crab Shack and she saw the rubber crab, she smiled.

The only item about which I might have anything at all negative to say would be number 6) Tolerance for me, and really only tolerance for me lately. She is "all in" about our move to Baltimore. If I "had doubts," I should have "said something before we bought the goddamn house and moved all our shit up here." I don't disagree with that. She just doesn't see that I am both all in, in the sense that I am sure she knows what's best, and not all in, in the sense that I am not sure what will happen next or that I'll like it.

*Service (bar)

And here we get to the crux of the issue. I don't know where Jerry hires his bar staff, but they are the rudest, most unpleasant people on the face of the earth.

I walked over to the bar and asked the bartender, politely, when our food might be ready. And this bartender, someone obviously on work release from a local prison or recently kicked out of his biker gang for being too obnoxious even for them, tells me It'll be ready when it's ready. Then, he rather grudgingly looked over at the order-up window and said, soon probably. I realize that doesn't sound so bad. In retrospect, it seems pretty reasonable. But I could not go back to the table and tell Janet that the food would be out "soon probably." I needed a timetable. Or a reason the food was being so slow. A kitchen fire, a death in the chef's family, a sudden crab shortage sweeping the Chesapeake. I had already screwed up dinner. I was going to be assertive. This was the one thing I could do right for her. So I said, Can you go back and check? Or find our waitress? And he said, I've got a bar to tend, dude. Unless you want a drink, I got other customers to worry about. The other men at the bar were starting to look at me. I could see them judging me, for my suit and the way I hold myself, which I know is a little awkward. I have unusually long arms. I said, This is simply unacceptable, again, not because I felt that it was that unacceptable but because I wanted to make Janet happy. I think I asked to speak to Jerry. My voice may have gone up in volume. That was when the bartender said that I should sit the fuck down in my faggy DC suit and wait like everyone else. The other men sitting at the bar laughed that rumbling masculine chuckle, as if something funny had happened, and they laughed again when the bartender accused me of "blushing." I did not say anything back because there isn't anything to say to that kind of behavior. I absolutely do not regret not saying anything at that moment and simply walking back to my table.

I don't know what people in this city have against DC. Not everyone from DC is an asshole. And I'm not even from DC. I'm from Ohio.

It feels good to have gotten that off my chest. I don't want to lie to you, future Yelp reader. I feel like we are connecting, unburdening ourselves. I'll tell you a few more things. I am drinking a beer right now, my third, and it is only beginning to help. My wife went to sleep hours ago. I am sitting with my computer, the empty bottles, and a little lamp on the wooden floor of what will be the living room because I don't have a desk yet and I don't want to go upstairs. This isn't where I hoped I would be. I was hoping to have "an extra special" night. And by extra special, I mean I was hoping I would be having sex. There, I said it. I don't have a problem talking about natural acts between a man and his wife. Unlike the bartender, I am not so insecure about my sexuality that I have to resort to homophobic, inappropriate name-calling. It did not make me feel good to be called "faggy" in front of my wife. In fact, it made me feel shitty. I do not like that bartender's comment repeating in my head, or testing out ways I might have responded, things I might have said. Because again, I'm absolutely not sorry that I walked away.

I actually do have a problem talking about sex sometimes. I could say that I used a euphemism for sex because I didn't want to shock more conservative Yelp users by talking about the birds and bees and the beast with two backs, but the truth is, there are moments like right now when being a person in a body seems impossible. All the parts working in chorus, repetitive involuntary rhythms, a near miracle of coordination. Bodies are strange, so fleshy and pierceable. Sometimes when I am on my endless commute I think about the parts of my car which, in an accident, would be most likely to run me through. The steering column. The parking brake. A shard from the other car. I don't like to think about how thin a membrane my skin actually is, but once I get it in my head, it's hard to get it out. This is why I am upset about the loss of my CDs.

Janet is "all in" for the move, but perhaps not the relationship. Gary is not "all in" for the move, but longs for his wife, even though she is right beside him. Like the rest of this hybrid short story, the conflict unfolds in two ways: the visit to the restaurant itself and the deeper currents of conflict running through the marriage. (Look back at the narrative arc discussion to see how both unfold at once.) Here, too, we read to see internal and external conflict.

As the situation in the restaurant becomes more and more tense, the external conflict builds. When, in an effort to keep Janet happy, Gary approaches the bartender asking to speak to the owner, the conflict at the restaurant itself reaches a climax: "That was when the bartender said that I should sit the fuck down in my faggy DC suit and wait like everyone else. The other men sitting at the bar laughed that rumbling masculine chuckle, as if something funny had happened, and they laughed again when the bartender accused me of 'blushing.'" In this same section, the other external conflict—the crisis point in this marriage—reaches its own crux with the revelation that Gary moved out of DC because Janet pressured him to move.

We see the inner conflict also climax in the service discussion when Gary's Yelp review turns to his sex life. Here he confesses to any Yelper willing to read, "but the truth is, there are moments like right now when being a person in a body seems impossible." Who writes that in a Yelp review? Gary does. And he writes it because his internal conflict drives him to it.

Looking at creative nonfiction, we will see both types of conflict, too. Though sometimes we have to remind ourselves that true stories also have narrative arcs. The arcs in narrative creative nonfiction may often be more subtle than in fiction, and the points may not always be as clearly defined, but where there is narrative, there is narrative arc. Ripe with conflict, the arc in "What You Learn in College" follows both the game and the narrator's inner landscape as she remembers her participation in and then escape from the strip spin the bottle game.

As we study this excerpt of "What You Learn in College," let's remember that what we discuss here can also be applied to other genres.

You learn that although you loathe the taste of beer, you love intoxication, and it is possible to quickly drink through the loathing. You love the daring of your intoxicated self, the way you're not stymied by your own naiveté. You feel brave and worldly when you join your new college friends in a bawdy exchange thick with sexual innuendo and brag. You laugh along with them, these people who welcomed your sober self before ever meeting your intoxicated self. You laugh when they close the door against dorm-mates attracted to the banter, and you sit right down on the floor in a circle with them to play strip-spin-the-bottle.

You learn you are having fun, and you revel in your bravery and the way you're unperturbed by the first round or two of the game, during which you peel off your sweatshirt and toss it over your shoulder.

The bottle spins.

You learn you are perhaps not so intrepid as your beer-bravado led you to believe. A few more spins, the last of the beer-foam winging away from the lip of the bottle, and this strip-spin-the-bottle game is requiring more stripping than you expected. (What did you expect?). By the time the game spins you out of your shoes, socks, and finally your t-shirt, you have realized you are not really drunk at all anymore.

Notice the different currents of conflict running throughout the essay. The internal conflict shows the narrator wanting to participate in game, explaining, "You love the daring of your intoxicated self, the way you're not stymied by your own naiveté," and later, as the bottle continues to spin and the participants continue to undress, realizing she cannot continue, even if part of her wants to be the kind of person who does.

The external conflict comes from the game as "the bottle spins," and the players, including the narrator, lose more and more clothing. As the essay continues, the conflict intensifies by the external pressure of the "pennied," door. The narrator cannot leave; neither can anyone else.

The bottle spins

You learn you couldn't leave even if you had the nerve, because the disgruntled wanna-be-party-goers in the hallway have pennied the door, tiny rounds of copper wedging door against frame. You watch Ed, in his briefs, try to yank the door open then shrug and return to the circle of strippers. No one is leaving.

The bottle spins.

You learn that if, immediately after your turn, you laugh, comment about your head swimming, and climb onto Ed's bed, you can credibly feign a drunken blackout. You hope this will keep you from losing more clothing or anything else. You lie frozen on Ed's bed, the only escape you can think of, fake slumber through the hubbub, the clink of the bottle, the giggles and wolf-calls, the throbbing of your heart.

The bottle spins.

The internal and external conflicts crisscross as the narrator pretends to sink into "a drunken blackout," and stays that way as the game continues, despite the friends who try to bring her back to the game. "You lie frozen on Ed's bed, the only escape you can think of, fake slumber through the hubbub, the clink of the bottle, the giggles and wolf-calls, the throbbing of your heart." These lines show both the external and internal conflict, intertwined.

Because reflection is a crucial part of memoir, the arc doesn't end when "the party breaks up and the participants redress, unjam the pennied door, and disperse." Or even when the narrator pretends to wake up, puts her own clothes on and, "with appropriate stumbling and giggling, wobble[s] out the door." Reading on, we see how the arc extends to include her reflection. This is still written in present tense, indeed is told in the context of walking home that night, but it brings in the perspective of the wiser narrator, looking back on the experience. Read the last paragraphs.

You learn this is the last time you will make this walk across campus from Ed's room to yours. And with this learning, that almost-sentient regret breaches like some black-backed sea creature glittering in the night. You do not see it behind you any more than you saw your friends' nakedness. But just the same, you sense it as it slides away into the deep, beyond your sight. But the regret isn't gone. It will never be gone, and you don't need to learn that. You already know it.

Here Donley-Hayes leaves the immediate narrative time of the game and moves forward, sliding seamlessly into the regret that "will never be gone." But what is it she regrets? Here we see the exploration of the narrator's inner landscape as part of the arc. Is it participating in the game she regrets? The way it changed her feeling for Ed? Or her decision to back out of the game before it changed her life? Because Donley-Hayes gives no answers to these questions, careful readers see that she may regret a bit or all of it or is at least unsure which part the regret stems from.

As readers, it isn't that we think she should have stayed with Ed, a guy who makes comments like "Nice headlights," but in this reflection, we see the short memoir is not only about playing strip-spin-the-bottle, but also about the loss of possibilities that comes with certain decisions. This is a different way of closing the story and tying up loose ends than we often see in fiction. But it is the final point on the narrative arc.

Non-narrative Forces

While most readers enjoy a good narrative, we enjoy a good non-narrative too. Reading to study the forces that hold together non-narrative literature may not be as intuitive as reading for plot and narrative arc, but it is just as important. The trick here is remembering that something holds the poem or piece of creative nonfiction together, and that something will be an overarching theme or concept or an image that resonates with the reader as central to the piece. Often, emotion will be tied to the concept, theme, or image that sustains the piece.

While we often think of non-narrative forces as applying to poetry, they are part of non-narrative creative nonfiction as well.

Central Theme and Concept

The words "theme" and "concept" ring of academic writing, don't they? While they do work in that area of writing, they work on the creative side too. One piece of creative writing can be about anything, but not about everything. When writers read for central theme or concept, we are reading to determine what a piece is about. Read asking yourself what concepts or themes guide the piece or run throughout it. If you find more than one answer to that question, you are probably reading a piece that has more than one theme or concept running through it. One piece of creative writing can be about more than one related theme. When this happens, the themes will be conceptually connected in some way. Reading for central theme or concept applies to creative nonfiction and often to poetry as well.

Reading strategies for central theme and concept work in ways similar to those for plot and narrative arc. In this case, though, the first step is putting words to the central theme or concept. From there, readers can map out how that theme/concept connects the different paragraphs or smaller ideas inside the piece. Some readers write out the central theme/concept, then, make additional notes as they read, explaining how each idea touches on the central concept. When related themes/concepts guide a piece, readers can map out the places those themes intersect making notes on the ways the concepts relate to one another.

Resonating Image, Sense, or Emotion

We often associate resonating image with poetry, and for good reason. Poetry is often saturated with image. Evoking one image that will stay with the reader after reading the last lines is no small part of the work many poems do (but remember, resonating image, sense, or emotion can be part of the glue that holds any non-narrative form together).

Part of your work as the reader is to notice that image, figure out why it resonates, and how that resonance matters for the entire piece. After you read a poem, for example, pause for a moment to think of the image that sticks with you then read the poem again to recognize the way that image is central to the emotional and conceptual thrust of the poem.

Try this with Mary Oliver's "Lead."

Lead

Here is a story
to break your heart.
Are you willing?
This winter
the loons came to our harbor
and died, one by one,
of nothing we could see.
A friend told me
of one on the shore
that lifted its head and opened
the elegant beak and cried out
in the long, sweet savoring of its life
which, if you have heard it,
you know is a sacred thing,
and for which, if you have not heard it,
you had better hurry to where
they still sing.
And, believe me, tell no one
just where that is.
The next morning
this loon, speckled
and iridescent and with a plan
to fly home

to some hidden lake,
was dead on the shore.
I tell you this
to break your heart,
by which I mean only
that it break open and never close again
to the rest of the world.

The image that resonates is the dying loon. Reading the poem, we can see it—the way this bird, already lost, moves as death begins to take it, the way it looks when it is still. But why is this the image that resonates? First, it is part of the central message of the poem. It is the loons who are dying for reasons the speaker cannot identify. What she does name is the death of a bird that should have been flying back to its nesting place.

The dying loon is also the heartbreaking story Oliver promises in the beginning of the poem. Without the image of the dying loon, what would there be to grieve? This is the image that sticks. It is also the image that lets us do what Oliver is asking us to do. Keeping the image of the dying loon allows us to recognize how much of the natural world is getting destroyed in ways we will notice only if we are willing to look and keep looking. The resonating image of the loon keeps us looking, even after we have finished reading the poem.

Poetry often draws on other senses too. Sometimes what resonates in a poem is a sensory message other than a visual one. Look again at "Lead." We can see the loon but also hear its cry. While the cry is a sound, not a visual image, it sticks to us too. Just as important, we hear the loon and then we do not hear the loon. The loon's cry and the loss of the loon's cry almost become part of the central image because it is part of the dying loon. Here Oliver gives us a sensory experience that reaches beyond image and works to accomplish what she tells us she is going to do.

Sensory promptings can also lead a reader to emotion and to central concept. Joy Harjo's "Grace," for example, evokes the sense of cold and freezing alongside the "epic search for grace," as seen in the excerpt below.

I think of Wind and her wild ways the year we had nothing to lose
and lost it anyway in the cursed country of the fox. We still talk
about that winter, how the cold froze imaginary buffalo on the stuffed
horizon of snowbanks. The haunting voices of the starved and mutilated
broke fences, crashed our thermostat dreams, and we couldn't stand it
one more time. So once again we lost a winter in stubborn memory, walked
through cheap apartment walls, skated through fields of ghosts into
a town that never wanted us, in the epic search for grace.

Like Coyote, like Rabbit, we could not contain our terror and clowned
our way through a season of false midnights. We had to swallow
that town with laughter, so it would go down easy as honey. And one
morning as the sun struggled to break ice, and our dreams had found us
with coffee and pancakes in a truck stop along Highway 80,
we found grace.

Careful readers will feel the winters of suffering and the search for grace in the following sentences form Harjo's prose poem:

"We still talk about that winter, how the cold froze imaginary buffalo on the stuffed horizon of snowbanks."
"And one morning as the sun struggled to break ice, and our dreams had found us with coffee and pancakes in a truck stop along Highway 80, we found grace."

In these lines, as in the rest of the poem, the physical senses bring the reader to the emotional stakes and the underlying concepts of displacement and prejudice.

Looking for resonating image, sense, or emotion can also be part of reading non-narrative creative nonfiction, particularly in lyric essay, which has roots in poetry, as we discussed in the first two lessons. If one image, sense, or emotion resonates in creative nonfiction, that resonance will be connected to the central theme.

Reading for Central Theme/Concept and Resonating Image, Sense, or Emotion

As a place-based photo essay, "Hestur" fits into the category of literary work. Plot doesn't drive the piece, but a central theme does. At first glance, the theme is obvious: Hestur, one of the "storm-swept," Faroe Islands. Ward introduces this central theme as she writes the paragraphs to introduce the photos, and the photographs and captions all convey some aspect of life on the island. Study this excerpt of "Hestur: A Photo Essay."

Anxious to disembark, I went about gathering my luggage into a manageable pile on the rumbling car deck of Teistin. The ferry's hydraulics made a shrill yelp when the hull opened and the ramp began to lower, jouncingly, toward Hestur's deserted quay. The final crash of the heavy ramp striking rain-soaked concrete made me flinch, and then it hit me: I was the only person going ashore that afternoon. The rest of the passengers were waiting for the ferry to resume its course across Skopunarfjørð to the more populated island of Sandur.

A closer reading will bring out the subtler and more specific concept: the daily life and deep-rooted customs of this declining, twenty-person village, a village kept alive, even as it is dying, by these twenty remaining inhabitants and their loyalty to life in the place itself. Notice how that concept begins in the opening paragraph as the narrator describes, "Hestur's deserted quay," and her realization that she is "the only person going ashore that afternoon."

Ward works the concept into each of the following paragraphs, too, touching on Hestur's vital statistics, the village's farming and fishing culture, the residents who sustain the village down to its infrastructure, and her own involvement in the life of the village, explaining her "most tender act of solidarity was simply turning on [her] kitchen light of an evening so people could see [she] was still there."

Ward touches nuanced concepts inside this theme in each photograph and photo caption throughout the rest of the essay, too. This is visible in the photo and caption excerpts below.

Ull er Føroya Gull

There are approximately 580 sheep grazing the island of Hestur. Long before the fishing industry emerged, woolen goods were one of the main staples of the Faroe Islands' economy. Wool, however, is no longer considered "Faroese gold"; its market value is so low that people often burn it rather than selling or processing it into yarn.

Tea for Two

Hjørleiv Poulsen is photographed in the kitchen of his home where he lives alone on Hestur. Fewer than 20 people live on the island year-round, and no more children attend school in the village.

The People's Church
Around 80% of the Faroese population belongs to the state's Evangelical Lutheran Church,
Fólkakirkjan. The village church in Hestur celebrated its centennial in 2011.

The photographs portray both the isolation of life on Hestur and the intense personal connections its inhabitants have to each other and to the ways of life on the island. The photographs depict vast windswept expanses of land and sea juxtaposed with a close up of one elderly man (a significant percentage of Hestur's population) and the sheep that are integral to village life. Studying the photos in the context of central theme, readers will see how each picks up on an aspect of the theme that guides the essay. Notice, too, how Ward uses the words in the captions to expand on those aspects giving the reader more information than is visible in the photographs, nuanced bits of information about Hestur, its inhabitants and traditions.

The photograph of the church, for example, shows the building against darkened land and a darkening ocean, its windows alight and outlines villagers gathered inside. Reading the caption, we understand further details about this church (it is Lutheran, it is the village church, and it is over one hundred years old) that provide context for the photo and explain more about the traditions of this desolate island village.

Central concept also provides a cohesive force in poetry. Central concept guides the poem "Sixteen Ways Old People Terrify the Young." The poem plays with the very idea that young people are afraid of old people, even as it pricks at the more serious idea of living in fear of our own aging. As a hybrid poem, its form itself engages with a concept because that's what top-ten lists do, explain ten aspects of whatever concept is named in the list. (Though in this case, the list is sixteen items long.)

Sixteen Ways Old People Terrify the Young

1. They have sex with each other.

2. They drive around.

3. They pretend they're thinking. They pretend they're not thinking about dying.

4. The vigor of diving through the waves (through time) or the splash of the body sprinting toward love. What's a sea, if not for swimming.

5. And what about those old people who walk—I don't know— like seventy-nine miles every morning on the beach? Skin cancer! Yo! They're going to die.

6. "Vex not his ghost: O, let him pass! he hates him

   That would upon the rack of this tough world

   Stretch him out longer" (*Lear*, 5.3.315-17).

7. It's a lie: they were never young.

8. Holidays were invented by old people to dress up and pretend they're all presents for young people.

9. The arc of Story graphed upon the axes of Love and Death.

10. They actually invented the computer.

11. Oh, and they wrote the poems.

12. Their whacked-out sense of sound. No guitars or headphones, no cars or guns; just TV commercials on MUTE, telephones, cats, and the sky.

13. It's like grout or glue or maybe gum. Whatever holds those bones together.

14. They like to die.

15. They like to die in big buildings surrounded by other people. Although occasionally, one of them will take off—to die in the woods or at the beach, some place far away—which accounts for the better old people movies.

16. Or they just die, one on the beach, just like today. With only three people there in the winter to see. A body.

See how each numbered entry lands on a new aspect of the concept ("1. They have sex with each other." "2. They drive around.") or takes a different look at an aspect already stated (10. "They actually invented the computer." 11. "Oh, and they wrote the poems.")

See too how a sensory message resonates in entries 4 and 16. Part image and part tactile feeling, these entries both take a different view of an aspect already stated and leave the reader with the image and the sense: "the vigor of diving through the waves," the "body" on the beach.

Lesson 4 Discussion Questions and Writing Prompts

Discussion Questions: Focus on Plot, Narrative Arc, Conflict, Central Theme, and Resonating Image

1. Draw the narrative arcs for Beth Uznis Johnson's "Negative Results" (found in Lesson 3, page 41) and Erin Pushman's "They Point at Her Face and Whisper" (found in the Readings section). Be as creative as you like and include as many details as you need to show the shape of the arc. Compare the narrative pieces, explaining how each arc unfolds on the page and exploring the differences.

2. Study the conflict in Chang-rae Lee's essay, "Sea Urchin," and Sophie Yanow's graphic novel, *The Contradictions* (both found in the Readings section). Consider what was different between exploring conflict in an essay and in a graphic narrative. Using these two readings as examples, identify the differences and similarities between reading for conflict in narrative prose and graphic narrative.

3. Reread Joy Harjo's "Grace" (found in Lesson 2, page 27). Name the central concept guiding this prose poem and identify the central image. Next, explain what the image accomplishes inside the poem. How does it move you, the reader, into a deeper understanding of the central concept? How does it work with the sensory detail Harjo uses in the poem? And why does the image stick to you even after you finish reading the piece? (If you think there is more than one important image that sticks, explain how they work together within the poem.)

Writing Prompts: Focus on Plot, Narrative Arc, Conflict, Central Theme, and Resonating Image

Generative Prompt

Option 1: Think about a character in a narrative you have in mind or one you are working on now. (In creative nonfiction, this character may also be the narrator.) First, write one sentence to describe a moment of intense conflict for a character. Now, make a list of the external pressures coming to bear on the character in this moment. Then write a list of internal pressures that will influence how the character acts and reacts. Now come back to the sentence you started with and widen that moment. As you write, use some of the conflict ideas you noted in the lists.

Option 2: Consider a central theme for a piece you'd like to write. Write it out in words. If you are writing poetry, experiment with using words that will evoke an image. Now narrow in to explore one aspect of that theme. Write one paragraph of prose or two lines of poetry dealing with that aspect. Next, write a paragraph or lines to develop another related aspect.

Revision Prompt

Option 1: Pull out a narrative for which you have completed a rough draft. Draw out its narrative arc. Study the arc reflecting on the way you have created the conflict and the plot. Consider these questions as you reflect: Are there any gaps? Are there places where points on the narrative arc are too close together? Is the conflict clear for each point? Does the reader know what is at stake throughout the narrative? Revise based on what you figured out while reflecting on the narrative arc.

Option 2: Pull out a poem or piece of non-narrative creative nonfiction in need of revision. Write out the central theme then map out the concepts in relationship to the theme. Revise to pull out any passages that do not connect to the central theme in compelling ways. Next, work to create a resonating image. (Do this even if you are writing prose instead of poetry. It will only make the piece stronger.)

LESSON 5
STRUCTURE

The Concept of Structure

Structure can be one of the most difficult concepts to wrap our minds around when we read—and one of the most difficult elements of the craft to get right when we write. Approaching structure as readers, we often forget that the writing didn't just fall out onto the page as we see it in published form. Reading like writers, though, we must remember how hard writers work to craft the structure of a piece. For writers, structural decisions are deliberate. So studying structure becomes a deliberate part of reading as writers, too.

In the simplest terms, structure is the way the writing appears on the page or screen. This includes the organization or order in which ideas present themselves, the shape of the piece, structural patterns or techniques, and structural mechanics.

Structural Mechanics and Devices

We are going to begin with the last item on the list above. This may be an unusual structural choice, but it is a deliberate one. Before we can discuss structure in larger ways, we need to start with structural mechanics writer use on the page and screen: whitespace, paragraphs, stanza breaks, section breaks, and chapters.

Whitespace

One of the most basic elements of structure is also the element most often ignored by readers: whitespace. Whitespace is the space on the page or screen in which there is neither text nor image. A simpler way to say this is that whitespace means the blank space on a page or screen. (Note that the same concept applies if you are reading page or screen that has a background appearing in color.)

Take a look at this page. Where do you see whitespace? If you are thinking margins, you are right. Margins make a page look neat but have more to do with printing than with structure. Where else is the whitespace?

Paragraph Breaks

Yes! What paragraph breaks do is provide whitespace. When we notice a paragraph break, we are not so much noticing the words as noticing the whitespace around them. Paragraphs are a signal to readers that one thought has finished or is about to change enough to need a pause before moving on. When writers give the reader a paragraph break, you know a shift in thought is taking place.

When a bigger shift happens, writers use more white space between paragraphs. Look at the whitespace between this paragraph and the one below it. More space. Longer pause. Bigger shift. Writers have many reasons for making bigger shifts. Indicating passages of or shifts in time, moving between points of view, and transitioning to new plot or character developments are only three examples. Another is what you see between this paragraph and the one below it: a conceptual shift. Regardless of the reason, what you must understand is this: Whitespace is crucial because it makes the reader pause and queues the reader to realize a shift of some kind is happening.

White Space in Graphic Narrative and Photo Essay

Whitespace is a part of visual hybrids, too. In visual work, though, the whitespace may be a different color. Remember that space surrounds photographs and separates them from the text. Also remember the term "gutter," from our graphic narrative discussion. While the gutters may not be white, they do separate panels from each other.

When you think about it, though, you already know how to identify the other structural mechanics creative writers use in poetry and prose. Poets often break poems into stanzas. Essayists and short story writers use larger section breaks when paragraph breaks aren't enough. Creative nonfiction and fiction writers often break books into chapters and sometimes break chapters into sections. Yes, yes, as a reader, you identify all of this. As a reading writer, you work to figure out why the paragraph, stanza, section, or chapter breaks come when they do and how the writer uses them and the white space that surrounds them to move the reader from one part to the next.

Stanza Breaks, Section Breaks, Chapter Breaks

Whitespace is also part of other structural devices that break up and organize text for the reader. Pay attention to the role whitespace plays in each. Think about the last book-length work of creative writing you have read. Chances are the writer organized the writing into more than paragraphs. Stanza, section, and chapter breaks all provide a way for writers to divide the text into smaller portions the reader can digest one at a time. This is another idea that seems so obvious, we often forget to pay attention to it as we read. But we need to pay attention anyway. When we do, we'll notice, for example, that the whitespace between this paragraph and the one above it is also accompanied by a heading that denotes a section break.

Overall Structure: The Order in Which the Writing Appears on the Page

Aside from the mechanics, we also think of structure as the order in which the writer puts the writing together. Often-given advice in creative workshops is that all narratives have a beginning, a middle, and an end, but not necessarily in that order. When writers read narrative work for structure, they are also reading to understand the way the plot or narrative arc unfolds on the page.

We discussed the narrative arc in Lesson 4. Even before reading the lesson, though, this traditional explanation of the narrative arc probably seemed familiar to you. While you want to grasp this concept of narrative arc as a cornerstone concept of structure, it is important to know that contemporary creative writers are working this arc in all sorts of compelling and nontraditional ways. Also, don't forget that the narrative arc can work for narrative poetry and creative nonfiction, too. Narrative structures are at work inside all narratives, regardless of the genre: fiction, creative nonfiction, poetry, and hybrid.

So we are back to the idea that all stories (in all genres) have a beginning, a middle, and an end, but not necessarily—or only—in that order. In other words, there are times when the parts of a narrative that seem like a beginning, a middle, and an end might not show up where you would expect to find them on a traditional narrative arc. As an example, think back to the opening sentences I played around with in Lesson 1. "When I was six years old, I killed my sister with a gun I did not know how to shoot." If this were the opening sentence of a novel, we might find that the writer was beginning with the middle of the story. A narrative that began here might also be expected to back up and tell the story of how the six-year-old found her way to the gun and later move on to the aftermath.

As writers shape their work, they select or invent a structure that guides the piece through the narrative arc. Structure can range from the simple to the complex, and, like genre, can run the gamut from easy to define to not-so-easy. While we can't discuss every structural possibility in one lesson, we can cover some common structures.

Let's remember that the following structures can be found in narratives in any genre, including hybrids. These structures can also be applied to non-narrative creative nonfiction and poetry (as we will briefly discuss later in this lesson).

Liner

In a linear structure, the story unfolds in one narrative arc and in a straightforward, beginning, middle, then end sort of a way. If a non-narrative essay or poem has a linear structure, the central concept will be presented in a straightforward, linear way. Many readings in this book have linear structures, including "Sea Urchin," "What You Learn in College," "Grace," "Cartography," "They Point at Her Face and Whisper," "Negative Results," "The Embassy of Cambodia," "Hestur: A Photo Essay," and *The Contradictions*. Others, like "Jerry's Crab Shack: One Star," take a linear structure even as they also borrow another. Notice how these readings represent each genre.

Linear structures are also often chronological, in that they follow the order of events happening in time. However, some narratives with linear structures unfold in one narrative arc but are not necessarily organized around the order of events happening in time. "They Point at Her Face and Whisper" is one example from the Readings. While chronology is present, the blog post come essay is not married to chronology. Instead, it is guided by a central theme presented in a linear way throughout the narrative. At the same time, some writers would say all linear structures have an element of chronology, which is true in most cases. Important to remember, though, is the idea that a linear structure does not always have to stick to chronology.

If we drew a linear structure, it might look something like this.

Figure 3 Linear Structure Drawing.

Chronological

Chronological structures are the most often used linear structure. They follow the order of time, beginning, middle, and end in that order. Though some chronological structures also have more than one narrative arc or move around in more than one chronology. These chronological structures will be more complex than those with one narrative arc or one chronology. Two examples of chronological structures in the readings for this book are "Sea Urchin" and "What You Learn in College."

Flashback is a structural technique writers sometimes use when they are working inside of a chronological structure and need to go backward in narrative time to show the reader something important. Narrative time is the clock or calendar as it is running from the beginning of the narrative to the ending. So flashbacks deal with important happenings that occurred before the current narrative time in the story or—often—before the story began. In "The Embassy of Cambodia," Zadie Smith employs flashback when Fatou remembers her time working in the Carib Beach hotel and the way she met the Devil there. If we drew a chronological structure, it might look something like this.

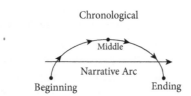

Figure 4 Chronological Structure Drawing.

Braided

Braided structures weave several narrative arcs together into one piece of writing. In non-narrative forms, the braided structure weaves several central concepts or images. Imagine braiding together three different lengths of string to make one bracelet. That is the idea behind braided writing structures. Braiding doesn't have to mean three strands. Braided writing can have as many strands as the writer can manage. Braided structures can also serve non-narrative creative nonfiction or prose poetry. When writers braid non-narrative work, they are braiding conceptual or emotional threads. In braided work, writers use whitespace to separate strands. Sometimes the whitespace is accompanied by brief text to help cue the reader. "Cuttings" is an example of a braided structure that

Braided – or – Braided

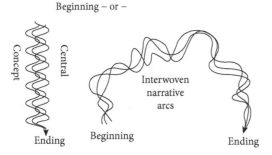

Figure 5 Braided Structure Drawing.

uses brief text (a,b,c,d) to cue the reader. If we drew a braided structure, it might look something like this. Braided structures are found more often in creative nonfiction.

Segmented

Segmented (or collage) structures pull segmented concepts or bits of narrative together to form a whole from diverse parts. Many writers would say that segmented structures are more push than pull because segmented prose often thrusts ideas or narratives up against each other. The very butting of ideas against each other helps make meaning in the segmented essay. Writers use whitespace in segmented structures too. The whitespace gives the reader a pause between segments and sometimes serves as a transition. As with braided work, the whitespace may or may not accompany bits of text. Many writers include braided structures under the umbrella of segmented structures. Segmented structures show up more in creative nonfiction than in other genres. (Check out the literary journals *The Fourth Genre*, *Creative Nonfiction*, *Zone 3*, and *Brevity* to read compelling prose in segmented structures.) If we drew a segmented structure, it might look something like this. Segmented structures are found more often in creative nonfiction.

Segmented or Collage

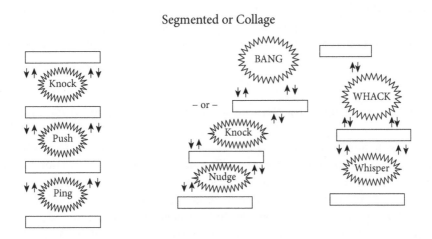

Figure 6 Segmented Structure Drawing.

Borrowed Structures

Some creative pieces, particularly hybrids, borrow their structures from other forms of writing or media. Since we've already discussed some of them in Lesson 2, you know "Jerry's Crab Shack: One Star," "Sixteen Ways Old People Terrify the Young," and "Cuttings" borrow structures from other forms of writing, Yelp reviews, lists, and outlines, respectively. Notice too, how "Cuttings" pulls from several structural concepts. Many borrowed structures use whitespace, including the list and outline forms. If we draw borrowed structures, they would probably take on the shape of whatever form they were borrowing, like this.

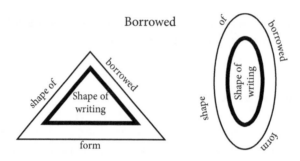

Figure 7 Borrowed Structure Drawing.

Other Structures

As you read beyond the pages of this book, you will encounter structures beyond those I've noted here. Some of them will be hard to define, like the spiraling structure Nick Flynn uses in *Another Bullshit Night in Suck City*. Some you may notice emerging on the literary scene, like the novel-in-stories approach Elizabeth Strout takes with *Olive Kitteridge*. When you read a piece structured in a way you cannot immediately name, pay attention to how it is working, and see if you can frame a definition in your own words.

Additional Considerations for Non-narrative Creative Nonfiction Structures

Reading for structure in non-narrative work means studying structure to see how the writer places concepts or emotions on the page. Non-narrative creative nonfiction, including creative nonfiction hybrids, often uses the structures noted above, arranging the structure around concept rather than narrative. Non-narrative prose will sometimes also borrow from structures we traditionally consider to be academic in nature, like argumentative or comparison and contrast. Sometimes non-narrative creative nonfiction borrows other non-narrative structures, including letters, field notes, reflections, and rants. To find non-narrative essays and graphic essays in a variety of structures, check out *Buzzfeed, Salon,* and *Creative Nonfiction,* or the *Modern Love* column from *The New York Times.*

Additional Considerations for Poetic Structures

Poetry may use any of the structures we have already discussed. Some writers would say that by poetry's nature, it often uses segmented structures. Narrative poetry will often follow linear or chronological structures. As you read through poems on your own, you will discover poems that follow braided structures or borrowed structures (like "Sixteen Ways Old People Terrify the Young").

Poetry also works in a number of structures specific to the type, or form, of the poem. We cannot cover each poetic structure in this lesson, but when writers read poetry, we should always be looking to see if the poem is structured into a specific form. When poets write according to a specific form of poetry, the structure dictates the form of the poem. For example, a poem can be a **sonnet** only if it is written in fourteen lines. And a sonnet can be a **traditional sonnet** only if those lines are written in iambic pentameter. To be a **hiku**, a poem must be written in three lines of five, seven, and five syllables. Some poetic structures, like villanelle, are so complicated that writing them becomes its own special challenge. Beautiful to read and tricky to write, **villanelle** contains nineteen lines with specific and strict rhyme scheme patterns and a series of repetitions and refrains.

Free verse poetry happens when a poem does not follow a specific poetic structure, rhyme scheme, or metrical rhythm. Though rhyming may emerge as organic to the poem. Mary Oliver's "Lead" (found on page 12) is an example of free verse poem with some rhyming. Free verse poetry can include as many or as few lines as the poet needs to convey the message. Free verse poems may also take on any of the structures discussed earlier in this lesson. Many contemporary poets write in free verse.

Line breaks serve as a critical part of poetic structure. When reading poetry, pay attention to the line breaks. If a poet is following a specific structure, like those mentioned above, the poet will break the lines accordingly. Poets writing in free verse break lines to emphasize ideas, images, and emotions or to work with patterns of sound or speech. At the same time, poetry written in the prose form needs a sort of inverse consideration of line breaks. In prose poetry, we read reflecting on how the lack of line breaks influences the poem. Line breaks or the lack of line breaks in prose poetry also create the shape of the poem on the page. Imagine a poem with line breaks that shape the lines to look like this: _____

The line breaks make the poem look neat, orderly, symmetrical, even smooth on the page. Now imagine a poem with line breaks like this looks sharp, uneven, and jagged on the page.

_____

_____

_____

_____

_____

_____

_____

Each poem's shape gives a feeling on the page. A jagged poem feels different than an orderly one.

In writing workshops, poets dedicate significant time to discussing the placement of line breaks. Reading poetry as writers, we need to do the same. This applies to the prose writers among us, too. Beyond appreciating this key structural aspect of poetry, reflecting on line breaks gives writers insight into structure for other genres. (When you do get to a piece of your own writing that needs work with structure, try taking a break from your own manuscript for a few days and studying the line breaks in poetry. While I cannot give you a step-by-step recipe for the alchemy that happens when writers study the line breaks in poetry and gain insight into structuring their work in other genres, it seems to help, nevertheless.) We will discuss reading for line breaks a little more thoroughly later in this lesson.

Authorial Choices about Structure

There is a relationship between the structure of a piece of creative writing and the content. Imagine, for example, a hiku. Writing a poem in only three lines and a total of seventeen syllables influences the poem's content. How a poet writes about a subject in seventeen syllables will be different than how a poet writes about a subject in free verse, where the form does not govern the number of lines or syllables.

The relationship between structure and content in prose works the same way. If a writer wants to bring more than one central concept into an essay or more than one narrative arc into a narrative, the writer will engage in braided or segmented structures. This is what Vivian Bikulege does in her essay "Cuttings." She pulls these seemingly disparate pieces together into one essay. She could not have done so with a linear structure. Braided and segmented (or collage) structures give writers space to bring together ideas or narratives they could not otherwise include in one piece.

Ditto for content and structure in hybrid works. Writing about a place in a photo essay, as Randi Ward does in "Hestur: A Photo Essay" structured with a textual introduction, photographs, and captions, influences the content. Gwen E. Kirby's hybrid story "Jerry's Crab Shack: One Star" is another stunning example of the relationship structure has to content. In the form of a Yelp review, Kirby has to follow a specific structure. Following the structure opens the piece into something unexpected. Notice what Kirby can accomplish in the structure of a Yelp review that she might not have been able to pull off in a traditional story of one evening.

Reading for Structure

Reading narrative work, we want to explore the relationship between plot, narrative arc, and overall structure. Reading non-narrative work, we want to study the relationship between concept or emotion and overall structure. One way to do this is to draw or map the structure of a piece. Your drawings may look similar to those included earlier in this lesson, or you may find your own ways to draw or map structures.

Drawing and mapping structure now as a reader will help you when you work on the structure of your writing, too. Many good writers also draw out the narrative arcs or map out the structures for their work. Though not always before we've started writing. Some of us, especially those who use non-linear structures, have even been known to print our work out, cut it up, and move the pieces around like a puzzle.

Structure will never be a one-size-fits-all sort of a thing, especially in literary work. Reading for structure means keeping an eye out for structures you have not seen before or have not seen often. As you make your own must-read list, try to incorporate pieces with funky structures then write those structures out. When drawing or mapping structure for a work you read leads you to create a nuanced image, you will know you are reading a piece with a nuanced structure—good for you.

Transitions

In writing terms, you may associate the word "transition" with academic essays, which is unfortunate because the academic writing concept of transitions leads writers to transitional words or phrases like "in addition to," "on the other hand," "furthermore," "conversely"—blah, blah, blah. These words provide connective material readers of academic work expect—a well-trodden bridge from here to there.

In creative writing, we think of transitions in a broader sense. Transitions in creative writing happen any time and in any way a writer moves the reader from one idea or space on the page to the next. Studying transitions in any genre will help us consider transitions in all genres.

Creative writers transition in ways that are more, well, creative and less formal. Creative writers also try to avoid all well-trodden bridges. The bridges will be narrow, bumpy, swinging, or interesting in some other way. Sometimes creative writers use transitions that involve whitespace with numbers, letters, words, or other textual markers. Look through "Jerry's Crab Shack: One Star" in our Readings section. In this hybrid short story, Kirby uses white space along with asterisks and other textual markers—the categories found in Yelp reviews—*Location, *Décor, *Cleanliness, *Service, *Food.

Sometimes writers use repetition to transition. A quick skim through the essay "What You Learn in College" (found in Lesson 3, page 39) will show you that Donley-Hayes uses a repeated phrase, surrounded by whitespace, to transition throughout most of her short essay, as shown in this excerpt.

The bottle spins

You learn you couldn't leave even if you had the nerve, because the disgruntled wanna-be-party-goers in the hallway have pennied the door, tiny rounds of copper wedging door against frame. You watch Ed, in his briefs, try to yank the door open then shrug and return to the circle of strippers. No one is leaving.

The bottle spins.

You learn that if, immediately after your turn, you laugh, comment about your head swimming, and climb onto Ed's bed, you can credibly feign a drunken blackout. You hope this will keep you from losing more clothing or anything else. You lie frozen on Ed's bed, the only escape you can think of, fake slumber through the hubbub, the clink of the bottle, the giggles and wolf-calls, the throbbing of your heart.

The bottle spins.

"The bottle spins." The next paragraph begins with, "You learn." And the reader moves seamlessly from one passage to the next, understanding that narrative time is moving as the game continues.

Sometimes writers decide to forgo bridges altogether and create transitions that do not involve text at all but use only white space. Look at the stanza breaks in poetry or at any paragraph break in prose where there is more than the usual amount of space between two paragraphs. Segmented essays often work this way. The transition is the whitespace. The essay woks because different ideas are pushed against each other.

Creative transitions will also use words that grow organically from the piece itself. Look again at "Jerry's Crab Shack: One Star." The Yelp categories are organic to the piece. So are the longer transitions. When the narrator transitions from reviewing the service to reviewing his wife, Kirby transitions with these two brief paragraphs.

(You know, Janet has a lot of good qualities. I want to say that right now. This is not a review of my wife.)

If this were a review of my wife, I might review her based on:

1. Supportiveness
2. Empathy
3. Stability
4. Sense of humor
5. Physical appearance
6. Tolerance for me

Here we see a transition that feels organic to the story. It is awkward, but its awkwardness is part of the story of the Yelp review it is pretending to be. (If you have trouble thinking of transitions beyond academic terms, imagine how much fun Kirby must have had writing the transitions for "Jerry's Crab Shack: One Star.")

Whatever the case, another part of reading for structure is reading to see how writers move the reader from one place in a text to the next. Those places may involve shifts in narrative time, scenes, concepts, emotions, strands, segments, or any other space that requires the reader to make connections between the end of one line or paragraph and the beginning of another.

Shape

In poetry and in some hybrid work, part of reading for structure is looking at shape. The shape a poem makes on the page is part of its structure. Flip or scroll through the pomes offered in a literary magazine to see how poems can be shaped into measured, even lines and stanzas (sonnets and villanelles are only two examples) or into lines and stanzas that are uneven or jagged. Whatever the shape, that shape is part of the poem's structure. Shape influences the way readers consume poems.

Look again at Mary Oliver's "Lead."

Lead

Here is a story
to break your heart.
Are you willing?
This winter
the loons came to our harbor
and died, one by one,
of nothing we could see.
A friend told me
of one on the shore
that lifted its head and opened
the elegant beak and cried out
in the long, sweet savoring of its life
which, if you have heard it,
you know is a sacred thing,
and for which, if you have not heard it,
you had better hurry to where
they still sing.
And, believe me, tell no one
just where that is.
The next morning
this loon, speckled
and iridescent and with a plan
to fly home
to some hidden lake,
was dead on the shore.
I tell you this
to break your heart,
by which I mean only
that it break open and never close again
to the rest of the world.

Reading poetry, we read the words and we read the shape of the lines. In Mary Oliver's "Lead," for example, the lines are jagged, even sharp. If the shape of a poem could wound, this one would. As the speaker of the poem shows us the dying birds and invites us to open ourselves to grieving them, the lines seem to prick the page. As we have discussed in previous lessons, the language of "Lead" is calm and written in complete sentences—a quiet, calm sadness. But in these jagged lines, we also see the sharp urgency. Read the shape of this poem to let it break you, the way Oliver invites you to be broken.

In a related, but different, way, prose poetry can raise emotional stakes with its paragraphed shape. Look again at Joy Harjo's "Grace," which remembers the racism inherent in the American academic system when Harjo was earning her MFA in creative writing.

"Grace"

I think of Wind and her wild ways the year we had nothing to lose
and lost it anyway in the cursed country of the fox. We still talk
about that winter, how the cold froze imaginary buffalo on the stuffed
horizon of snowbanks. The haunting voices of the starved and mutilated
broke fences, crashed our thermostat dreams, and we couldn't stand it
one more time. So once again we lost a winter in stubborn memory, walked
through cheap apartment walls, skated through fields of ghosts into
a town that never wanted us, in the epic search for grace.

Like Coyote, like Rabbit, we could not contain our terror and clowned
our way through a season of false midnights. We had to swallow
that town with laughter, so it would go down easy as honey. And one
morning as the sun struggled to break ice, and our dreams had found us
with coffee and pancakes in a truck stop along Highway 80,
we found grace.

I could say grace was a woman with time on her hands, or a white
buffalo escaped from memory. But in that dingy light it was a promise
of balance. We once again understood the talk of animals, and spring
was lean and hungry with the hope of children and corn.

I would like to say, with grace, we picked ourselves up and walked
into the spring thaw. We didn't; the next season was worse. You went
home to Leech Lake to work with the tribe and I went south. And, Wind,
I am still crazy. I know there is something larger than the memory
of a dispossessed people. We have seen it.

(For Wind and Jim Welch)

Notice the images Harjo writes into the poem and the way she creates them with emotionally charged language paired with everyday terms: "The haunting voices of the starved and mutilated broke fences, crashed our thermostat dreams, and we couldn't stand it one more time." She packs this language and these images into paragraphs. Written paragraphs, themselves, are an inherent part of the academic system. Paragraphs are the structural opposite of broken fences. See how the prose structure and paragraph shape change the way you read the poem and heighten, even bring into focus, the theme of Native American writers struggling in an academic system that privileges the majority? As a reader, you may want to break out of the lines, but because they are structured into a paragraph, you cannot.

Image and Text

When hybrid work pairs image and text, savvy readers study both the arrangement of the images and the arrangement of the text and the images together. In photo essay, notice whether the writer organizes the essay into paragraphs of text punctuated by photographs or a textual introduction followed by images. In "Hestur: A Photo Essay," Ward writes a textual introduction to the series of images. She also writes captions for the photos. The structure keeps the photo essay closer to the roots of photojournalism, which is to say the images are given a lot of room to stand on their own. Notice, too, how the captions often provide just a little more information than is visible in the photographs. Ward allows the images to do most of the work, while using the structure of a brief introduction followed by photographs with captions also gives Ward the space she needs to give the reader enough words to understand.

In graphic prose, pay attention to the way the panels are arranged, where the text appears, and how much text accompanies each image. Notice the differences in the excerpts of three different pages of *The Contradictions*.

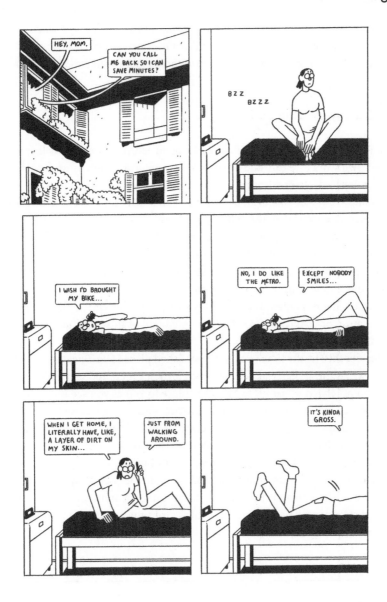

Some panels take an entire page, and some are arranged in several tiers on one page. Some panels are framed, and some are open. Some are circular while most are not. Some panels have captions; some have speech bubbles; some include no words at all. These are all part of the structural choices Yanow is making.

Sophie Yanow pulls her readers into this graphic novel with a large panel that consumes the entire first page, enveloping the reader in the stark, black and white image without any words. By the third page, one panel with two separate images divides the space of the page, and captions begin to reflect Sophie's thinking. Notice the way images and words accumulate on the page as the narrative continues. By page six, three tiers of panels show one conversation Sophie has with her mother. Here we engage in the details—one framed panel per detail. The details come to us in the drawings, including different parts of the figure of Sophie, the speech bubbles, and sound effects. See how we move from a broad picture of where Sophie is and her mindset to a specific series of actions and details during a phone conversation with her mother? This shows us the authorial and artistic choices Yanow makes about structure.

Reading Strategy for Structure

As writers, we read for structure because studying structure as we read will teach us how to structure our own work. We can study structure by paying attention as we read, but even more important is going back after we finish a reading to look again at its structure. Only after we finish an entire reading can we see all the parts inside the whole. To learn about structure from the work we read, we have to see how the breaks, the white space, the overall structure, the transitions, the shape, the arrangement on the page, and all of the other parts inside the whole fit together.

If rereading for structure doesn't work with your mojo, try reading for structure by first skimming the piece and looking *only* for the structure. Without reading enough to understand what the piece is about, skim to see where the whitespace shows up, where there are textual transitions, where there is repetition (especially surrounded by whitespace), and whether there are section, stanza, or chapter breaks. Make a note of all of this and then read the piece fully, paying attention to structure as you go.

Also, consider this: by the time you read a published piece of writing, the parts are no longer moving, but while the writer was writing, each structural component was fluid. The writer made a myriad of related decisions to bring the piece to you as you see it shaped on the page.

Let's explore reading for structure by studying two works from our Readings section, Vivian I. Bikulege's "Cuttings," which appears in its entirety, and a long excerpt of Zadie Smith's "The Embassy of Cambodia." We will look at portions of the works here.

We've already discussed Vivian I. Bikulege's "Cuttings" as an example of a braided essay, which can also be called a segmented essay. Bikulege divides her essay into four strands then braids those strands together evenly, weaving back and forth and back, as you would do if you were braiding strands of hair. The effect of this word braiding is lovely and complicated, as evidenced in the excerpt below.

---

1 Bits

A.

There is a snapshot in the archives of the *New York Daily News* of Leiby Kletzky waiting on the street for Levi Aron to pay his dental bill. The Brooklyn boy got lost walking home from camp and the moment was captured by a surveillance camera on July 11, 2011. Leiby waited seven minutes before getting into Aron's 1990 Honda Accord trusting the next stop would be home.

B.

I walk my beagle Toby on a path beside the Coosaw River. A tidal creek splits from the river cutting into the marsh forest. We play a running game to the top of a sandy ridge in the South Carolina lowcountry. As I wait for my chubby friend, I catch sight of a white heron wading on stilt legs in the pluff mud, quiet and focused.

C.

Mary Oliver, the poet, hears a voice in the weeds. She is headed to blueberry fields and wonders if the voice is from a June beetle or a toad. Her imagination gives life to an image of elves bearing a dead elf away in a casket made of a flower petal.

D.

Videos of Islamic State beheadings are available on-line. I consider watching because seeing may help me process what I do not understand. As the brutality becomes part of the global topography in 2014, I remember Leiby. I ask myself, "Why do we cut one another into bits?"

2 Grids

A.

Borough Park is a neighborhood inside greater Brooklyn Borough and home to one of the largest Jewish populations in the United States. The heart of the community is inside a grid between 11th and 18th avenues, and 40th and 60th streets. Leiby met Aron on 18th Avenue. The boy was supposed to meet his mother at the corner of 13th Avenue and 50th Street.

B.

On July 12, I drive south on Interstate 95 to the Savannah/Hilton Head International Airport. I will fly to Newark and take a train into Manhattan for business the following day. The one o'clock news reports the murder and dismemberment of an eight-year-old boy in Brooklyn. The newscaster is exact and remote in his delivery of the story. My breath catches in my throat and I turn off the radio.

C.

In The Journey, Oliver delivers a prophesy. She predicts coming days, wisdom-filled, when I will know what I have to do. In spite of bad advice, and the clamor of naysayers, she gives me permission to begin, encourages me through the finality of days.

D.

Hervé Gourdel, a French mountaineering guide, was kidnapped shortly after his fifty-fifth birthday while hiking the mountains in Djurdjura National Park in Algeria. Gourdel is beheaded by ISIS in retaliation for French government air strikes against them. The name Djurdjura comes from the word Jjerjer which means "great cold" or "elevation". Confronting cold-blooded murder with art, with pencil, or pen and paper, I can elevate beauty over brutality. Disconnected people and places find common ground in poetry.

"Cuttings" weaves together four seemingly disparate strands: The narrator's walking and travels, her listening to the news; the murder and dismemberment of a young Jewish boy; Mary Oliver and her poetry; terrorism and the ISIS beheadings.

Why bring these four strands of thought together? Because this is how life works. These disparate strands come together, some strands, however much unwanted, force themselves into the rest. Unspeakable violence happens to a child. News reports speak it anyway. As human beings living in an increasingly violent and chaotic world, we hope the violence doesn't touch our own lives, but the news of violence may still reach us in personal ways. This is part of the inner landscape of Bikulege's essay. The violence isn't happening in her own life, but it touches her, nonetheless.

As noted earlier, this essay also borrows the structure of outline in it's A, B, C, D pattern. Unlike outlines though, those letters are repeated. They serve the piece as textual transition markers. As Bikulege put it in a recent conversation we had about her essay, "A equals A equals A, etcetera. The letters cue the reader." Cueing the reader is, after all, why writers use structural markers. Markers, in this case the letters, give the reader a way to keep up with the complicated structure and know immediately which strand we are following. Along with the whitespace around them, the letters provide the transitions without other connective words or phrases. Notice, too, how the numbers, 1,2,3,4, and the subheadings provide additional breaks and transitional markers between larger sections.

In Zadie Smith's story, "The Embassy of Cambodia," we see a linear structure with small sections broken by whitespace and numbers. The sections aren't exactly chapters, but the numbering and the significant amount of whitespace between them gives the reader a larger pause between sections. The pauses, or breaks, are important in a story of this length as evidenced in the excerpt below.

---

0 – 1

Who would expect the Embassy of Cambodia? Nobody. Nobody could have expected it, or be expecting it. It's a surprise, to us all. The Embassy of Cambodia!

Next door to the embassy is a health center. On the other side, a row of private residences, most of them belonging to wealthy Arabs (or so we, the people of Willesden, contend). They have Corinthian pillars on either side of their front doors, and—it's widely believed—swimming pools out back. The embassy, by contrast, is not very grand. It is only a four- or five-bedroom North London suburban villa, built at some point in the thirties, surrounded by a red brick wall, about eight feet high. And back and forth, cresting this wall horizontally, flies a shuttlecock. They are playing badminton in the Embassy of Cambodia. Pock, smash. Pock, smash.

The only real sign that the embassy is an embassy at all is the little brass plaque on the door (which reads, "*the embassy of cambodia*") and the national flag of Cambodia (we assume that's what it is—what else could it be?) flying from the red tiled roof. Some say, "Oh, but it has a high wall around it, and this is what signifies that it is not a private residence, like the other houses on the street but, rather, an embassy." The people who say so are foolish. Many of the private houses have high walls, quite as high as the Embassy of Cambodia's—but they are not embassies.

0 – 2

On the sixth of August, Fatou walked past the embassy for the first time, on her way to a swimming pool. It is a large pool, although not quite Olympic size. To swim a mile you must complete eighty-two lengths, which, in its very tedium, often feels as much a mental exercise as a physical one. The water is kept unusually warm, to please the majority of people who patronize the health center, the kind who come not so much to swim as to lounge poolside or rest their bodies in the sauna. Fatou has swum here five or six times now, and she is often the youngest person in the pool by several decades. Generally, the clientele are white, or else

South Asian or from the Middle East, but now and then Fatou finds herself in the water with fellow-Africans. When she spots these big men, paddling frantically like babies, struggling simply to stay afloat, she prides herself on her own abilities, having taught herself to swim, several years earlier, at the Carib Beach Resort, in Accra. Not in the hotel pool—no employees were allowed in the pool. No, she learned by struggling through the rough gray sea, on the other side of the resort walls. Rising and sinking, rising and sinking, on the dirty foam. No tourist ever stepped onto the beach (it was covered with trash), much less into the cold and treacherous sea. Nor did any of the other chambermaids. Only some reckless teen-age boys, late at night, and Fatou, early in the morning. There is almost no way to compare swimming at Carib Beach and swimming in the health center, warm as it is, tranquil as a bath. And, as Fatou passes the Embassy of Cambodia, on her way to the pool, over the high wall she sees a shuttlecock, passed back and forth between two unseen players. The shuttlecock floats in a wide arc softly rightward, and is smashed back, and this happens again and again, the first player always somehow able to retrieve the smash and transform it, once more, into a gentle, floating arc. High above, the sun tries to force its way through a cloud ceiling, gray and filled with water. Pock, smash. Pock, smash.

Here too, the white space and numbers provide transitions. Often, the transitions happen between small passages of narrative time or shifts in Fatou's understanding. But notice the other shifts too. While the overall structure is linear, the story still holds structural complexities. Notice the Point of View shifts from the Greek-chorus-like "I/we," speaking for the people of Willesden and the close third narrating from Fatou's point of view. Those shifts happen after whitespace, and all but one of those shifts happen in their own numbered sections, separating the chorus-like narration from the rest.

These transitions would not work without the whitespace and the numbered sections. Notice how this way of transitioning carries the story. Smith writes no transitions beyond those. When we read creative writing, we tend only to notice transitions when they do *not* work. If you didn't notice the white space and section breaks as transitions on your first read, that's because they are working. So go back and reread a few sections looking for the spaces and noticing the way that nothing more is needed to move you from one paragraph or section to the next.

Lesson 5 Discussion Questions and Writing Prompts

Discussion Questions: Focus on Structure

1. Look through the works in this book to find three different structures. (For example, you might read Beth Uznis Johnson's "Negative Results," found in Lesson 3, page 41; Alan Michael Parker's "Sixteen Ways Old People Terrify the Young," found in Lesson 2, page 31; and Vivian I. Bikulege's "Cuttings," found in the Readings section.) Explain or draw the structure of each piece then discuss why you think the authors made the structural choices they did for each piece. What do the structures bring to the pieces? How do they influence the way you read each piece? Do the structures have any special relationship to the subject matter of the writing?

2. Read Mary Oliver's "Lead" (found on page 79) and Chang-rae Lee's "Sea Urchin" (found in the Readings section). Study the transitions. First explain how the writers use white space, repetition, line or paragraph breaks, and other structural markers to transition. Next, explain what it is that those transitions move the reader between (chunks of narrative time, concepts, emotions, etc.).

3. Study Sophie Yanow's *The Contradictions* and Randi Ward's "Hestur: A Photo Essay." Explore the structural relationship between the images and the text. How are the images and text arranged on the page? Where do you see more text, and where do you see more image? How do you encounter the text—part of a caption, a paragraph, a sound effect, a speech bubble, etc.? Why do you think the author made these choices?

Writing Prompts: Focus on Structure

Generative Prompt

Draft a piece that follows a borrowed or nonlinear structure. If you are not sure how to begin, write your own story or essay in the structure of an Amazon product review or select three narrative ideas and begin writing them out in three strands.

Revision Prompt

Option 1: Take some time to play around with transitions in a current draft of a story, poem, or essay. Try using whitespace in different ways, textual transition markers, repetition, or a combination of all three. Don't be afraid to experiment. After you play with the transitions, read the piece again. If you like the changes, keep them. If not, remember that playing around with different ways to transition can help make you a better writer.

Option 2: Changing the structure of a manuscript can allow you to rework a piece that isn't quite getting where you want it to with other revisions. Sometimes, playing with structure can show you how to break open a piece and bring in fresh ideas. Engage in structural play with one of your manuscripts-in-progress. Change the structure completely. Try bringing in new threads of idea or narrative and braiding those ideas/narratives into your current piece. Or skip the braiding, but try bringing in new ideas to write a collage. Or turn an easily identifiable piece into a hybrid by borrowing a structure. What happens if you turn your poem or essay into a list piece? What happens if you borrow a different form? Can a short story turn into a math equation? A review? An application letter? Or try rearranging the beginning, middle, and end. As you work, print out your work and cut it up. If you can't get to a printer or don't have any paper, cut it up on your screen.

LESSON 6
CHARACTER DEVELOPMENT

Getting Acquainted: Discovering Depth and Nuance

Have you ever seen those awkward questions about your personal feelings for literary characters pop up from time to time on social media? If you could go on a date with a literary character, who would it be? If you could get coffee with a literary character, who would it be? If you could eat lunch/go shopping/go bowling/be friends with a literary character, who would it be? Character development is the reason questions like these are answerable. When a reader knows a character well enough to imagine going on a date or a shopping excursion, a reader knows the character well.

At its essence, character development is a process during which this acquaintance happens. Good writers don't just introduce characters to the reader; they make sure readers know the characters (at least the main ones) in intimate and nuanced ways.

When thinking of character development, all readers—and writers—have to remember that character development applies to narratives in all genres.

This fundamental part of narrative writing is a fundamental part of narrative reading, too. Character development can also be easy to overlook as a reader: When character development is done well, it enters the narrative seamlessly, often contributing to plot and conflict. Well-written character development usually comes in a series of small but specific details that accumulate. This accumulation of character detail leads readers to know the character enough to make the story work. Sometimes these details acquaint readers so well they begin to feel they know the character almost as a friend or would-be lover.

Perhaps you've already encountered a character you feel this way about. (I have, but I'm not naming any names.) If you have, think about the details the writer wrote that led you to feel this way. If you have not, looking for characters you'd like to know outside the story isn't a bad way to read for character development.

About those details that accumulate, well-written character development doesn't happen in blizzard form. It's more a gentle-but-lasting snowfall sort of thing. When we read for character development, we aren't looking for information dumps. We are looking for details that add up. As an example, let's peek at Gary, the Yelp review writer in "Jerry's Crab Shack: One Star." Studying character development in any genre will help you become a better reader and writer in any genre. In this part of the lesson, we are going to study character development in two works of fiction, but the discussion applies to character development in narrative creative nonfiction and poetry too.

Jerry's Crab Shack: One Star
Gary F.
Baltimore, MD
Yelp member since July 14, 2015
Review: Jerry's Crab Shack
Review posted: July 15, 2015, 2:08am
1/5 stars

After perusing the restaurant's website and reading the positive reviews on Yelp, my wife and I went to Jerry's Crab Shack this evening. We did not have a good experience. It was not "a home run," as another reviewer suggested. I don't know where these reviewers usually go to dinner, and I won't post the speculations I typed and then deleted because they were unflattering and, dare I say, so accurate as to be hurtful and it is not my intention to be hurtful. I simply want to correct the record.

I'm going to review Jerry's Crab Shack in a methodical, fair-minded way so that other people who use this site, people like my wife and I who are new to Baltimore and rely on this site to make informed dinner plans, can know what they are getting into and make their own decisions. If you are going to take the time to do something, as my dear wife says, take the time to do it right or don't bother with it and let her do it like she does everything else (ha ha).

*Location

Jerry's Crab Shack is near Fell's Point (not in historic Fell's Point, as their website leads one to think). In fact, the "shack," which is not a shack but a regular storefront wedged between a hair salon and a mattress store, is several blocks to the east, in a less-than-savory bit of neighborhood. If after reading this, you, future Yelp user, still plan to go to Jerry's Crab Shack, I would suggest that you do not park your car near Jerry's. Park it in Fell's Point proper and walk. Even if you are mugged, the criminals will only take your wallet and not, as happened to us, your front right window (shattered), your Garman navigation system, and five CDs, including a Smithsonian Folkways 2-CD set, Rhythms of Rapture: Musics of Haitian Vodou, that you were looking forward to listening to on your commute.

Within the Yelp setup and first three paragraphs, we learn these telling details about Gary: He has only been a Yelp member for one day. He just moved to Baltimore. He thinks his wife does "everything," and he wants to make a joke of it, "(ha ha)." He has a long commute—at least since his move—and an interesting, eclectic taste in music, which he listens to on CD during his long commute.

See how we get acquainted as we read? We learn these details here and there, not all dumped into one passage. Despite his attitude on Yelp, we even begin to feel sorry for Gary. The feeling sorry might not happen if we received all this information in one breath, as it were. Nor would we find him at all interesting if these details were not nuanced. A less interesting way to explain Gary might have been something like this: Recently relocated to Baltimore, Gary, who is experiencing some tension in his marriage, has started reading restaurant reviews on Yelp and listening to music during his long commute. That would be a character-information dump. It would also include details that, while specific, are not nuanced. Lucky for us, we are in the hands of a good writer when we read "Jerry's Crab Shack: One Star," and we can learn a lot about character development form reading the first few paragraphs.

As we delve into this lesson, it's important to remember what we've discussed here: character development in the form of small, specific, nuanced details that accumulate, as seen in the example Kirby provides as she crafts Gary's character development in the beginning of her story.

Physical Characteristics

We are all living in physical bodies, and we all notice the physical bodies of the people (and creatures) around us. That's why physical characteristics are one part of character development. I mention creatures because every now and then, main characters are not people or even people-like life forms from other universes. (Read Lalinie Paull's novel *The Bees* or search the internet for small excerpts to see brilliant physical character development along non-human lines. You'll never think of antennae in the same way again.) Human or otherwise, getting a sense of a character's physicality is a basic part of character development.

Reading about a character's physical characteristics is part of getting acquainted because in reading physical details, we can imagine what the character looks, smells, sounds, and feels like. We also appreciate knowing a character's age and other vital stats that will orient us to who this character is in fundamental, physical ways. The writers represented in this book work to acquaint their readers with the characters in their stories. Zadie Smith, for example, uses subtle but detailed strokes while developing characters in "The Embassy of Cambodia."

In section 0–2, physical character details begin to emerge.

---

0 – 2

On the sixth of August, Fatou walked past the embassy for the first time, on her way to a swimming pool. It is a large pool, although not quite Olympic size. To swim a mile you must complete eighty-two lengths, which, in its very tedium, often feels as much a mental exercise as a physical one. The water is kept unusually warm, to please the majority of people who patronize the health center, the kind who come not so much to swim as to lounge poolside or rest their bodies in the sauna. Fatou has swum here five or six times now, and she is often the youngest person in the pool by several decades. Generally, the clientele are white, or else South Asian or from the Middle East, but now and then Fatou finds herself in the water with fellow-Africans. When she spots these big men, paddling frantically like babies, struggling simply to stay afloat, she prides herself on her own abilities, having taught herself to swim, several years earlier, at the Carib Beach Resort, in Accra. Not in the hotel pool—no employees were allowed in the pool. No, she learned by struggling through the rough gray sea, on the other side of the resort walls. Rising and sinking, rising and sinking, on the dirty foam. No tourist ever stepped onto the beach (it was covered with trash), much less into the cold and treacherous sea. Nor did any of the other chambermaids. Only some reckless teen-age boys, late at night, and Fatou, early in the morning. There is almost no way to compare swimming at Carib Beach and swimming in the health center, warm as it is, tranquil as a bath. And, as Fatou passes the Embassy of Cambodia, on her way to the pool, over the high wall she sees a shuttlecock, passed back and forth between two unseen players. The shuttlecock floats in a wide arc softly rightward, and is smashed back, and this happens again and again, the first player always somehow able to retrieve the smash and transform it, once more, into a gentle, floating arc. High above, the sun tries to force its way through a cloud ceiling, gray and filled with water. Pock, smash. Pock, smash.

By describing where Fatou swims and contrasting her with the other people in this particular pool, Smith creates physical character development. "Fatou has swum here five or six times now, and she is often the youngest person in the pool by several decades. Generally, the clientele are white, or else South Asian or from the Middle East, but now and then Fatou finds herself in the water with fellow-Africans." In these lines you read about Fatou's ethnicity and her youth, and both in contrast to the wealthy, health club clientele. These bits of character development serve the plot, even as they acquaint the reader with Fatou.

Later, in section 0–11, Smith writes details about both of the main characters, Fatou and Andrew.

---

0 – 11

Andrew and Fatou sat in the Tunisian coffee shop, waiting for it to stop raining, but it did not stop raining, and at 3 *p.m.* Fatou said she would just have to get wet. She shared Andrew's umbrella as far as the Overground, letting him pull her into his clammy, high-smelling body as they walked. At Brondesbury station Andrew had to get the train, and so they said goodbye. Several times he tried to press his umbrella on her, but Fatou knew the walk from Acton Central to Andrew's bed-sit was long and she refused to let him suffer on her account.

"Big woman. Won't let anybody protect you."

"Rain doesn't scare me."

Fatou took from her pocket a swimming cap she had found on the floor of the health-club changing room. She wound her plaits into a bun and pulled the cap over her head.

"That's a very original idea," Andrew said, laughing. "You should market that! Make your first million!"

"Peace be with you," Fatou said, and kissed him chastely on the cheek. Andrew did the same, lingering a little longer with his kiss than was necessary.

Notice the small, telling details about Fatou's hair. As Smith describes an action, something Fatou did—"wound her plaits into a bun and pulled the cap over her head"—we get a solid, sensory description of her hair.

We learn details about Andrew's body too. Smith writes of Andrew's, "clammy, high-smelling body." Again, this up-close (even uncomfortable) information about Andrew's body comes in the midst of an action. Read the entire sentence again: "She shared Andrew's umbrella as far as the Overground, letting him pull her into his clammy, high-smelling body as they walked."

It's also worth paying attention to the fact that these details about Andrew's body in section 0–11 come *after* a series of carefully panted details in section 0–10:

"But, Fatou, you're forgetting the most important thing. Who cried most for Jesus? His mother. Who cries most for you? Your father. It's very logical, when you break it down. The Jews cry for the Jews. The Russians cry for the Russians. We cry for Africa, because we are Africans, and, even then, I'm sorry, Fatou"—Andrew's chubby face creased up in a smile—"if Nigeria plays Ivory Coast and we beat you into the ground, I'm laughing, man! I can't lie. I'm celebrating. Stomp! Stomp!" He did a little dance with his upper body, and Fatou tried, not for the first time, to imagine what he might be like as a husband, but could see only herself as the wife, and Andrew as a teen-age son of hers, bright and helpful, to be sure, but a son all the same—though in reality he was three years older than she. Surely it was wrong to find his baby fat and struggling mustache so off-putting. Here was a good man! She knew that he cared for her, was clean, and had given his life to Christ. Still, some part of her rebelled against him, some unholy part.

In this passage, we can see the way Smith incorporates Andrew's physical details throughout a conversation: First his "chubby face creased up in a smile"; then the fact that "he was three years older" than Fatou; then, "his baby fat and struggling mustache."

For both characters, Fatou and Andrew, the details accumulate. As the story continues, we receive important but subtle physical descriptions that end up allowing us to see, feel, and smell these characters. Notice, too, the nuancing in these character details. Through describing what Fatou does with her hair, we understand that her hair is long and worn in plaits. We are not simply told Andrew has a chubby face; we see it as he smiles. The mustache is "struggling." The "clammy body" is "high-smelling." These aren't details you could read anywhere about anyone. This is what writers mean when we talk about nuanced details.

Emotional, Mental, and Spiritual Characteristics

Just as there is more to a person than meets the eye, so too there is more to a well-developed character than physical details. Good writers develop their characters from the inside as well, crafting characters who are complete. Look at sections 0–10 and 0–11 from "The Embassy of Cambodia" in their entirety to see the way Smit crafts details of the characters' internal lives.

0 – 10

It was the Sunday after Fatou saw the Cambodian that she decided to put a version of this question to Andrew, as they sat in the Tunisian café eating two large fingers of dough stuffed with cream and custard and topped with a strip of chocolate icing. Specifically, she began a conversation with Andrew about the Holocaust, as Andrew was the only person she had found in London with whom she could have these deep conversations, partly because he was patient and sympathetic to her, but also because he was an educated person, currently studying for a part-time business degree at the College of North West London. With his student card he had been given free, twenty-four-hour access to the Internet.

"But more people died in Rwanda," Fatou argued. "And nobody speaks about that! Nobody!"

"Yes, I think that's true," Andrew conceded, and put the first of four sugars in his coffee. "I have to check. But, yes, millions and millions. They hide the true numbers, but you can see them online. There's always a lot of hiding; it's the same all over. It's like this bureaucratic Nigerian government—they are the greatest at numerology, hiding figures, changing them to suit their purposes. I have a name for it: I call it 'demonology.' Not 'numerology'—'demonology.' "

"Yes, but what I am saying is like this," Fatou pressed, wary of the conversation's drifting back, as it usually did, to the financial corruption of the Nigerian government. "Are we born to suffer? Sometimes I think we were born to suffer more than all the rest."

Andrew pushed his professorial glasses up his nose. "But, Fatou, you're forgetting the most important thing. Who cried most for Jesus? His mother. Who cries most for you? Your father. It's very logical, when you break it down. The Jews cry for the Jews. The Russians cry for the Russians. We cry for Africa, because we are Africans, and, even then, I'm sorry, Fatou"—Andrew's chubby face creased up in a smile—"if Nigeria plays Ivory Coast and we beat you into the ground, I'm laughing, man! I can't lie. I'm celebrating. Stomp! Stomp!" He did a little dance with his upper body, and Fatou tried, not for the first time, to imagine what he might be like as a husband, but could see only herself as the wife, and Andrew as a teen-age son of hers, bright and helpful, to be sure, but a son all the same—though in reality he was three years older than she. Surely it was wrong to find his baby fat and struggling mustache so off-putting. Here was a good man! She knew that he cared for her, was clean, and had given his life to Christ. Still, some part of her rebelled against him, some unholy part.

"Hush your mouth," she said, trying to sound more playful than disgusted, and was relieved when he stopped jiggling and laid both his hands on the table, his face suddenly quite solemn.

"Believe me, that's a natural law, Fatou, pure and simple. Only God cries for us all, because we are *all* his children. It's very, very logical. You just have to think about it for a moment."

Fatou sighed, and spooned some coffee foam into her mouth. "But I still think we have more pain. I've seen it myself. Chinese people have never been slaves. They are always protected from the worst."

Andrew took off his glasses and rubbed them on the end of his shirt. Fatou could tell that he was preparing to lay knowledge upon her.

"Fatou, think about it for a moment, please: what about Hiroshima?"

It was a name Fatou had heard before, but sometimes Andrew's superior knowledge made her nervous. She would find herself struggling to remember even the things she had believed she already knew.

"The big wave ..." she began, uncertainly—it was the wrong answer. He laughed mightily and shook his head at her.

"No, man! Big bomb. Biggest bomb in the world, made by the U.S.A., of course. They killed five million people in *one second*. Can you imagine that? You think just because your eyes are like this"—he tugged the skin at both temples—"you're always protected? Think again. This bomb, even if it didn't blow you up, a week later it melted the skin off your bones."

Fatou realized that she had heard this story before, or some version of it. But she felt the same vague impatience with it as she did with all accounts of suffering in the distant past. For what could be done about the suffering of the past?

"O.K.," she said. "Maybe all people have their hard times, in the past of history, but I still say—"

"Here is a counterpoint," Andrew said, reaching out and gripping her shoulder. "Let me ask you, Fatou, seriously, think about this. I'm sorry to interrupt you, but I have thought a lot about this and I want to pass it on to you, because I know you care about things seriously, not like these people." He waved a hand at the assortment of cake eaters at other tables. "You're not like the other girls I know, just thinking about the club and their hair. You're a person who thinks. I told you before, anything you want to know about, ask me—I'll look it up, I'll do the research. I have access. Then I'll bring it to you."

"You're a very good friend to me, Andrew, I know that."

"Listen, we are friends to each other. In this world you need friends. But, Fatou, listen to my question. It's a counterpoint to what you have been saying. Tell me, why would God choose us especially for suffering when we, above all others, praise his name? Africa is the fastest-growing Christian continent! Just think about it for a minute! It doesn't even make sense!"

"But it's not him," Fatou said quietly, looking over Andrew's shoulder at the rain beating on the window. "It's the Devil."

0 – 11

Andrew and Fatou sat in the Tunisian coffee shop, waiting for it to stop raining, but it did not stop raining, and at 3 *p.m.* Fatou said she would just have to get wet. She shared Andrew's umbrella as far as the Overground, letting him pull her into his clammy, high-smelling body as they walked. At Brondesbury station Andrew had to get the train, and so they said goodbye. Several times he tried to press his umbrella on her, but Fatou knew the walk from Acton Central to Andrew's bed-sit was long and she refused to let him suffer on her account.

"Big woman. Won't let anybody protect you."

"Rain doesn't scare me."

Fatou took from her pocket a swimming cap she had found on the floor of the health-club changing room. She wound her plaits into a bun and pulled the cap over her head.

"That's a very original idea," Andrew said, laughing. "You should market that! Make your first million!"

"Peace be with you," Fatou said, and kissed him chastely on the cheek. Andrew did the same, lingering a little longer with his kiss than was necessary.

Study the details to glimpse the emotional, mental, and spiritual sides of character development for Andrew and Fatou. Andrew is "studying for a part-time business degree at the College of North West London." Understanding which kind of college degree a character is working on reveals a key part of the character's mentality: Andrew wants to be a businessman. Notice the other details too. We know where he is studying for the degree. We know he is studying part-time. Studying character development, it is important to consider what these additional details reveal about Andrew and why they matter in the story.

These lines about Fatou are just as telling in different ways: "… but sometimes Andrew's superior knowledge made her nervous. She would find herself struggling to remember even the things she had believed she already knew." Here we glimpse Fatou's intelligence and her uncertainty about her own hard-gained knowledge. Revealing in other ways is Fatou's reflection on her unromantic feeling toward Andrew, "Still, some part of her rebelled against him, some unholy part." Notice how this window into Fatou's feeling about her own moral character both stirs the conflict and gives a sense of her mental state. It isn't just the rebelling; it's that she considers these feelings to be wrong.

Fatou's spiritual beliefs also stir the conflict while revealing aspects of her character. See what happens at the end of section 0–10 when Andrew asks Fatou why God would choose them for suffering: " 'But it's not him,' Fatou said quietly, looking over Andrew's shoulder at the rain beating on the window. 'It's the Devil.'" By the end of section 0–10 we understand that the Devil is real for Fatou, and she feels his evil in the world. See the conflict intensify. See the character grow in her depth on the page.

A close reading of the mental, emotional, and spiritual aspects of character development will show us how a writer has worked to make characters like Fatou and Andrew complete on the inside as well as the outside.

Habits, Interactions, Reactions

Other parts of character development good writers include are character's habits, interactions with other characters, and reactions. As with the other aspects of character development, habits, interactions, and reactions can stir the conflict and influence the plot.

Study the character details about Fatou in section 0–4:

Since August 6th (the first occasion on which she noticed the badminton), Fatou has made a point of pausing by the bus stop opposite the embassy for five or ten minutes before she goes in to swim, idle minutes she can hardly afford (Mrs. Derawal returns to the house at lunchtime) and yet seems unable to forgo. Such is the strangely compelling aura of the embassy.

Now, add another detail, this time from section 0–7:

And on Mondays Fatou swam. In very warm water, and thankful for the semi-darkness in which the health club, for some reason, kept its clientele, as if the place were a night club, or a midnight Mass. The darkness helped disguise the fact that her swimming costume was in fact a sturdy black bra and a pair of plain black cotton knickers.

Now add the details we have already studied from section 0–11:

Rain doesn't scare me.

Fatou took from her pocket a swimming cap she had found on the floor of the health-club changing room. She wound her plaits into a bun and pulled the cap over her head.

Fatou's habits tell the reader a lot in relatively few words—words that accumulate throughout the story over several sections. As we read, we learn more and more about Fatou's habits: Fatou can't "afford" the "idle minutes," while she pauses across from the embassy, but she pauses anyway. And she is not just pausing, she "seems unable" to give up those minutes. She cannot afford a bathing suit either, so she improvises with the underwear she has. She also pockets a swim cap discarded by a stranger. For Fatou, the value of the cap is great enough to take it, to put it upon her own head. As readers, we empathize with her, but we also see her as industrious and un-self-conscious enough to swim in her underwear, to wear the swim cap home in the rain. See the way these habits and reactions accumulate to help make Fatou into the complex and compelling character she is? You may feel sorry for her, but there is more than sorry too. Feeling sorry for someone (character or otherwise) is never enough.

Andrew's habits make his character a fully realized person as well. Read through section 0–10 again. This time, notice the series of details describing Andrew's habits:

Andrew "put the first of four sugars in his coffee."
"Andrew pushed his professorial glasses up his nose."
"Andrew took off his glasses and rubbed them on the end of his shirt."

Planted throughout the section, these descriptions of Andrew's habits show the reader how he acts as he is having coffee with the woman he desires. Notice how much he touches his glasses. Notice the nuancing in the writing—not just that he takes coffee with sugar but that he adds "the first of four sugars."

Also important to study are the habits that connect these two characters to each other. Read this passage from section 0–7:

On Sunday mornings, for example, Fatou regularly left the house to meet her church friend Andrew Okonkwo at the 98 bus stop and go with him to worship at the Sacred Heart of Jesus, just off the Kilburn High Road. Afterward Andrew always took her to a Tunisian café, where they had coffee and cake, which Andrew, who worked as a night guard in the City, always paid for.

This passage is stepped in character development—steeped. Notice how the passage is crafted as a list of habits and what these habits reveal about the characters and their relationship. We see where they worship, which kind of café they visit, what they eat and drink there, who pays. Each of these habits adds to what we already know about the characters and makes a ripe space for further meaning as we learn more character details in later sections.

Remembering the list of habits, read these two interactions from section 0–11: "Several times he tried to press his umbrella on her, but Fatou knew the walk from Acton Central to Andrew's bed-sit was long and she refused to let him suffer on her account." And " 'Peace be with you,' Fatou said, and kissed him chastely on the cheek. Andrew did the same, lingering a little longer with his kiss than was necessary." A close reading of these lines will lead you to ask if this is part of the conflict or part of the character development. The answer is yes. In writing about these interactions, Smith is crafting conflict as she crafts character development. Notice, too, the subtlety—the chaste kiss from Fatou versus Andrew's kiss that lingers beyond necessity.

Reading these passages like a writer demonstrates how habits, interactions, and reactions also form an important part of character development.

Speech/Dialogue

We think of the way characters speak as being part of dialogue, which it certainly is. But the way characters speak is also part of character development. We have already looked at dialogue in the other discussions of this chapter. Character development can be written into dialogue because dialogue is how characters communicate their thoughts and feelings to each other. A character's use of specific phrases can also reveal character development. For example, when Fatou says, "Peace be with you," she is speaking a phrase of Christian fellowship. From this line of dialogue, we know she has embraced this custom of the Christian church, and we see her practicing her faith. That's a lot to learn about a character in four words of dialogue.

That Fatou is speaking these words to Andrew, right before he kisses her cheek longer than needed shows us more about her feelings for Andrew—which develops her character while stirring the conflict.

Read these two other lines of dialogue form section 1–10:

"But more people died in Rwanda," Fatou argued. "And nobody speaks about that! Nobody!"
"Yes, I think that's true," Andrew conceded …

Fatou and Andrew speak like the intelligent people they are. Through the lines they speak to each other, we get a better sense of who they are. In Fatou's case this is important in ways greater than this story itself. Fatou's ability to speak the way she does reminds us that victims of human trafficking are as intelligent as the rest of us and often know truths about the world that many people ignore.

Whole-Character Development

Wait, though, aren't the lines between these types of character details blurring a bit. Yes.

They are. This is what happens when writers create nuanced details and craft characters into fully recognizable people. For purposes of our discussion, we have separated four kinds of character details, but writers develop whole characters. When you read for character development, notice the ways writers work different types of character details together.

By now, for example, you have probably noticed that these little bits of character development we are studying from "The Embassy of Cambodia" all come from the same several sections of the story, and many of them come from the same passages within those sections. When you read one of the sections looking for character development, you can see how Smith develops both characters as whole people. Reread this passage from section 0–10:

It was the Sunday after Fatou saw the Cambodian that she decided to put a version of this question to Andrew, as they sat in the Tunisian café eating two large fingers of dough stuffed with cream and custard and topped with a strip of chocolate icing. Specifically, she began a conversation with Andrew about the Holocaust, as Andrew was the only person she had found in London with whom she could have these deep conversations, partly because he was patient and sympathetic to her, but also because he was an educated person, currently studying for a part-time business degree at the College of North West London. With his student card he had been given free, twenty-four-hour access to the Internet.

"But more people died in Rwanda," Fatou argued. "And nobody speaks about that! Nobody!"

"Yes, I think that's true," Andrew conceded, and put the first of four sugars in his coffee. "I have to check. But, yes, millions and millions. They hide the true numbers, but you can see them online. There's always a lot of hiding; it's the same all over. It's like this bureaucratic Nigerian government—they are the greatest at numerology, hiding figures, changing them to suit their purposes. I have a name for it: I call it 'demonology.' Not 'numerology'—'demonology.' "

"Yes, but what I am saying is like this," Fatou pressed, wary of the conversation's drifting back, as it usually did, to the financial corruption of the Nigerian government. "Are we born to suffer? Sometimes I think we were born to suffer more than all the rest."

Andrew pushed his professorial glasses up his nose. "But, Fatou, you're forgetting the most important thing. Who cried most for Jesus? His mother. Who cries most for you? Your father. It's very logical, when you break it down. The Jews cry for the Jews. The Russians cry for the Russians. We cry for Africa, because we are Africans, and, even then, I'm sorry, Fatou"—Andrew's chubby face creased up in a smile—"if Nigeria plays Ivory Coast and we beat you into the ground, I'm laughing, man! I can't lie. I'm celebrating. Stomp! Stomp!" He did a little dance with his upper body, and Fatou tried, not for the first time, to imagine what he might be like as a husband, but could see only herself as the wife, and Andrew as a teen-age son of hers, bright and helpful, to be sure, but a son all the same—though in reality he was three years older than she. Surely it was wrong to find his baby fat and struggling mustache so off-putting. Here was a good man! She knew that he cared for her, was clean, and had given his life to Christ. Still, some part of her rebelled against him, some unholy part.

Most of the passage works to develop Andrew's character, though it is written from Fatou's point of view. Though Andrew has been little more than introduced before the beginning of this section, we learn volumes about him in six paragraphs. Reading these paragraphs in their entirety, we see how Smith weaves character details together. We also see the way the details accumulate, and we see the nuancing. Andrew's habits with his glasses come in throughout the passage. Fatou sees Andrew's baby fat and struggling mustache. Her perspective adds the nuancing even as her perceptions of his physicality reveal her feelings about him. We also hear him talk and appreciate his patient, even dialogue, which he allows, once, to break into silliness. The same silliness makes Fatou uncomfortable, and in her reaction to it, we learn vital stats: Andrew is several years older than Fatou, but she somehow sees him as younger. Throughout the passage, as he talks with Fatou, we feel his eagerness to learn and study, his desire to look up all he can and pass it on.

When the Narrator Is Also a Character

If paying attention to character development is difficult in general, it is even harder when the narrator is also a character. This happens when a story is narrated by a character who is part of the story. Being complicated and interesting people, writers can make the concept of narrator-characters complicated and interesting too. Most of the time, characters who are narrating the story are doing so from a first person ("I") point of view. Sometimes, though, narrator-characters tell the story from a second person ("you") point of view. We will dig deeper into points of view in the next lesson. The main point here is to remember that sometimes main characters are called, "I," or "you," and tell the story themselves.

Narrator-Characters in Fiction and Creative Nonfiction

When a piece of fiction or creative nonfiction is narrated by a main character, the narrator is also a critical part of the story. This means the writer develops that narrator into a full-fledged character. Writers in both genres can learn about developing narrator-characters by reading to study the development of narrator-characters in both genres.

First, look at this excerpt from "What You Learn in College," a piece of creative nonfiction by Karen Donley-Hayes. Donley-Hayes calls herself "you" in this essay, and the "you" is both the main character and the narrator.

You learn you are perhaps not so intrepid as your beer-bravado led you to believe. A few more spins, the last of the beer-foam winging away from the lip of the bottle, and this strip-spin-the-bottle game is requiring more stripping than you expected. (What did you expect?). By the time the game spins you out of your shoes, socks, and finally your t-shirt, you have realized you are not really drunk at all anymore.

You learn you are still naive when Ed says, "Nice headlights, Karen," and you are reasonably certain he is not talking about your eyes. You laugh along with everyone else, but you don't look at Ed, or at any of your other friends. You keep smiling, keep acting intoxicated, realizing you passed your comfort level with the game one spin ago, when you lost your t-shirt. You want to leave. You want to bolt into the cold dark of the night, but you don't.

In these two paragraphs, we see the narrator-character change over the time of the game as she becomes uncomfortable and realizes she is no longer drunk. We also learn about her mental state and her beliefs and values. This "you" is a woman who did not know to expect this game to lead to so much stripping, and she is uncomfortable with it. She is "still naïve" and, just as important, she is realizing she is still naïve. The details about this narrator accumulate to show the reader how she is changing during the game and also to show you the kind of person she is. Without this character development for the "you" narrator, the essay would not work because as a reader, you wouldn't know enough about her to care what she did during a strip-spin-the-bottle game while she was in college. To care about this narrator-character, we would need to know these details about her, regardless of whether she were narrating a piece of creative nonfiction (as she is) or fiction.

In the second paragraph we also get a little information about this character's physical appearance, at least as others see her in this essay. It comes through another character's perspective via Ed's dialogue. Given that this essay is about a stripping game and the narrator's escape from it, seeing her only through the "eyes" of another character matters for the story she is telling.

Now look again at "Jerry's Crab Shack: One Star." We know the narrator's name is Gary because it is listed in the Yelp review. But Gary refers to himself as "I," throughout the story, which makes him a first-person narrator. In "Jerry's Crab Shack," as in all well-written stories (fiction or creative nonfiction) with a first-person narrator, we get the character development form what the character says about himself or how he thinks others see him. As you read this excerpt, study the way the writer manages to work in solid character development without breaking away from the character's perspective.

---

*Service (bar)

And here we get to the crux of the issue. I don't know where Jerry hires his bar staff, but they are the rudest, most unpleasant people on the face of the earth.

I walked over to the bar and asked the bartender, politely, when our food might be ready. And this bartender, someone obviously on work release from a local prison or recently kicked out of his biker gang for being too obnoxious even for them, tells me It'll be ready when it's ready. Then, he rather grudgingly looked over at the order-up window and said, soon probably. I realize that doesn't sound so bad. In retrospect, it seems pretty reasonable. But I could not go back to the table and tell Janet that the food would be out "soon probably." I needed a timetable. Or a reason the food was being so slow. A kitchen fire, a death in the chef's family, a sudden crab shortage sweeping the Chesapeake. I had already screwed up dinner. I was going to be assertive. This was the one thing I could do right for her. So I said, Can you go back and check? Or find our waitress? And he said, I've got a bar to tend, dude. Unless you want a drink, I got other customers to worry about. The other men at the bar were starting to look at me. I could see them judging me, for my suit and the way I hold myself, which I know is a little awkward. I have unusually long arms. I said, This is simply unacceptable, again, not because I felt that it was that unacceptable but because I wanted to make Janet happy. I think I asked to speak to Jerry. My voice may have gone up in volume. That was when the bartender said that I should sit the fuck down in my faggy DC suit and wait like everyone else. The other men sitting at the bar laughed that rumbling masculine chuckle, as if something funny had happened, and they laughed again when the bartender accused me of "blushing." I did not say anything back because there isn't anything to say to that kind of behavior. I absolutely do not regret not saying anything at that moment and simply walking back to my table.

I don't know what people in this city have against DC. Not everyone from DC is an asshole. And I'm not even from DC. I'm from Ohio.

It feels good to have gotten that off my chest. I don't want to lie to you, future Yelp reader. I feel like we are connecting, unburdening ourselves. I'll tell you a few more things. I am drinking a beer right now, my third, and it is only beginning to help. My wife went to sleep hours ago. I am sitting with my computer, the empty bottles, and a little lamp on the wooden floor of what will be the living room because I don't have a desk yet and I don't want to go upstairs. This isn't where I hoped I would be. I was hoping to have "an extra special" night. And by extra special,

I mean I was hoping I would be having sex. There, I said it. I don't have a problem talking about natural acts between a man and his wife. Unlike the bartender, I am not so insecure about my sexuality that I have to resort to homophobic, inappropriate name-calling. It did not make me feel good to be called "faggy" in front of my wife. In fact, it made me feel shitty. I do not like that bartender's comment repeating in my head, or testing out ways I might have responded, things I might have said. Because again, I'm absolutely not sorry that I walked away.

I actually do have a problem talking about sex sometimes. I could say that I used a euphemism for sex because I didn't want to shock more conservative Yelp users by talking about the birds and bees and the beast with two backs, but the truth is, there are moments like right now when being a person in a body seems impossible. All the parts working in chorus, repetitive involuntary rhythms, a near miracle of coordination. Bodies are strange, so fleshy and pierceable. Sometimes when I am on my endless commute I think about the parts of my car which, in an accident, would be most likely to run me through. The steering column. The parking brake. A shard from the other car. I don't like to think about how thin a membrane my skin actually is, but once I get it in my head, it's hard to get it out. This is why I am upset about the loss of my CDs.

Have you ever listened to Haitian Vodou music? It's not what you would expect. A low patter of rain beat out on the drum. The song a chant, one woman leading, the village following. Call and response. They invite the spirits to come and ride them. But in the end, it's the music that rides you.

I don't know how I got here.

Janet has an outie bellybutton. It's cute, like a little pigtail on her stomach. She hates it. Like it's an inefficiency she wants to eliminate. And she doesn't like when I touch it. She says it "feels weird," as if I am poking a sensitive cord that sends shocks to a place in her body she can't name, a secret nestling between her uterus and stomach. It is hard to fuck someone and not rub up against their outie bellybutton. Also, because I know I can't touch it, sometimes touching it is the only thing I can think about.

Janet doesn't use sites like Yelp. She isn't like me and you. She doesn't trust "random" people's opinions. She reads food critics, peruses "Best of" lists. Since we moved here, she has started to read the Baltimore Sun. I like this about her. She does her research and she has high standards.

If Janet were reviewing me, I wonder what criteria she would use. I think she would say that I make her laugh. I think she would say she finds me handsome instead of saying that I am handsome. I think she would use the word frustrated and point to the small things: taking out the trash, removing expired food from the refrigerator, planning dates. I hope she would say that I am loyal and that she would rank that quality above all others, because I think it's the best one I have. I think if she understood that, she'd see why I didn't raise a fuss about moving here, why I go along when maybe I should speak up. I worry that perhaps she likes this quality in me least of all.

Gary gives his own physical details in humorous but poignant sentences like this one: "I could see them judging me, for my suit and the way I hold myself, which I know is a little awkward. I have unusually long arms." To do this, Gary explains how he thinks the people sitting at the bar see him and reveals two insecurities he has about his own appearance and posture. Notice the nuancing too and the way those nuanced details make you feel sorry for him—he feels himself as, "awkward," in his own body; he finds his own arms to be, "unusually long." In this short passage, we also get a sense of what he is wearing and that he feels self-conscious in it. Notice how much character information we read in these two sentences. We understand Gary in physical and emotional ways. And we get all of this in two sentences.

Later, Gary explains this about his wife's perceptions of his physical appearance: "I think she would say she finds me handsome instead of saying that I am handsome." Here too, we can see how an I narrator can explain his physical appearance by reflecting on what he thinks someone else sees.

In this same section, Gary provides insight into his feelings about sex, and he does it through contradicting himself: "I don't have a problem talking about natural acts between a man and his wife. Unlike the bartender, I am not so insecure about my sexuality that I have to resort to homophobic, inappropriate name-calling." And in the next paragraph, "I actually do have a problem talking about sex sometimes." Here the narrator discloses facts about himself that let the reader know his emotional and mental state intimately. In these character details and others planted throughout the story, we get to know Gary much more intimately than we—or any Yelp readers—would want to know him, which is, of course, why the character development for this first-person narrator is working so well.

In both "What You Learn in College" and "Jerry's Crab Shack: One Star," we see a narrator-character giving us details we need to know if we are going to care about what happens to the character. Notice, too, how the same types of details are present—we get a sense of what the narrator-character looks like; we understand the character's emotional and mental state; we glimpse the character's values. In both, we also get a sense of the character's physicality through dialogue spoken from another character's perspective. Studying character development in these two readings together helps us remember how character development can work the same ways in both creative nonfiction and fiction.

Special Complexities for Narrator-Characters in Creative Nonfiction

Creative nonfiction does offer some additional complexities for narrator characters. These come back to the creative nonfiction discussion we had in Lesson 1. The narrator's character details have to be true, and only those aspects of the narrator's life that are pertinent to this story—the one the writer is telling now in this book or essay—need to be included. Here is the tricky thing about narrator-characters in creative nonfiction. Usually, the "I" narrating the story is also the writer. Those who plan to write creative nonfiction need to pay special attention to the way creative nonfiction writers create themselves as characters on the page. Even my use of the word, "create," is tricky here. In creative nonfiction, "create," cannot mean "to make up." When writers create themselves as characters, what they are doing is remembering that readers need character details then figuring out which details about themselves matter for the story they are telling. For example, Donley-Hayes does not need to tell us everything about her physical appearance. Ed's perspective after she loses her tee shirt is enough for the story she is telling.

Now take a look at Chang-rae Lee's character development in this passage from "Sea Urchin":

July, 1980. I'm about to turn fifteen and our family is in Seoul, the first time since we left, twelve years earlier. I don't know if it's different. My parents can't really say. They just repeat the equivalent of "How in the world?" whenever we venture into another part of the city, or meet one of their old friends. "Look at that–how in the world?" "This hot spell, yes, yes–how in the world?" My younger sister is very quiet in the astounding heat. We all are. It's the first time I notice how I stink. You can't help smelling like everything else. And in the heat everything smells of ferment and rot and rankness. In my grandfather's old neighborhood, where the two- and three-room houses stand barely head-high, the smell is staggering. "What's that?" I ask. My cousin says, "Shit."

"Shit? What shit?"

"Yours," he says, laughing. "Mine."

On the wide streets near the city center, there are student demonstrations; my cousin says they're a response to a massacre of citizens by the military down south in Kwangju. After the riot troops clear the avenues, the air is laden with tear gas–"spicy," in the idiom. Whenever we're in a taxi, moving through there, I open the window and stick out my tongue, trying to taste the poison, the human repellent. My mother wonders what's wrong with me.

I don't know what's wrong. Or maybe I do. I'm bored. Maybe I'm craving a girl. I can't help staring at them, the ones clearing dishes in their parents' eateries, the uniformed schoolgirls walking hand in hand, the slim young women who work in the Lotte department store, smelling of fried kimchi and L'Air du Temps. They're all stunning to me, even with their bad teeth. I let myself drift near them, hoping for the scantest touch.

What succinct and compelling ways for a writer to describe himself. More to the point, see how much character development is packed into these lines, and see how much these lines show you about the "I" who is both narrator and main character in this memoir. Each aspect of character development is here: We know his vital stats—his age and ethnicity and the fact that he is returning to Seoul for the first time since he was a toddler. We know other physical details—he stinks. We see his habits as they pertain to the story Lee is telling in this memoir— here in Seoul he is trying to lick the tear gas from open taxi windows. Here, he wants to sample everything. We know his mental state and understand he is in the throes of puberty.

In Lee's writing, too, we see character development work in nuanced and accumulating ways. Notice, for example, how he reports what his mother wonders about him and counters by reflecting on his own feelings during that trip. Go back to the story itself and see how Lee has placed these details throughout the essay.

Another complexity of narrator-character development in creative nonfiction is the difference between the writer who is writing the piece and the person the narrator was then, living the experience. As creative nonfiction writers develop themselves as characters on the page, they have to develop those characters as they were then, at the time of the experience they are writing about. At the same time, they have to show us the perspective of the person looking back. That sounds as complicated as it is. So let's look again at this paragraph from Lee's narrative.

I don't know what's wrong. Or maybe I do. I'm bored. Maybe I'm craving a girl. I can't help staring at them, the ones clearing dishes in their parents' eateries, the uniformed schoolgirls walking hand in hand, the slim young women who work in the Lotte department store, smelling of fried kimchi and L'Air du Temps. They're all stunning to me, even with their bad teeth. I let myself drift near them, hoping for the scantest touch.

We've already discussed the idea that Lee portrays himself as a fifteen-year-old caught in the grip of puberty. Look at the way he explains this though. The boy at that time was feeling all of this, but he probably would not have been able to articulate his feelings in this way. Here we have the experienced narrator looking back, telling us what he understands now. In creative nonfiction, this is called **reflection**.

Karen Donley-Hayes uses reflection too, as she narrates "What You Learn in College." Look at these two paragraphs, one from earlier in the narrative and one from the ending, looking for the reflection.

You learn you are perhaps not so intrepid as your beer-bravado led you to believe. A few more spins, the last of the beer-foam winging away from the lip of the bottle, and this strip-spin-the-bottle game is requiring more stripping than you expected. (What did you expect?). By the time the game spins you out of your shoes, socks, and finally your t-shirt, you have realized you are not really drunk at all anymore.

You learn this is the last time you will make this walk across campus from Ed's room to yours. And with this learning, that almost-sentient regret breaches like some black-backed sea creature glittering in the night. You do not see it behind you any more than you saw your friends' nakedness. But just the same, you sense it as it slides away into the deep, beyond your sight. But the regret isn't gone. It will never be gone, and you don't need to learn that. You already know it.

The "(What did you expect?)" question is a reflection, the experienced narrator looking back, wondering what her naïve, college self expected that night. The reflection comes back in the ending paragraph. Like Lee's reflection in "Sea Urchin," this articulation comes from the POV of the experienced narrator, looking back. Here she reflects on this early experience with regret. We know from the essay that she has made smart choices, both to stop stripping and to walk away from Ed, but sometimes even making smart choices leaves us with regrets. It takes most of us a while to learn that. The narrator of "What You Learn in College" has learned this lesson, and she reflects on the lesson here.

Here is what all this boils down to: Narrator-characters in creative nonfiction have to create themselves as characters on the page as they were then (at the time the experience took place) and show us the POV of the narrator now, reflecting on how the experience mattered.

Exploring Character Development in Non-narrative Forms

I'd be remiss if I did not point out that a bit of character development can also enhance non-narrative creative writing. True, non-narrative creative writing doesn't usually need the in-depth character development central to narrative. But savvy readers should notice character details when writers include them because these details will influence the central theme or the resonating image. Our example is "Hestur: A Photo Essay." Reading one of the opening paragraphs, we will learn little facts about the life of the narrator, who, in this case, is also the photographer.

It was rather inevitable that I too would become subject to the roiling social currents of the village of Hestur. As a newcomer to the island, its youngest resident, an independently employed, single female and a foreigner to boot, my life was ripe for interpretation; it wasn't long before my daily routines and social interactions came under all kinds of scrutiny. Yet it was this complex configuration of intense proximity and solitude that made my time in Hestur, where I spent my last 6 months in the Faroe Islands, exquisitely vivid. I experienced an incredible spectrum of life and humanity and often participated in it to near-overwhelming extremes. Whether I was assisting at the sheepfold, raking freshly mown hay, enjoying a colorful conversation with Hjørleiv, teaching Jørmund how to use email, or borrowing Ebbe's clothesline for an afternoon, perhaps my most tender act of solidarity was simply turning on my kitchen light of an evening so people could see I was still there.

Here are some of the details we learn about the narrator/photographer:

- She is a woman.
- She is an outsider.
- She is spending six months in Hestur.
- She is self-employed.
- She is the youngest resident of the island.

This is not much information, and we learn it in few words. Because "Hestur: A Photo Essay" is more about the place than the narrator, we do not need to know any more than this. But see the way this information influences the way we read the rest of the piece, including the way we read the photographs. If any one of these pieces of information were different, the reader would come away with a slightly different perspective. If, for example, the narrator had been living on Hestur since her birth seventy years ago, we would read the words and photographs knowing they were coming from an insider, one whose entire life and existence had been shaped by the island. Instead, we read about the island as Ward writes it, an outsider with intimate knowledge of the place, a youthful visitor determined to take part in life there for a while, even as she documents it.

This digression into character development in non-narrative work is all by way of explaining that little touches of character information can affect the way a reader understands any piece of creative writing. So even as you read non-narrative creative writing, stay on the lookout for those tasty bits of character development that make a real difference in the piece.

Reading for Character Development: Further Considerations

Character development is a crucial part of all forms of narrative, which means reading for character development is crucial in reading all forms too. As you read to study character development, notice how techniques change depending on the type of piece. In flash and micro forms, for example, writers can accomplish character development in few words and brief strokes. Read this sentence from Beth Uznis Johnson's "Negative Results." "Not really, but you have a husband and three children, a life that's mostly good. The baby is out of diapers and your team won the bowling league." Brief strokes. Few words. But in them, the reader gets a glimpse into "you," the main character who is narrating this story.

In graphic narrative, readers need to look for character development in one more way—a way that is at the crux of graphic work. Yes, look for visual character development. And read looking to see which character details the writer/illustrator shows with visuals and which details the writer shows with words. In the Readings section, for example, Sophie Yanow's *The Contradictions*, literally, shows us what Sophie (the character) looks like, how she holds herself, how she moves her body. Look at Sophie in the excerpt below.

The figure of Sophie shows us key physical details—Sophie wears glasses and hunches her shoulders but walks in long strides. In the same panels, the captions tell us more about Sophie's character—she really wishes she had her bike with her in Paris; she feels she cannot connect with most of her fellow study-abroad students. Sophie's speech bubbles show us what Sophie says—the polite face she puts on—as she realizes she doesn't fit in.

Some Strategies in Reading for Character Development

Regardless of the genre, reading for character development can be interesting and fun, too, if you do it right. Try some of these strategies to read for character development.

- Sketch out the physical details you've read about a character.
- Make columns for each type of character development (physical, mental/emotional/spiritual, habits/interactions/reactions, and speech/dialogue) and list character development details for each column.
- Highlight character developing information and details as you read. Note which type of character development the detail is.
- After reading a creative work once, do a character development scavenger hunt. Find character development details for each of the four categories: physical, mental/emotional/spiritual, habits/interactions/reactions, and speech/dialogue.

Lesson 6 Discussion Questions and Writing Prompts

Discussion Questions: Focus on Character Development

1. If you *could* eat lunch with a main character from one of the narrative works in this book, who *would* it be and why? For that matter, what kind of a lunch would it be? Friendly? Romantic? A heavy meal? Nothing but salad? Served with drinks? Served indoors? Home-cooked? In your answer, make sure to include the details you discover about this character in the story and what it is about the writer's conveyance of those details that makes you want to eat lunch with this character.

2. Study the character development in Poornima Laxmeshwar's prose poem "Cartography" (found in Lesson 3, page 42) and Beth Uznis Johnson's micro fiction "Negative Results" (found in Lesson 3, page 41). List the types of character development these writers use, citing the details you learn about the characters. How do these writers develop characters in so few words? And how does the character development influence each narrative?

3. Read Karen Donley-Hayes's essay "What You Learn in College" (found in Lesson 3, page 39) and Sophie Yanow's graphic narrative *The Contradictions*. Using one of the strategies listed at the end of this chapter, study the character development in each. Then compare the character development you see in the different pieces. Where do the writers use similar techniques? Where do they differ?

Writing Prompts: Focus on Character Development

Generative Prompt

Keeping in mind the various aspects of character development, make a character-sketch list for a main character. Get as specific as possible and have fun. Here is an example template to help you get started:

Character Name:
Race/Ethnicity:
Gender Identity:
Age:
Physical description/drawing:
Occupation/school:
Feelings/Attitudes about occupation/school:
Religion/Spiritual Preferences:
Hobbies:
Habits:
Fears:
Goals:
Things that prompt laughter:
Favorite Foods:
Foods only eaten in the morning:

Foods tried only once:

Foods that prompt gage reflex:

Coffee, tea, or juice?

Dairy, ricemilk, or almond milk?

Sparkling or still?

Paper, plastic, or reusable tote?

Briefcase, purse, messenger bag, pockets, backpack, or book bag?

Secrets willing to tell one person:

Secrets unwilling to tell:

Reasons to get up in the morning:

Last thought before falling asleep:

Anything else:

Revision Prompt

Option 1: Write a personal advertisement for one of your main characters. In the ad, be sure to use details that touch on various aspects of the character. Using the plot or narrative arc to inform your ad, include what the character would be in search of (a pet sitter, a roommate, a date, etc.). After you have finished the ad, select the details from it that are important to your story, pull them from the ad, and work them into the story.

Option 2: Select a main character from a narrative you are already writing. Reread the narrative with an eye to your character development. First, rewrite the character details already present to make them more nuanced. Next, write new details. Remember to make your character full. Include habits and beliefs. Finally, drop these details throughout the story, so they will accumulate. For example, in the beginning of the story, show the main character engaging in a habit. In the middle, write the character engaging in that habit but show how the conflict might change what the character is doing. If the character drinks decaffeinated coffee every morning in the beginning, adding a detail about the character switching to caffeinated coffee as the conflict is growing in the middle will tell your reader a lot about how the character is changing because of the conflict.

LESSON 7
POINT OF VIEW

Point of View as a Lens

To keep things interesting—as writers must—let's begin our Point of View lesson with a two-part activity.

Activity Part 1: Stand (or imagine standing) on your roof or the roof of your building: Look down at the street. Now come down off the roof (or imagine coming down) and crouch on the ground. Look out at the street. What is the difference?

The answer lies in Point of View, or, as it is affectionately known to writers everywhere, POV. Unless it took a long time to get down off the roof and onto the ground, nothing much on the street should have changed. What has changed is the perspective from which you saw the street. Things look different from street-level than from a roof-top.

Activity Part 2: Imagine a person walking along a crowded sidewalk, carrying a cat in a pet carrier. Imagine the sidewalk from the person's perspective. There are people to walk around, uneven pavement to step over, obstacles to avoid knocking the pet carrier into. Now change the perspective to that of the cat inside the carrier: Bump, swoosh, bump. Don't hit that signpost. Ouch, meow, hiss.

Just as things look different from the rooftop than from street-level, things look different holding the pet carrier than riding inside it. Now, change the POV one more time to imagine the perspective of someone else, say a person standing on the sidewalk, watching the pet-owner struggle along. Again, from the vantage point of someone else watching, things look a little different.

As in the other elements in the craft of creative writing, POV is a fundamental part of writing in any genre, including hybrids. Look, for example, at this excerpt from Joy Harjo's prose poem "Grace."

Like Coyote, like Rabbit, we could not contain our terror and clowned
our way through a season of false midnights. We had to swallow
that town with laughter, so it would go down easy as honey. And one
morning as the sun struggled to break ice, and our dreams had found us
with coffee and pancakes in a truck stop along Highway 80,
we found grace.

The POV here is a first-person plural, a *we*. The speaker is speaking not as one person but as part of a pair of people, people who find themselves in the position of being marginalized outsiders in the town and in the university community. Imagine how the poem would be changed if the speaker were presenting the perspective of an "I" instead of a "we." The poem, with its details of struggle, would be the same. But the depiction of the struggle and the spring morning would be centered on the voice of one—an *I*. The *we* POV changes the gravity of the poem and of the speaker. There is more than one voice here. There is more than one person having the same experience of marginalization and prejudice.

Reading writers study POV to figure out why a writer narrates (in fiction and creative nonfiction) or speaks (in poetry) from a certain perspective. Reading writers also analyze how narrating or speaking from that perspective works within the piece. To place this idea into the context of this book, study these two paragraphs from "Jerry's Crab Shack: One Star," by Gwenn E. Kirby, which is included in the Readings section.

Jerry's commits to its nautical theme. The bar has a charming fishing net draped above it, and caught in the net are plastic starfish and a cardboard mermaid. On the walls are pictures of sailboats, not framed but tacked to the plaster, the edges curled and yellowing as they might do in a more briny environment. At the end of the bar is a rubber crab, lovingly cuddled up to a Bud Light. A sign next to it says: No One Feels Crabby with a Bud Light! (You can feel crabby with a Bud Light. I would say, considering all the better beers out there in the world, that you should feel crabby with a Bud Light. I would also say that since the staff of Jerry's Crab Shack seems so invested in their status as "native" Baltimoreans, they might consider supporting Maryland businesses and serving only local beers.)

There are eight tables, each covered with a laminated red-and-white-check tablecloth, the kind that has holes through which you can feel the soft white polyester fuzz. We were expecting more of a "restaurant restaurant" (my wife's words), and less of a "bar with some tables" (also my wife). The pictures on the website do not accurately reflect the interior, so this was not my fault. I was lead to expect more of a nautical bistro atmosphere, which my wife later suggested was "not a thing." The point is, I promised my wife a special dinner. I told her this place would be quintessentially "Baltimore." I hoped that we would finally be able to unwind and enjoy an evening out of the house, away from the half unpacked boxes and nearly empty rooms.

This hybrid short story is narrated from Gary's POV. Notice the details that can only come from his perspective. He explains what his wife said about this Jerry's Crab Shack. He notes that selecting a restaurant with this ambiance is not his "fault." He explains the simple but important hopes he'd had for the evening. Even his musing about the staff being "invested in their status as 'native' Baltimoreans" is an important observation from Gary's angle—an observation that will have layered meaning as the reader moves through the story.

POV is the lens through which the reader sees. Consider how this story might change if we saw it through the lens of Janet, Gary's wife. Even if some of the same details were included—the unfortunate décor, the need for a night out—we'd be seeing Jerry's Crab Shack and the couple in it differently than we see them through Gary's eyes.

Narrator/Speaker

If POV is the lens, an important part of studying POV is thinking about who is holding the lens. Every story has a narrator. The narrator is holding the lens. In other words, the narrator is the voice telling the story. In "Jerry's Crab Shack: One Star," Gary is holding the lens himself. We see the events at the restaurant/bar with tables from his perspective and in his words. Study this paragraph from "Jerry's Crab Shack: One Star."

I walked over to the bar and asked the bartender, politely, when our food might be ready. And this bartender, someone obviously on work release from a local prison or recently kicked out of his biker gang for being too obnoxious even for them, tells me It'll be ready when it's ready. Then, he rather grudgingly looked over at the order-up window and said, soon probably. I realize that doesn't sound so bad. In retrospect, it seems pretty reasonable. But I could not go back to the table and tell Janet that the food would be out "soon probably." I needed a timetable. Or a reason the food was being so slow. A kitchen fire, a death in the chef's family, a sudden crab shortage sweeping the Chesapeake. I had already screwed up dinner. I was going to be assertive. This was the one thing I could do right for her. So I said, Can you go back and check? Or find our waitress? And he said, I've got a bar to tend, dude. Unless you want a drink, I got other customers to worry about. The other men at the bar were starting to look at me. I could see them judging me, for my suit and the way I hold myself, which I know is a little awkward. I have unusually long arms. I said, This is simply unacceptable, again, not because I felt that it was that unacceptable but because I wanted to make Janet happy. I think I asked to speak to Jerry. My voice may have gone up in volume. That was when the bartender said that I should sit the fuck down in my faggy DC suit and wait like everyone else. The other men sitting at the bar laughed that rumbling masculine chuckle, as if something funny had happened, and they laughed again when the bartender accused me of "blushing." I did not say anything back because there isn't anything to say to that kind of behavior. I absolutely do not regret not saying anything at that moment and simply walking back to my table.

Notice how Gary directs the lens. Through Gary's eyes, we see the embarrassing scene begin at the bar. We see the bartender glance back at the order-up window and hear his response. We also get a window into Gary's thoughts—his sarcastic but inconsequential opinion of the bartender. His quickly-growing-desperate need to appease Janet. Gary shows us his internal and external conflict, both brewing at the bar. We hear Gary explaining all of this to us himself.

This concept of the narrator being the one holding the lens and the voice telling the story is true for poetry, too, with one exception: In poetry, that voice behind the lens is called the speaker, and often the speaker is doing something other than telling a story.

Consider these lines from Alan Michael Parker's hybrid poem "Sixteen Ways Old People Terrify the Young."

---

1. They have sex with each other.
2. They drive around.
3. They pretend they're thinking. They pretend they're not
    thinking about dying.

4. The vigor of diving through the waves (through time) or the splash of the body sprinting toward love. What's a sea, if not for swimming.

5. And what about those old people who walk—I don't know— like seventy-nine miles every morning on the beach? Skin cancer! Yo! They're going to die.

The observations in this list come through the speaker's lens and in the speaker's voice. Notice how this lens combines annoyance with humor (the "sex," the "driv[ing] around) and brings the idea of approaching death up against details of a lively swim ("diving," "splashing," "sprinting"). Reading the first five reasons on the list, we realize we are reading through the lens of a speaker who is not among the "old" of this poem.

Most of the poem is written in third person, with the speaker referring to "old people," often using the third-person pronoun, "they." But in 5, the speaker inserts the first-person. "And what about those old people who walk—I don't know—/like seventy-nine miles every morning on the beach? Skin/cancer! Yo! They're going to die." Here, the "I don't know—like" is a colloquialism, and it's a bit sarcastic. We know the speaker doesn't really think those old people are walking seventy-nine miles. But see how bringing in this "I" phrase changes the lens a little bit. It is through the speaker that we get this list about "old people" and explore our feelings about them. We aren't just seeing these sixteen reasons through the lens of an anonymous list-writer, the way most top-ten lists work, we are seeing these reasons through the lens of this particular speaker. We appreciate the sarcasm and the humor, but running beneath it, there is a specific someone noticing these old people on the beach. Knowing that changes everything. Without the "I," the final item in the list, the death on the beach, would not hit us the way it does: "With only/three people there in the winter to see. A body."

First, Second, Third

We talk about narrators or speakers as being in first person, second person, or third person. First-person and third-person narrators are most common, but second-person narrators happen too. The works in this book include examples of each.

Now let's get technical. A pronoun is a word we use to refer to people, places, or things without giving them a name or any other specific identity: she, he, they, we, you, I, it, her, him, them, us, me, that, etcetera, etcetera.

Think again about Gary, the narrator in "Jerry's Crab Shack: One Star." What does Gary call himself? "I." Gary, the narrator, calls himself "I." "I" is a first-person pronoun, so are "I's" close relatives: me, my, mine, and myself. Narrators or speakers who use these words to refer to themselves are always first-person narrators. The same is true on the rare occasions a speaker or narrator uses plural first-person pronouns: we, us, our, etcetera. In these cases, the speaker in the prose poem "Grace" among them, the narration is coming from a first-person plural: a "we" not an "I."

Second-person narrators or speakers call themselves, "you," and use the other second-person pronouns: your and yours. In second-person narration, the "you" is almost always a replacement for "I." "You" narrators or speakers are usually still explaining from their own perspective, but the writers have made the choice to employ a second-person narrator/speaker to make the piece work differently than it would in first-person.

Third-person narrators or speakers do not refer to themselves because third-person narrators/speakers are not personally involved in the story. Third-person narrators/speakers name characters and explain what happens to them using the characters' names or any of the third-person pronouns (she/he/it/they, etcetera).

Within third-person narration, there are three more-specific points of view. Limited third happens when a narrator/speaker closely follows one character and knows that character's thoughts and feelings. While "limited third" is the term often used to discuss literature, many writers use the term "close third" instead because the narration gives a close perspective on one character. An omniscient narrator knows everything about everyone in the piece and can speak to the thoughts and feelings of any of the characters—even minor ones. An objective narrator or speaker is pretty much what it sounds like: a narrator/speaker who reports what is happening in an objective manner without commenting on the thoughts or feelings of any of the characters. In general, writers use this POV less often than the other third-person points of view.

In terms of studying narrators or speakers, reading the way writers read means more than recognizing whether the voice telling the story or poem is narrating from first, second, or third person. Reading writers consider how different lenses work and why a particular lens is used.

First Person

First-person narrators or speakers are also characters. Often, they are main characters.

Look again at Gary, the first-person narrator of "Jerry's Crab Shack: One Star." (We know his name is Gary from the beginning of his Yelp review, but he calls himself, "I.") Gary is a main character in this story. His character development and the explanation of what happens to him and his internal and external conflicts, all come to us through his lens and in his voice.

Reading for POV in this hybrid short story, it is important to notice that the I narrator is crucial to the way the story works. Yelp reviews are first-person. (If you have seen a Yelp review from any other POV, send it to me, or tag me in a social media post about it!) To work in the Yelp review form, the narrator has to be first-person.

Gary's first-person narration makes the story work in other ways too. Read this section from "Jerry's Crab Shack: One Star."

Janet has an outie bellybutton. It's cute, like a little pigtail on her stomach. She hates it. Like it's an inefficiency she wants to eliminate. And she doesn't like when I touch it. She says it "feels weird," as if I am poking a sensitive cord that sends shocks to a place in her body she can't name, a secret nestling between her uterus and stomach. It is hard to fuck someone and not rub up against their outie bellybutton. Also, because I know I can't touch it, sometimes touching it is the only thing I can think about.

Janet doesn't use sites like Yelp. She isn't like me and you. She doesn't trust "random" people's opinions. She reads food critics, peruses "Best of" lists. Since we moved here, she has started to read the Baltimore Sun. I like this about her. She does her research and she has high standards.

If Janet were reviewing me, I wonder what criteria she would use. I think she would say that I make her laugh. I think she would say she finds me handsome instead of saying that I am handsome. I think she would use the word frustrated and point to the small things: taking out the trash, removing expired food from the refrigerator, planning dates. I hope she would say that I am loyal and that she would rank that quality above all others, because I think it's the best one I have. I think if she understood that, she'd see why I didn't raise a fuss about moving here, why I go along when maybe I should speak up. I worry that perhaps she likes this quality in me least of all.

Wow, that paragraph about Janet's belly button is intense. It's also uncomfortable on several levels. 1: It's a Yelp review. Reading about someone's sex life—especially the pathetic details part—is not what we signed up for. 2: The pathetic-ness for Gary—his wanting to touch that bellybutton and not. being allowed to. 3: The first-person POV in regard to the bellybutton and the sex—"Sometimes touching it is the only thing I can think about." The first-person POV makes this section.

Notice, too, how the elements we have discussed in previous lessons, the conflict and character development, for example, come together in smart and penetrating ways from Gary's first-person POV. Remember, first-person narrators are also characters in the story, characters who must be fully realized. See the smart ways Kirby writes Gary's character development from Gary's own POV. Reading the way Gary describes himself through what he imagines to be Janet's eyes, feels honest (even though we know we are reading fiction) and makes Gary a sympathetic character, even as it shows us more about him. As Gary finishes listing his traits as he imagines Janet sees them, he deepens the conflict, showing us what is on the line here— from his perspective: he hopes Janet would see his loyalty as an important quality, but worries she values it "least of all."

Imagine how this section of the story would change if written from Janet's POV. Maybe she would not discuss her belly button at all. Maybe she would say they had an epic date-night fail. Maybe she would say she was exhausted by both the experience and by her husband who can never get things right, so she went to bed early—and alone. We do know that if this story were written from Janet's POV, we would not be reading it as a Yelp review, because, as Gary puts it, "Janet doesn't use sites like Yelp."

On rare occasions, writers will use first-person plural narrators—we, us, our, ours, etcetera. A plural narrator is difficult to pull off for the obvious reason that it is hard to narrate from the POV of more than one. This is the reason plural, first-person narrators (we narrators) are rare. When we do find "we" narrators, we tend to find them in shorter works or in shorter sections of longer works. Zadie Smith's "we" narrator in "The Embassy of Cambodia" is an example of the latter. In Smith's narrative, the "we" narrates brief sections of the work. Look, for example, at the first paragraph from section 0–3 below.

---

0 – 3

When the Embassy of Cambodia first appeared in our midst, a few years ago, some of us said, "Well, if we were poets perhaps we could have written some sort of an ode about this surprising appearance of the embassy." (For embassies are usually to be found in the center of the city.

This was the first one we had seen in the suburbs.) But we are not really a poetic people. We are from Willesden. Our minds tend toward the prosaic. I doubt there is a man or woman among us, for example, who—upon passing the Embassy of Cambodia for the first time—did not immediately think: "genocide."

When a "we" is holding the lens, what does the reader see? And who is that "we"? Both are important questions to ask when reading a first-person plural narrator. In "The Embassy of Cambodia," the "we" is the people of Willesden. In many reviews of the story, the "we" narrator, when it comes in, is compared to a Greek chorus—a collective body commenting on the events of the narrative. Smith uses the "we" lens sparsely, and its perspective provides a contrast to the close, third-person narrator who explains what is happening to Fatou and what she thinks and feels about these circumstances.

In "The Embassy of Cambodia," the "we" lens gives the reader a broader perspective, a context in which to understand the Embassy from the view of the people who live in the neighborhood surrounding it. Because the "we" is a form of first person, the narrator can say what the "we" is thinking—"genocide"! But because of its collective lens, the perspective seems distant. The "we" narrator cannot tell us about Fatou's struggles as an enslaved servant, only that the people of Willesden, many of whom are struggling in their own right, recognize many evils happening in the world but cannot do anything to stop them. Do the "people of Willesden" realize what is happening to Fatou any more than Fatou realizes what is happening to the Cambodian woman?

With these questions in mind, now consider how the "we" narrator is working in the story. The "we" narrator shows us how people like Fatou and the Cambodian woman continue to be victims of human trafficking, even as they are living in a large city in a free county.

Switching gears—or genres—let's think about first-person speakers in poetry. Joy Harjo uses a first-person plural speaker for much of her prose poem "Grace." Earlier in this chapter, we discussed the "we" narrator. In this poem, though, Harjo also moves seamlessly between "we," and "I." The speaker, whom we know to be Joy Harjo herself, is part of a larger identity of Native American students, specifically the friends in her graduate program. Read the poem's second paragraph again.

> Like Coyote, like Rabbit, we could not contain our terror and clowned
> our way through a season of false midnights. We had to swallow
> that town with laughter, so it would go down easy as honey. And one
> morning as the sun struggled to break ice, and our dreams had found us
> with coffee and pancakes in a truck stop along Highway 80,
> we found grace.

See how the plural speaker—the "we" applies to Harjo and to her friends. Like "we" narrators, "we" speakers are speaking for a group, in this case the other Native American students in this graduate program. In this way, the poem becomes about more than her own individual experience. The "we" changes the stakes.

Now read the third paragraph.

I could say grace was a woman with time on her hands, or a white
buffalo escaped from memory. But in that dingy light it was a promise
of balance. We once again understood the talk of animals, and spring
was lean and hungry with the hope of children and corn.

The "we" stays as Harjo explains the experience that is common between her and her friends. Notice how the "I" comes in when Harjo is trying to explain the way she describes "grace." Here, she is not ascribing the description of "grace" as "a woman with time on her hands, or a white buffalo escaped from memory," to the "we" POV. This description belongs only to her. Then the "we" comes back in to explain a collective understanding and experience of spring.

Moving between the "I" and the "we" means Harjo is moving between two different first-person points of view. In doing so, she brings a layering to the speaker that would not otherwise be there. Moving between the "I" and the "we" also allows Harjo to differentiate between the common experience and the language she chooses as an individual. Notice how this makes the poem feel more true in the literal sense. Because the speaker is willing to say when an articulation is hers alone, we feel we can believe her when she is communicating a shared experience.

Second Person

Like first-person, second-person or "you" narrators/speakers are also characters. In narrative forms (whether fiction, creative nonfiction, or poetry,) a second-person narrator is usually a main character. As such, their writers need to render them fully. That is one reason second-person narrators are tricky. The other is that in narrative-writing, the second-person "you" narrator almost always translates into "I." (This last sentence exemplifies how very complex POV can be.) How, exactly, can a "you" translate into an "I?"

The answer can be found in Karen Donley-Hayes's short memoir, "What You Learn in College." Consider this sentence: "You watch Ed, in his briefs, try to yank the door open then shrug and return to the circle of strippers." The "you" in this sentence is not a "you" that can apply to anyone. There is one, specific person who is watching Ed, clad in his underpants, try and fail to open the door. The person is the narrator of this true story.

In this short essay, Donley-Hayes is writing about one of her own experiences—the night she played a stripping game in college. She is using the pronoun "you" to tell her own story. (This is a technique fiction writers use, too, except that in fiction a "you" narrator is telling a fictional narrator's own story. For an example, read Beth Uznis Johnson's micro fiction "Negative Results," found in Lesson 3, page 41.) The "you" in this short memoir is written from Donley-Hayes's perspective. Changing the POV to second-person, however, changes the way we read the narrative. Let's take a closer look at a passage from "What You Learn in College."

The bottle spins.

You learn you are perhaps not so intrepid as your beer-bravado led you to believe. A few more spins, the last of the beer-foam winging away from the lip of the bottle, and this strip-spin-the-bottle game is requiring more stripping than you expected. (What did you expect?).

You learn you are still naive when Ed says, "Nice headlights, Karen," and you are reasonably certain he is not talking about your eyes. You laugh along with everyone else, but you don't look at Ed, or at any of your other friends. You keep smiling, keep acting intoxicated, realizing you passed your comfort level with the game one spin ago, when you lost your t-shirt. You want to leave. You want to bolt into the cold dark of the night, but you don't.

The bottle spins.

You learn you couldn't leave even if you had the nerve, because the disgruntled wanna-be-party-goers in the hallway have pennied the door, tiny rounds of copper wedging door against frame. You watch Ed, in his briefs, try to yank the door open then shrug and return to the circle of strippers. No one is leaving.

In this passage, as in the rest of the essay, the "you" narrator continues to mean one specific person—the person narrating the "you" who had this experience. Notice the ways the conflict and character development unfold for the "you" narrator. We read the order she strips off clothing. We get a concrete detail about her naivety and her own realization that she is still naive. We see the conflict: She becomes uncomfortable in the game, but the door is "pennied" shut. All of this comes from Karen's perspective. In this narrative, Karen calls herself "you," not "I."

The second-person narrator provides a little more distance. We could almost say "you" narrators are distant-first narrators, except that the term "distant-first" doesn't exist in narration, and "you" is a second-person pronoun. Still, the distance is there, and the "you" puts it there.

When I asked Karen Donley-Hayes about the "you" narrator in her essay, she told me this: "The second person POV was pretty much an experiment, just to try it on … but in a way, that POV also made an easier, less personal way to examine the issue, to tell this story." What Donley-Hayes is speaking to here is the distance. She used the distance of the "you," to tell this story. Finding this kind of distance can help creative nonfiction writers tell a true story in a way they may otherwise not be able to.

Of course, Donley-Hayes is also talking about experimenting—playing around with ways to tell a story, the way writers do. Playing with second-person narration may be a sort-of common experiment for memoir writers, though making the second-person POV work is less so. Why does the second-person POV work in "What You Learn in College"?

Part of the reason is the less-personal, more distant lens for the stripping game. It's nice to read the essay without an "I" telling us what clothing I took off or how I got embarrassed and didn't want to keep playing. We trust this you narrator to tell us the truth about the unsavory details and about backing out of the game by faking a "blackout." Just as important, we trust this less-personal you to explain what she learned about regret—the giving up of whatever possibilities might have happened if the narrator had acted differently.

The other way second-person POV works—in this essay and beyond—is inserting the reader behind the lens. It is the narrator doing these things; we know it is the narrator deciding to join this game. But the "you" narrator puts us (those reading this essay) into the game in a way we would not be if the story were narrated from a different POV. "By the time the game spins you out of your shoes, socks, and finally your t-shirt, you have realized you are not really drunk at all anymore." You. You have just been spun out of your t-shirt. As a reader, you find yourself in this stripping game, whether you expected to or not (kind of like Donley-Hayes herself.)

This memoir, with its second-person POV, also speaks to an experience common to many a college student. (It's okay, you don't have to raise your hand if you've been there.) Not everyone has played strip spin the bottle, but learning what it feels like to get drunk, or to undress in front of other people, or to join a small party in a dorm room, or to give up the crush after an awkward night, to realize regret—these are common experiences. The "you" POV in this essay reminds us of exactly what the title promises it will: "What You Learn in College."

Not often, but sometimes a "you" narrator or speaker will translate into a "you" that means people in general or the reader specifically. When this kind of a "you" is narrating or speaking, the work is probably not narrative. Speaking from the POV of people in general or putting the reader in the POV of the speaker, is tricky and does not work in many contexts. In non-narrative creative nonfiction, second-person narrators/speakers are rare enough to be almost nonexistent. In poetry and some non-narrative creative nonfiction, the second-person "you" shows up often enough as part of the essay or poem, but is rarely working as the speaker or narrator.

For an example of a second-person "you" that is present in a piece but not coming from the POV of the narrator or speaker, look at the "you" in Mary Oliver's poem "Lead."

Look again at Mary Oliver's "Lead."

Lead

Here is a story
to break your heart.
Are you willing?
This winter
the loons came to our harbor
and died, one by one,
of nothing we could see.
A friend told me
of one on the shore
that lifted its head and opened
the elegant beak and cried out
in the long, sweet savoring of its life
which, if you have heard it,
you know is a sacred thing,
and for which, if you have not heard it,
you had better hurry to where
they still sing.
And, believe me, tell no one
just where that is.
The next morning
this loon, speckled

and iridescent and with a plan
to fly home
to some hidden lake,
was dead on the shore.
I tell you this
to break your heart,
by which I mean only
that it break open and never close again
to the rest of the world.

In this poem, the speaker is not the "you." The speaker is speaking to the "you." The "you" is us, the reader. As readers, our hears should open to the loons and the rest of the natural world. But the POV of the speaker is not the "you." The speaker already knows the story told in this poem. The speaker has seen the loons and grieved for them already.

Poems spoken entirely from a second-person POV are hard to come by. You—as in you, the person reading this book—can find some examples by searching The Poetry Foundation's website or typing "The Poetry Foundation Second Person POV" into your search bar.

Third Person

Third-person POV can happen three ways, and in each of them, the narrator or speaker is outside the story or poem. The third-person narrator/speaker does not become a character in the narrative, but the narrator can tell the reader what is happening from a character's perspective.

Can? Or will? That is an important question. So is this: From which character's perspective? This is where the three ways come in. Remember, third-person narration includes three POV options:

1. Limited—or close—third
2. Omniscient third
3. Objective third

Sometimes, early on in our education, we learn that the difference is whether a narrator is all-knowing or not. That's true enough, but when we start thinking, reading, and writing like writers, the differences between third-person points of view become more nuanced.

An important part of the difference among them is closeness and distance. To compare them, let's look back at the opening line examples I offered in Lesson 1. Let's examine them as fiction and change them to third person.

When Carla was six years old, she killed her sister with a gun she did not know how to shoot. Reading this, we could say the POV is close/limited third or omniscient because we know the character did not know how to shoot the gun. If we add a few more sentences, we can make a clear distinction.

When Carla was six years old, she killed her sister with a gun she did not know how to shoot. Carla does not remember this, only that one day her sister was there, and the next day her sister was not. Sometimes, Carla thinks her mother remembers every day, even though it has been ten years. Even though Carla has been trying to make up for being the only child ever since her sister stopped being a child too. Sometimes Carla sees her mother see her, and the look on her mother's face feels all wrong. Now we are sure we have a limited, or close, third. Even though the narrator tells us information about what Carla's mother may be thinking, the information all comes through Carla's eyes.

Now, read this version:

When Carla was six years old, she killed her sister with a gun she did not know how to shoot. Carla does not remember this, only that one day her sister was there, and the next day her sister was not. It has been ten years, but Carla's mother remembers every day. Her mother tries not to do this remembering in the presence of her remaining child, but sometimes, she cannot help it. Now we have an omniscient third. The narrator knows what is going on inside the heads of both Carla and her mother. We see from Carla's perspective and from her mother's.

Now, read the last version: *When she was six years old, Carla killed her sister with a gun no one had taught her how to shoot. Ten years later, Clara is an only-child. Sometimes Clara's mother watches her.* Now we have an objective third. The narrator reports the happenings of the story—just the facts. Notice the lack of commentary on what Carla or her mother are thinking. As readers, we are left on our own to figure out how the characters are dealing with the past.

Changing the POV for a third-person narrator is not just a matter of how much the narrator knows. Changing the POV is also a matter of changing the distance. Notice how close the narrator is in the first two examples and how distant in the third. Notice how the narrator knowing what both characters are thinking (in the second example) makes the narration feel less close to Carla than when the narrator knew only what Carla was thinking.

Many writers refer to limited third as close third because of how close we feel to one character when the narrator follows all the inner workings of one character. Even in the brief example above, we can see how every part of the narrative comes through Carla's filter—including what her mother may be thinking. Another aspect of close third is the fact that the narrator does not know what is going on in the minds of the other characters. In this way, close third is as limited as first-person.

In the omniscient example, the narrator is inside the heads of both characters. This is a close perspective, but it is close to all the characters. The events of the story can be viewed through the filter of any character. Writers apply these filters in varied ways though. At any given moment in a story, the writer may or may not write from a specific character's POV.

In the objective third, the narrator is so distant that the narrator does no more than report or record. In objective third, the story usually works because of the distance.

Studying Third-Person POV across Genres

Of all the Point of View, we tend to think of third person applying almost exclusively to fiction. But we can find third person in poetry and creative nonfiction and poetry too. To round-out our discussion, we will study examples of each. As we look at third-person POV in each genre, we will also examine the three different types of third-person POV: close/limited, omniscient, and objective.

Let's start with fiction. Most of Zadie Smith's fictional story, "The Embassy of Cambodia" is written in close third, including this passage below.

But, looking again at the bags the Cambodian woman carried, Fatou wondered whether they weren't in fact very old bags—hadn't their design changed? The more she looked at them the more convinced she became that they contained not food but clothes or something else again, the outline of each bag being a little too rounded and smooth. Maybe she was simply taking out the rubbish. Fatou stood at the bus stop and watched until the Cambodian woman reached the corner, crossed, and turned left toward the high road. Meanwhile, back at the embassy the badminton continued to be played, though with a little more effort now because of a wayward wind. At one point it seemed to Fatou that the next lob would blow southward, sending the shuttlecock over the wall to land lightly in her own hands. Instead the other player, with his vicious reliability (Fatou had long ago decided that both players were men), caught the shuttlecock as it began to drift and sent it back to his opponent—another deathly, downward smash.

To study close-third in this passage, first answer this question: What happens beyond what is directly happening to Fatou? Leaving the embassy, the Cambodian woman walks to the corner carrying her bags. And the men in the embassy continue to play badminton. Now reread the passage to see how these happenings are shown through Fatou's eyes.

Fatou watches the woman walking away with her shopping bags, and Fatou watches the shuttlecock. Fatou also begins to wonder about the woman's shopping bags. The narrator is so close to Fatou that we see Fatou notice the pages and begin to think about them, first wondering if the bags were "very old," and asking herself "hadn't their design changed?" As Fatou keeps thinking about the Cambodian woman, she starts to approach a realization. As readers we can figure out the woman may be in a situation similar to Fatou's. Fatou turns away at the brink of the realization, though, and we stay with her perspective. "Maybe she was simply taking out the rubbish." Here, the close-third raises the stakes. In this section, we cannot see beyond what Fatou can see, and she cannot see herself in this woman.

At the same time, the close-third perspective from Fatou's POV reminds us how isolated victims of human trafficking can be. Remember, at this point in the narrative, Fatou has begun to wonder if she is a slave. Fatou cannot recognize the Cambodian woman as a victim like herself. The Cambodian woman does not even see Fatou—or if she does, Fatou is not aware. What Fatou does see is the shuttlecock, moving in a game that continues to be played behind the gates of the embassy. As the stakes rise, we see this game the way Fatou sees it, from behind a gate she cannot pass through.

These are important observations to make when reading to see how close third works in fiction. But we would study the way close third works in the same ways if the piece was creative nonfiction or poetry. Two online literary journals that publish compelling close third POV pieces outside of fiction are *Brevity* for creative nonfiction and *Plume* for poetry. (Check out Kwame Dawes's Bodies on the Margins in *Plume* and Imprint in *Brevity*. You won't be sorry.)

Poornima Laxmeshwar's prose poem "Cartography" has an omniscient third narrator. As you read the excerpt below, think about the different points of view entering the poem.

Their eighth anniversary was on its way, just like a cheesy pizza. Just that it came every year on 26th Feb even if they didn't want it. This year they spoke about unexplored Europe.

She was excited about Amsterdam. The infamous Red light district, the coffee shops, she was already preparing her to-do list while he wanted Venice—a boatman singing, the flowing romance and her.

They slept with their own set of dreams and the map led them to places where they wanted to go.

At first, the omniscient third is plural—"even if they didn't want it." The couple begins by talking together about a trip to Europe. In the next paragraph, though, the third-person omniscient moves to hers and his. As we read the details each envisions for a trip to Europe, we see how she and he want different things. In the next paragraph, the omniscient third moves back to plural, as the two people in the poem diverge from each other.

Like first-person plural POV, third-person plural is a tricky perspective for a writer to pull off. Laxmeshwar does it well by interspersing the plural perspective—they—with the individual perspective of the she and he in the poem. Her desires conflict with his. His desires conflict with hers. Because the narrator is omniscient, we see from both lenses. The lens revealing what happens to both of them (together and alone) as they diverge from each other heightens the emotional impact: "They slept with their own set of dreams."

Vivian I. Bikulege narrates part of her hybrid essay "Cuttings," a work of creative nonfiction, in third-person objective. The excerpt below contains the first two segments of the "Grids" section. Segment A has an objective third POV.

---

2. Grids

A.

Borough Park is a neighborhood inside greater Brooklyn Borough and home to one of the largest Jewish populations in the United States. The heart of the community is inside a grid between 11th and 18th avenues, and 40th and 60th streets. Leiby met Aron on 18th Avenue. The boy was supposed to meet his mother at the corner of 13th Avenue and 50th Street.

B.

On July 12, I drive south on Interstate 95 to the Savannah/Hilton Head International Airport. I will fly to Newark and take a train into Manhattan for business the following day. The one o'clock news reports the murder and dismemberment of an eight-year-old boy in Brooklyn. The newscaster is exact and remote in his delivery of the story. My breath catches in my throat and I turn off the radio.

In segment A, Bikulege records the facts. From part one of the essay, we know Leiby was murdered after losing his way back to his mother and finding Aaron instead. Knowing what we do, this section is devastating. The objective third POV adds to the devastation. Bikulege reports this information not unlike news reporters report the information about murders— including the murder of this child. Bikulege doesn't tell us how to feel about these facts, nor do news reporters. The objective third POV mimics that remoteness of news reportage, developing one of the essay's central themes and reminding us all of the remote ways we receive news of violence.

Not telling us how to feel here works for the essay because in reading (as in the rest of life) no one likes being told how to feel. Instead of telling us how to feel, Bikulege juxtaposes the objective third in segment A. with first-person in segment B. In B, Bikulege is the first-person narrator, immersed in the story as a character. This character shows the reader how she feels— what it is like—to be driving to an airport, en route to Manhattan and to hear the "exact and remote" report of Leiby's murder on the news.

When the Narrator Is Also the Writer: Special Complexities of POV in Creative Nonfiction

A complex part of narrative POV in creative nonfiction is that the writer is behind the narrator. When we read creative nonfiction, we know the words we are reading are true. We are seeing true events through the lens of the writer. When creative nonfiction is written in first- or second person, with narrators who call themselves "I" or "you," the writer has developed that "I" or "you" into a character on the page. When creative nonfiction is written in third-person, the writer is usually describing events that have happened to someone else. Though it's also true that some creative nonfiction writers choose to use third person to narrate their own experiences. When reading for POV in creative nonfiction, remember that creative nonfiction writers are making the same POV choices writers do in other genres.

Whatever the POV or the reason for using it, when we read creative nonfiction, we read knowing the writer is part of the lens. Read this excerpt from "Sea Urchin" by Chang-rae Lee.

What does it taste like? I'm not sure, because I've never had anything like it. All I know is that it tastes alive, something alive at the undragged bottom of the sea; it tastes the way flesh would taste if flesh were a mineral. And I'm half gagging, though still chewing; it's as if I had another tongue in my mouth, this blind, self-satisfied creature. That night I throw up, my mother scolding us, my father chuckling through his concern. The next day, my uncles joke that they'll take me out for some more, and the suggestion is enough to make me retch again.

But a week later I'm better, and I go back by myself. The woman is there, and so are the sea urchins, glistening in the hot sun. "I know what you want," she says. I sit, my mouth slick with anticipation and revulsion, not yet knowing why.

Lee admits he isn't "sure" what the sea urchin tastes like, but he goes on to give details we wouldn't normally associate with taste. We trust Lee not to make something up but to give us what he can. And what he gives us a clear and unusual idea of what it was like to have a sea urchin in his mouth.

The next paragraph is also the last in Lee's essay. Notice how the perspective changes a little. Lee is still narrating in first-person, but look at the last sentence. In the last sentence, the narrator's lens includes reflection. By the end of the sentence, the narrator realizes something Lee did not in those moments as he waited for his second taste of sea urchin. The "I" narrator is a young teenager, not yet fifteen. He could not, at that age, at that moment of waiting for another plate of sea urchin, have understood what Lee, the narrator looking back, realizes about this experience—the "not yet knowing why."

When the Lens Includes Actual Images: POV in Graphic and Photographic Narrative

We already know that reading hybrid work requires thinking in hybrid ways. In Lesson 2, we discussed the importance of reading both the text and the images in graphic and photographic creative writing. This holds true for reading for POV in graphic and photographic creative writing as well. In our Readings section, both Sophie Yanow's graphic novel *The Contradictions* and Randi Ward's "Hestur: A Photo Essay" are written in first-person POV. This is to say (of course) they both have "I" narrators. The images add another filter to the lens though.

Look at this excerpt from "Hestur: A Photo Essay." The excerpt includes the last paragraph of the introduction and one of the photographs and accompanying caption.

It was rather inevitable that I too would become subject to the roiling social currents of the village of Hestur. As a newcomer to the island, its youngest resident, an independently employed, single female and a foreigner to boot, my life was ripe for interpretation; it wasn't long before my daily routines and social interactions came under all kinds of scrutiny. Yet it was this complex configuration of intense proximity and solitude that made my time in Hestur, where I spent my last 6 months in the Faroe Islands, exquisitely vivid. I experienced an incredible spectrum of life and humanity and often participated in it to near-overwhelming extremes. Whether I was assisting at the sheepfold, raking freshly mown hay, enjoying a colorful conversation with Hjørleiv, teaching Jørmund how to use email, or borrowing Ebbe's clothesline for an afternoon, perhaps my most tender act of solidarity was simply turning on my kitchen light of an evening so people could see I was still there.

Ull er Føroya Gull

There are approximately 580 sheep grazing the island of Hestur. Long before the fishing industry emerged, woolen goods were one of the main staples of the Faroe Islands' economy. Wool, however, is no longer considered "Faroese gold"; its market value is so low that people often burn it rather than selling or processing it into yarn.

In the introduction, Ward's "I" narrator explains her presence in Hestur, but the photos are not about her. We know Ward is literally behind the lens herself. While she is behind the camera, she is not a part of the photograph. None of the compositions include her at all. The "I" narrator makes the photo essay more personal by showing the reader the person behind the camera. Notice, though, how the POV changes once the photographs begin. While Ward's eye is part of taking the photographs, her "I" is not inside them.

See, too, how the narration in the photo captions comes in an objective third POV. In this part of the photo essay, Ward is an observer, taking the photographs, explaining the facts. In ways similar to the way Vivian I. Bikulege juxtaposes first-person and omniscient third, Ward juxtaposes the first-person introduction with objective-third captions. The photos meet somewhere in between. They connect the personal introduction with all its quirky tenderness to the facts Ward wants her readers to understand about this old, isolated island and its dwindling population and culture of sheep husbandry. Only by reading for POV in the layers of this photo essay (introduction, photographs, captions) can we understand what Ward accomplishes in these pages.

Now look at the excerpt from Sophie Yanow's graphic novel *The Contradictions*, written in first-person POV.

In the captions and narratory blocks (or voice-overs) of this graphic novel, Yanow creates a first-person narrator. "In a daze I had walked to the study abroad office and asked for any option without a language requirement," Sophie's voiceover tells the reader. In this excerpt the "I" narrator remembers the troubled circumstances surrounding her decision to study abroad.

Reading the image *with* the text in the panels on this page, we see Sophie entering an art museum, walking through its corridors, and sitting down to sketch. Sophie's dialogue "One student, si'l vous plait" and the onomatopoeia sound effects "rip, pluck, flop" pair with what we see in the graphics. We hear the sounds Sophie makes, and the words she says.

Just as the photographs add another layer to POV in photo essay, the drawings add a POV layer in graphic narrative. We don't exactly see through Sophie's eyes, as though she were holding a camera and we were looking through her lens. Instead we see Sophie drawn as a figure—a figure living Sophie's life during her study abroad time in Paris.

It's worth noticing how the panels in the first tiers on this page include borders, while the second tier moves from borders to an open panel, and the third tier includes open panels. (Remember, open panels are panels without one or more border lines.) Opening the panels brings us a little closer to Sophie's character, doesn't it? The open panels invite us into the POV. We might describe this as a first-person POV in words meeting a close-third in graphics. Whatever words we might use to describe the POV, the point in reading for POV in graphic narrative is to notice how the words and the images work together to form—or alter—the lens.

Lesson 7 Discussion Questions and Writing Prompts

Discussion Questions: Focus on Point of View

1. Study the tweeted micro essays by Chris Galvin Nguyen (found in Lesson 3, page 46). Identify the points of view used in each and explain why you think Nguyen chose the particular POV for the particular micro essay. What does each POV allow Nguyen to accomplish?

2. Read the selection "Negative Results" (found in Lesson 3, page 41) and explain why you think Beth Uznis Johnson wrote this story in second person. How would a first-person or third-person narrator change this micro story?

3. Imagine the story "Jerry's Crab Shack: One Star" (found in the Readings section) narrated in third person and from the waitress's POV. How would the story change? Would it be as compelling? Would the main conflict still be between Gary and Janet?

Writing Prompts: Focus on Point of View

Generative Prompt

Select a POV from which you have not written (or not written much) before. From this POV, draft the beginning of a story, essay, poem, graphic narrative, or photo essay.

Revision Prompt

Get out a piece of writing you have already worked on. Notice the POV. Now rewrite the piece in a different POV or add a narrative layer that brings a different POV into the piece. (Using the piece you started for the generative prompt is fair game for this revision.)

LESSON 8
SETTING

Two questions: Where? When?

In creative writing, setting answers these questions.

Where a story, poem, or essay takes place (in a Colorado State University dorm room, in London, on the moon) and when it takes place (now, in 1752, in the distant future) are fundamental parts of the writing. Think, for example, about setting in fiction and narrative creative nonfiction. Setting affects other elements of the narrative, like character development. Setting a story during a specific period of history, for example, means characters will have some different habits than they would in a story set right now. Similar ideas hold true for the settings of poem. Setting a poem in a specific location will influence the content of the poem.

Where and when seem like simple concepts at first glance. As we read to study setting—and the ways writers construct setting on the page—we need to look more closely at the where and when of setting.

Place

Place means geographical place. Where on the globe, or the universe, or the made-up vortex beyond space, is this story, poem, or essay happening? And not just where but specifically where? In our Readings section, for example, Chang-rae Lee's essay, "Sea Urchin," is set in Seoul, South Korea. Writers in any genre can learn from the way Lee crafts setting in this narrative essay.

The first paragraphs of "Sea Urchin" describe many of the key details of the setting. Notice how these paragraphs go beyond naming the specific place, Seoul, South Korea, to cover other important aspects of place.

July, 1980. I'm about to turn fifteen and our family is in Seoul, the first time since we left, twelve years earlier. I don't know if it's different. My parents can't really say. They just repeat the equivalent of "How in the world?" whenever we venture into another part of the city, or meet one of their old friends. "Look at that–how in the world?" "This hot spell, yes, yes–how in the world?" My younger sister is very quiet in the astounding heat. We all are. It's the first time I notice how I stink. You can't help smelling like everything else. And in the heat everything smells of ferment and rot and rankness. In my grandfather's old neighborhood, where the two- and three-room houses stand barely head-high, the smell is staggering. "What's that?" I ask. My cousin says, "Shit."

"Shit? What shit?"

"Yours," he says, laughing. "Mine."

On the wide streets near the city center, there are student demonstrations; my cousin says they're a response to a massacre of citizens by the military down south in Kwangju. After the riot troops clear the avenues, the air is laden with tear gas–"spicy," in the idiom. Whenever we're in a taxi, moving through there, I open the window and stick out my tongue, trying to taste the poison, the human repellent. My mother wonders what's wrong with me.

As far as setting goes, other physical aspects of place can also be key: the geography, the topography, the architecture, the landmarks, the layout. These are the elements that help make a place what it is, and often they influence a story—or the writer's telling of the story. In these paragraphs from "Sea Urchin," Lee describes the small houses in his "grandfather's old neighborhood," and the "wide streets near the city center." In doing so, Lee puts the reader there with him, showing us what Seoul is like as he experienced it in 1980, as part of a family returning.

Environment

In setting, part of the "where" is the physical environment, the climate, the weather, the air, the landscape, the cityscape. What is the environment in Lee's essay? It is summer in Seoul, and the city is having a hot spell. As Lee writes, "And in the heat everything smells of ferment and rot and rankness." The heat inside the city—and the smell—becomes part of setting too.

Describing what life is like for the characters who occupy the place is another important part of setting. What is the social and political climate? What are people doing? What historical or political events are happening? In "Sea Urchin," "there are student demonstrations" after a "massacre of citizens." There is "tear gas" in the air. In these lines, Lee gives us to understand what life is like for the people in Seoul, those who live there and those who are visiting.

Time

Just as place has many complexities when we are talking about setting, so does time. Time means when the story is happening. When in history, when on the calendar. When in relation to events and characters. The year, the season, the month. But time means more than that, too. Look again at the first paragraph from "Sea Urchin." Notice how much it tells you about time.

July, 1980. I'm about to turn fifteen and our family is in Seoul, the first time since we left, twelve years earlier. I don't know if it's different. My parents can't really say. They just repeat the equivalent of "How in the world?" whenever we venture into another part of the city, or meet one of their old friends. "Look at that–how in the world?" "This hot spell, yes, yes–how in the world?" My younger sister is very quiet in the astounding heat. We all are. It's the first time I notice how I stink. You can't help smelling like everything else. And in the heat everything smells of ferment and rot and rankness. In my grandfather's old neighborhood, where the two- and three-room houses stand barely head-high, the smell is staggering. "What's that?" I ask. My cousin says, "Shit."

The year on the calendar is 1980. But there is more to the year than that. This is the first time in twelve years that Lee's family has been back to Seoul. So we also get a sense of a year in terms of what it means to the characters in the narrative. Time has elapsed—not as part of the story, but before the story has begun—and those elapsed years change the way this family experiences Seoul.

In setting, we think about when the story is happening in the year, in the week, in the day. In the first paragraph of "Sea Urchin," for example, Lee tells us when on the calendar we are in this story—July. While the month is part of place in that it indicates season, it is also part of time—the time of year.

The passage of time within a story is also part of setting, whether the time passing is minutes or years, the fact that time is passing is important. Passing time is often part of conflict and plot and the way characters change. Study the last paragraph of "Sea Urchin."

But a week later I'm better, and I go back by myself. The woman is there, and so are the sea urchins, glistening in the hot sun. "I know what you want," she says. I sit, my mouth slick with anticipation and revulsion, not yet knowing why.

One week has passed. By noting this change in setting, Lee lets us know that enough time has passed for something to change for the characters. In this case, the narrator has recovered from his sickness after eating the sea urchin. In the world of this narrative, one week is enough time for the narrator to realize he wants to go back for more.

Constructing Setting

Considering the importance of where and when, though, is only part of what writers study when they study setting. Even more important than where and when a story happens is the way a writer conveys details about the setting to the reader.

Before we go on here, let me pause to remind us about the genre of "Sea Urchin." This is a piece of creative nonfiction. I mention this because it is easy to think of setting as part of fiction, but writers of both fiction and creative nonfiction narratives work to develop setting. Remember, setting is often a part of poetry too, and poets who read to study setting learn to bring striking details about place and time into their own work. Joy Harjo's prose poem "Grace" is an example of a poem that includes details about setting. Read the first paragraph from "Grace."

I think of Wind and her wild ways the year we had nothing to lose
and lost it anyway in the cursed country of the fox. We still talk
about that winter, how the cold froze imaginary buffalo on the stuffed
horizon of snowbanks. The haunting voices of the starved and mutilated
broke fences, crashed our thermostat dreams, and we couldn't stand it
one more time. So once again we lost a winter in stubborn memory, walked
through cheap apartment walls, skated through fields of ghosts into
a town that never wanted us, in the epic search for grace.

Notice the setting details: "cursed country of the fox," "winter," "how the cold froze imaginary buffalo on the stuffed horizon of snowbanks," "cheap apartment wall."

Whatever the genre, setting can add depth, nuance, and interest to a piece of creative writing. Setting also becomes part of the writing (as opposed to being dropped in for no other reason than to explain the where and when). When reading for setting, read to study how the writer constructs the setting and what this construction brings to the piece.

Of course, part of constructing setting means the writer gives the reader all the necessary information about place and time—information like we have studied in "Sea Urchin." Good writers, like Chang-rae Lee, do this information-giving in compelling ways that also become a meaningful part of the narrative.

Here is another way to think about what writers do when they construct setting:

They provide specific **location details.**

They provide concrete, **physical details.**

They explain **vital info.**

They show the **characters occupying space.**

They indicate **time, elapsed time, and passing time.**

They do all this in ways that are **interesting to read.**

They make setting a **part of the story.**

Let's look at key passages of "Sea Urchin" again, this time studying the beginning paragraphs, a passage from the middle, and the ending paragraph.

Beginning Paragraphs

July, 1980. I'm about to turn fifteen and our family is in Seoul, the first time since we left, twelve years earlier. I don't know if it's different. My parents can't really say. They just repeat the equivalent of "How in the world?" whenever we venture into another part of the city, or meet one of their old friends. "Look at that–how in the world?" "This hot spell, yes, yes–how in the world?" My younger sister is very quiet in the astounding heat. We all are. It's the first time I notice how I stink. You can't help smelling like everything else. And in the heat everything smells of ferment and rot and rankness. In my grandfather's old neighborhood, where the two- and three-room houses stand barely head-high, the smell is staggering. "What's that?" I ask. My cousin says, "Shit."

"Shit? What shit?"

"Yours," he says, laughing. "Mine."

On the wide streets near the city center, there are student demonstrations; my cousin says they're a response to a massacre of citizens by the military down south in Kwangju. After the riot troops clear the avenues, the air is laden with tear gas–"spicy," in the idiom. Whenever we're in a taxi, moving through there, I open the window and stick out my tongue, trying to taste the poison, the human repellent. My mother wonders what's wrong with me.

Passage from the Middle

As it is, the days are made up of meals, formal and impromptu, meals between meals and within meals; the streets are a continuous outdoor buffet of braised crabs, cold buckwheat noodles, shaved ice with sweet red beans on top. In Itaewon, the district near the United States Army base, where you can get anything you want, culinary or otherwise, we stop at a seafood stand for dinner. Basically, it's a tent diner, a long bar with stools, a camp stove and fish tank behind the proprietor, an elderly woman with a low, hoarse voice. The roof is a stretch of blue poly-tarp. My father is excited; it's like the old days. He wants raw fish, but my mother shakes her head. I can see why: in plastic bins of speckled, bloody ice sit semi-alive cockles, abalones, eels, conchs, sea cucumbers, porgies, shrimps. "Get something fried," she tells him, not caring what the woman might think. "Get something cooked."

Ending Paragraph

But a week later I'm better, and I go back by myself. The woman is there, and so are the sea urchins, glistening in the hot sun. "I know what you want," she says. I sit, my mouth slick with anticipation and revulsion, not yet knowing why.

We've already discussed how Lee provides specific details about place and time. But Lee does more than show us where and when. Lee pulls us into the setting, and he pulls us by constructing setting in the ways outlined in the list (providing location details and physical details, explaining vital info, showing the characters in this space, indicating time, and making all of this compelling). Let's look again at Lee's construction of setting, this time studying how he does it.

Lee accomplishes a lot with setting in a little space. Often, Lee constructs more than one part of setting with only a sentence or two: "July, 1980. I'm about to turn fifteen and our family is in Seoul, the first time since we left, twelve years earlier." As he explains where they are, Lee shows us how this family visits Seoul—for the first time since leaving.

Now notice how, within one essay, Lee shows his readers three different locations inside of Seoul: his "grandfather's old neighborhood," the "city center," "Itaewon." See the ways Lee depicts concrete location, physical details, and vital stats about these places.

In my grandfather's old neighborhood, where the two- and three-room houses stand barely head-high, the smell is staggering.

On the wide streets near the city center, there are student demonstrations; my cousin says they're a response to a massacre of citizens by the military down south in Kwangju.

In Itaewon, the district near the United States Army base, where you can get anything you want, culinary or otherwise, we stop at a seafood stand for dinner.

With each of these details of the city, Lee plunges us further into Seoul. We learn about the place and see Lee and his family and the other inhabitants of the city.

Lee also shows how the characters occupy space in these places. He writes of how the characters behave in the heat—and how they smell. "My younger sister is very quiet in the astounding heat. We all are. It's the first time I notice how I stink. You can't help smelling like everything else. And in the heat everything smells of ferment and rot and rankness." In his "grandfather's old neighborhood," Lee and his cousin talk about the "shit," smell of this environment, too. Here, Lee uses dialogue to construct setting.

A paragraph later, describing the protests in "the wide streets near the city center," Lee writes of the tear gas, both what the locals call it and his own reaction to it: "Whenever we're in a taxi, moving through there, I open the window and stick out my tongue, trying to taste the poison, the human repellent."

Later, in Itaewon, Lee brings the readers into a very specific setting, the place where he tastes the sea urchin. "Basically, it's a tent diner, a long bar with stools, a camp stove and fish tank behind the proprietor, an elderly woman with a low, hoarse voice. The roof is a stretch of blue poly-tarp." In these two sentences, Lee puts us there. He does not give every detail of this establishment—only the important ones—the ones that bring the reader in.

The next sentences show how the characters occupy the space: "My father is excited; it's like the old days. He wants raw fish, but my mother shakes her head. I can see why: in plastic bins of speckled, bloody ice sit semi-alive cockles, abalones, eels, conchs, sea cucumbers, porgies, shrimps."

In the very next sentence, Lee uses dialogue again to help construct setting, as his mother tells his father what kind of seafood to order: " 'Get something fried,' she tells him, not caring what the woman might think. 'Get something cooked.'" Notice the subtle setting detail. This is the kind of place where not-cooked somethings are an option.

Of course, the dialogue here is also part of the conflict—should Lee eat the sea urchin or not. This is one reason Lee's construction of setting works so well. As Lee creates the setting, he also weaves setting into the rest of the story. Setting becomes part of the narrative arc, the character development, the central theme.

As Lee depicts time—what the passage of time has meant for the characters and how much time has passed in the story—he is not only writing about the when but writing part of the narrative. At the beginning, in giving details of time, Lee explains how long his family has been away and tells us his parents' reaction to the changes—"how in the world?" As the narrative approaches the resolution and Lee explains time again, noting the week that has passed and the heatwave that has not, Lee also brings the piece to its resolution: "But a week later I'm better, and I go back by myself. The woman is there, and so are the sea urchins, glistening in the hot sun." Here the passage of time is part of the ending.

Setting also touches the central theme of tasting. Notice all of the setting details about food or taste. "The streets are a continuous outdoor buffet of braised crabs, cold buckwheat noodles, shaved ice with sweet red beans on top." In describing the city streets, Lee lists some of the foods that can be found. Even the tear gas is "spicy."

As the narrative arc rises, Lee wants to taste everything, and some of what he wants to taste is part of the setting, the tear gas in the streets. Remember, too, how we discussed Lee's wanting to taste the tear gas as part of his character development in Lesson 6? The tear gas is a vital detail of the setting, but it is also a vital part of the story.

Setting in Place-Based and Environmental Literature

In some creative work, particularly place-based narrative and some environmental literature, setting often becomes part of the plot or functions almost as a type of character. "Place-based narrative" and "environmental literature" are fairly broad terms that mean writing in which place plays a significant role and literature that deals with the environment and what is happening to it. Place-based and environmental literature can be found in any genre. Randi Ward's "Hestur: A Photo Essay" (found in the Readings section) is a place-based narrative, and Mary Oliver's "Lead" (found in Lesson 7, page 122) is environmental literature.

Look that the following excerpt from "Hestur: A Photo Essay," paying attention to place. Then take a close look at the following excerpts, a passage from the text introduction and two of the photographs and captions.

Excerpt from the Text Introduction

Hestur, which literally means "Horse," is one of 18 storm-swept islands situated north-northwest of Scotland, approximately halfway between Iceland and Norway, in the North Atlantic Ocean. As a self-governing territory of the Danish Kingdom, the have their distinct language, culture, parliament, and flag. The capital city of Tórshavn, along with the surrounding villages incorporated into its municipality, is home to nearly 20,000 of the archipelago's 52,000 inhabitants. Hestur's 20 residents joined Tórshavn's municipality in 2005, but the population of the village itself continues to decrease. Those who remain, most of whom are at or well-beyond retirement age, divide their days between farming/fishing and part-time jobs in the public sector providing services that keep the island habitable.

Though many people have labeled Hestur a "dying village," I witnessed firsthand the traditions and various acts of kindness and reserved devotion that sustain the community's infrastructure and morale. These touching deeds seem even more remarkable in the face of the subtle tensions between families or individuals, resentments that have simmered for generations and occasionally threaten to disturb the village's delicate balance.

Excerpt of two photographs and accompanying captions

Ull er Føroya Gull

There are approximately 580 sheep grazing the island of Hestur. Long before the fishing industry emerged, woolen goods were one of the main staples of the Faroe Islands' economy. Wool, however, is no longer considered "Faroese gold"; its market value is so low that people often burn it rather than selling or processing it into yarn.

Hjørleiv & Jørmund

Hjørleiv Poulsen and Jørmund Zachariassen grew up together in the village of Hestur and have remained friends and neighbors. Hjørleiv was the village postman for 37 years. Jørmund assumed the position shortly after Hjørleiv's retirement, and he also serves as organist in Hestur's church.

Like the rest of the photo essay, these excerpted paragraphs, photographs, and captions are steeped in place. The photo essay is about this place, and while Hestur is certainly the setting, Hestur becomes almost a character—a character we end up routing for, even though, as Ward writes, "many people have labeled Hestur a 'dying village' … " Hestur is a living, breathing, sheep-rearing part of this photo essay. The village is everywhere in the essay. By the end, we know Hestur as well and as intimately as we would hope to know any main character. We know its ways. We know its shape. We know its struggles.

See, too, how the photographs are anchored in the place, even when people or sheep appear as the main subjects of the frame. In the *Ull er Føroya Gull* photograph, we see the sheep in their stone fold, but we see them against the backdrop of the windswept island on which Hestur sits. In the *Hjørleiv & Jørmund* photograph, the two old friends are looking out over the landscape—a landscape we can see in the photograph. In "Hestur: A Photo Essay," Ward does not separate the place from the people or animals there. Indeed, she shows us how the people and the sheep are a part of the place, and the place is part of them.

Setting in Graphic and Photographic Writing

It is just as important to read for setting in graphic and photographic prose as it is in other creative work. The difference, of course, is that we read for setting visually, too. Really, we've already discussed this just now, as we looked to see how the images of place are essential in the composition of "Hestur: A Photo Essay." Without even discussing it first, when you *read* the photographs to see how Hestur itself figured into them, you were also *reading* them to see how much Ward depicts setting through the photographs.

Reading graphic prose for setting works in similar ways. Read Sophie Yanow's *The Contradictions* from our Readings section, then take a close look at the excerpt below.

In Yanow's graphic novel, we see setting, literally almost entirely in the graphics. Paris, as Sophie experiences it, is depicted visually. Here Yanow uses a splash page to show the figure of Sophie inside the setting. In this page-size panel, we see setting in the objects Yanow has drawn—the buildings, the sidewalks, and the streets. Notice, though, how little details of setting come through in the text: "No one smiles here." "I need to buy some black clothes." Both of these sentences add a little more vital information about setting—just a little more than we can see in the graphics. Notice, too, how, Yanow forgoes thought bubbles for Sophie's internal dialogue. Instead, she draws the text into the images of the city itself. The text details about setting literally become part of the visual setting.

We have already covered (and covered again) the concept that reading graphic and photographic prose means reading the image and text as two pars of a whole. Reading for setting works the same way. Setting will show up in the images and in the words. Even if setting shows up more dramatically in one than in the other, as in Yanow's novel, reading the words and the images together will show the ways setting becomes an important part of the story.

Lesson 8 Discussion Questions and Writing Prompts

Core Reading Discussion Questions: Focus on Setting

1. Setting is key in Chang-rae Lee's "Sea Urchin" (found in the Readings section). What sensory experiences (smell, taste, sound, sight, touch) does Lee offer as he introduces the reader to this place? Which character has these sensory experiences, and why are these sensory details important in Lee's construction of setting?

2. Explore the ways the speaker experiences setting in Joy Harjo's prose poem "Grace" (found in Lesson 5, page 80). How do these depictions of setting heighten the emotional experience for the reader and clarify what is at stake in this poem?

3. Read Randi Ward's "Hestur: A Photo Essay" (found in the Readings section). Which details of setting does Ward place in the text, and which details of setting does Ward show through the camera lens? Why does Ward draw the reader's focus to these setting details? Are there any details that overlap from the text to the photographs?

Writing Prompts: Focus on Setting

Generative Prompt

Consider a setting you find compelling. Write three sentences to describe the setting. Now write three sentences to describe the setting at close-range. (For example, if the setting is a city street, focus on the cracks in the asphalt or the smell from the gutter.) Now write three sentences from a great distance. (For example, describe something happening just beyond the street, describe the architecture or the size of the buildings, or imagine the aerial view.)

Revision Prompt

Revise a manuscript in progress by exploring two ways the characters experience the setting:

Option 1: Describe how the main character experiences setting through his or her senses. Where does the character walk, drive, or ride? What does the character hear and see while she does these things? Where does the character sleep? What does she smell as she closes her eyes there? What else does the character do in specific places? What are the sensory experiences she has as she inhabits these places? (Remember, if you are working on a visual piece, you can include these details in photographs or illustrations.)

Option 2: Revisit the setting of a poem-in-progress. Work to bring the setting into focus for the reader by including specific details. What season is the poem set in? Does it take place indoors or outdoors? What color are the walls or what kind of surface is the ground? What does the speaker smell or taste? What sounds are important for the reader to experience through words? What other details of setting might come into the poem?

LESSON 9
SCENE

When most of us read the word "scene," we think of movies or plays. Scenes are not just for those genres, though. Scenes are an important part of most narratives, and scenic rendering can be a part of poetry, too. When we read for pleasure, we tend to overlook the craft of writing scenes. This happens in part because scenes are so engaging for readers that we forget we are reading at all. Reading writers, however, always reread those pages to figure out how writers render the scenes that pull their readers into the page.

What Is Scene?

That's an important question. Here is the answer. Scene happens when a piece of creative writing slows down and narrows in on a specific action or interaction, and the writer conveys what is happening moment-to-moment, or nearly so. Scenes include sensory details, characters' actions, and often dialogue. Scenes also happen when a writer is working in specific time, instead of explaining what happens in general.

In the narratives in this book, you will find many examples of scenes. While scene is an important part of narrative prose writing, scenic rendering often enters poetry and non-narrative prose, too. In other words, writers in all genres and forms use scene, but they don't always write full-blown scenes. When this happens, writers work with scene in abbreviated ways, slowing the piece a bit, using some parts of scene writing mentioned above, and moving from writing about what happens in general time to what happens in a specific moment.

Studying scenic rendering in poetry, where scene often happens in brief, can be a helpful introduction to reading for scene. To that end, take a look at this excerpt from Joy Harjo's "Grace."

Like Coyote, like Rabbit, we could not contain our terror and clowned
our way through a season of false midnights. We had to swallow
that town with laughter, so it would go down easy as honey. And one
morning as the sun struggled to break ice, and our dreams had found us
with coffee and pancakes in a truck stop along Highway 80,
we found grace.

I could say grace was a woman with time on her hands, or a white
buffalo escaped from memory. But in that dingy light it was a promise
of balance. We once again understood the talk of animals, and spring
was lean and hungry with the hope of children and corn.

In this poem, Harjo engages in brief moments of scenic rendering. Read these two paragraphs. Where does she engage in scene? In the first two sentences, Harjo is speaking about what happened during the winter. She is writing in general time about the entire season of "false midnights." The next brings us to "one morning"—specific time. Harjo slows the poem here as the "sun struggled to break ice," and the speaker and her friend end up at a truck stop. See the way we are suddenly inside this moment with the characters in the poem? The "coffee and pancakes," the "woman with time on her hands," the "dingy light." While Harjo does not move moment-to-moment, she does slow the poem enough to let us sit with them in the truck stoop for a while, feeling the "promise of balance." After this, Harjo moves back into general time, but now the time is spring. Harjo also uses this scene to transition through time—from the end of winter to the coming of spring.

Now let's move on to study a scene in a piece of narrative prose, the climax of Chang-rae Lee's essay "Sea Urchin." Study the excerpt below. While this is a piece of creative nonfiction, writers in any narrative genre can learn about scene from studying this excerpt.

A young couple sitting at the end of the bar order live octopus. The old woman nods and hooks one in the tank. It's fairly small, the size of a hand. She lays it on a board and quickly slices off the head with her cleaver. She chops the tentacles and gathers them up onto a plate, dressing them with sesame oil and a spicy bean sauce. "You have to be careful," my father whispers, "or one of the suction cups can stick inside your throat. You could die." The lovers blithely feed each other the sectioned tentacles, taking sips of soju in between. My mother immediately orders a scallion-and-seafood pancake for us, then a spicy cod-head stew; my father murmurs that he still wants something live, fresh. I point to a bin and say that's what I want—those split spiny spheres, like cracked-open meteorites, their rusty centers layered with shiny crenellations. I bend down and smell them, and my eyes almost water from the intense ocean tang. "They're sea urchins," the woman says to my father. "He won't like them." My mother is telling my father he's crazy, that I'll get sick from food poisoning, but he nods to the woman, and she picks up a half and cuts out the soft flesh.

What does it taste like? I'm not sure, because I've never had anything like it. All I know is that it tastes alive, something alive at the undragged bottom of the sea; it tastes the way flesh would taste if flesh were a mineral. And I'm half gagging, though still chewing; it's as if I had another tongue in my mouth, this blind, self-satisfied creature. That night I throw up, my mother scolding us, my father chuckling through his concern. The next day, my uncles joke that they'll take me out for some more, and the suggestion is enough to make me retch again.

Some of the essay explains what happens in general time during this family's trip in sentences like this: "Whenever we're in a taxi, moving through there, I open the window and stick out my tongue, trying to taste the poison, the human repellent." While this is a sentence loaded with sensory detail, it conveys what Lee does during the trip in general—"whenever" they are in a taxi. Study the difference between this sentence and the excerpt above. In the excerpt, the narrative slows down and opens up to explain a series of moments in detail.

See how the actions happen, almost moment to moment and movement by movement. Reading the scene, we can see the "old woman" and what she does to the octopus. Read all of the actions in those three sentences: "nods," "hooks," "lays," "slices," "chops," "gathers," "dressing." These actions also evoke the senses. As we read, we can see what the woman is doing. But Lee draws on more than sight here. These words also draw on the sense of touch. This is another important part of scene. Scenes provide readers with sensory descriptions of what is happening. And remember, he is explaining what the woman is doing before she serves the octopus to a pair of lovers. (If this is not an enthralling scene, tell me what is.)

As the scene continues, Lee writes both direct and indirect dialogue. (Direct dialogue means words spoken as a quotation by characters. In-direct dialogue means the narrator tells what is said without putting words into quotations.)

> "You have to be careful," my father whispers, "or one of the suction cups can stick inside your throat. You could die." The lovers blithely feed each other the sectioned tentacles, taking sips of soju in between. My mother immediately orders a scallion-and-seafood pancake for us, then a spicy cod-head stew; my father murmurs that he still wants something live, fresh.

In these lines we hear the characters—specifically the father—talking to his son. Through direct dialogue, we hear the words he uses, and in them, we hear his excitement. In the indirect dialogue, we hear his determination to eat the "fresh" seafood he wants.

Interspersed with the lines of dialogue, are sentences that describe the action—"the lovers blithely feed each other the sectioned tentacles ... " and "my mother immediately orders a scallion-and-seafood pancake for us ... " We see and hear the scene unfold almost as we would in a movie or play. The characters talk and act, almost beat by beat. Reread the rest of the scene. It continues to play out in dialogue and action. The dialogue continues to vary between indirect and direct, and this time the dialogue happens in a triangle: the narrator (indirect), the mother (indirect), and the old woman (direct). And between those words are the actions. We can see and feel Lee bending to smell the sea urchins. Lee gives us the physical sensation of eyes "almost" watering and the smell: "the intense ocean tang."

In this passage, Lee also brings in description of an object central to the piece: "I point to a bin and say that's what I want—those split spiny spheres, like cracked-open meteorites, their rusty centers layered with shiny crenellations." Any reader who has never seen a sea urchin cracked on culinary display can see it now, through these words.

Reread the scene again to see the way we experience this as Lee does, from one moment or action to the next. He sees the sea urchins; he points to them, he smells them. But he does not name them. Unlike the octopus, he does not have a name for them—until the old woman speaks:

> "They're sea urchins," the woman says to my father. "He won't like them."
> Part of the brilliance in the way Lee renders the scene here is that it unfolds for the reader as it unfolded for Lee. Other than reading it in the title, we do not read the word "sea urchin," until Lee learns that a sea urchin is what he wants to taste. He learns this after he sees them, "those split spiny spheres ..."

As the scene continues to the next paragraph, Lee finally eats the sea urchin. Again, notice the slowing of time—the sensory description of that taste, the way "flesh," a word we do not normally associate with taste, enters the scene. Here, too, Lee pauses to show us what it feels like to be tasting this urchin: "And I'm half gagging, though still chewing; it's as if I had another tongue in my mouth, this blind, self-satisfied creature." Again, notice how as readers we are pulled into the scene—moment-by-moment, dialogue, action, sensory experience.

When Writers Use Scene

Now we know what a well-rendered scene is and how it works. But when do scenes happen? An entire story cannot be made up of scene. If everything happened in-scene, the narrative would move too slowly. Writers use scene during important moments, including important conversations. In "Sea Urchin," the moments of Lee pointing out and eating the sea urchin are an important part of the story. In this particular narrative, in fact, these sea-urchin-tasting moments make up the climax of the narrative arc.

Scenes can—and often do—unfold around other important moments too. Look, for example, at section 0–12 of Zadie Smith's "The Embassy of Cambodia," found in the Readings section. While this is a work of fiction, narrative writers in any genre can study this excerpt to see the way scenes unfold around critical moments in a narrative.

---

0 – 12

By the time Fatou reached the Derawals', only her hair was dry, but before going to get changed she rushed to the kitchen to take the lamb out of the freezer, though it was pointless—there were not enough hours before dinner—and then upstairs to collect the dirty clothes from the matching wicker baskets in four different bedrooms. There was no one in the master bedroom, or in Faizul's, or Julie's. Downstairs a television was blaring. Entering Asma's room, hearing nothing, assuming it empty, Fatou headed straight for the laundry bin in the corner. As she opened the lid she felt a hand hit her hard on the back; she turned around.

There was the youngest, Asma, in front of her, her mouth open like a trout fish. Before Fatou could understand, Asma punched the huge pile of clothes out of her hands. Fatou stooped to retrieve them. While she was kneeling on the floor, another strike came, a kick to her arm. She left the clothes where they were and got up, frightened by her own anger. But when she looked at Asma now she saw the girl gesturing frantically at her own throat, then putting her hands together in prayer, and then back to her throat once more. Her eyes were bulging. She veered suddenly to the right; she threw herself over the back of a chair. When she turned back to Fatou her face was gray and Fatou understood finally and ran to her, grabbed her round her waist, and pulled upward as she had been taught in the hotel. A marble—with an iridescent ribbon of blue at its center, like a wave—flew from the child's mouth and landed wetly in the carpet's plush.

Asma wept and drew in frantic gulps of air. Fatou gave her a hug, and worried when the clothes would get done. Together they went down to the den, where the rest of the family was watching "Britain's Got Talent" on a flat-screen TV attached to the wall. Everybody stood at the sight of Asma's wild weeping. Mr. Derawal paused the Sky box. Fatou explained about the marble.

"How many times I tell you not to put things in your mouth?" Mr. Derawal asked, and Mrs. Derawal said something in their language—Fatou heard the name of their God—and pulled Asma onto the sofa and stroked her daughter's silky black hair.

"I couldn't breathe, man! I couldn't call nobody," Asma cried. "I was gonna die!"

"What you putting marbles in your mouth for anyway, you idiot," Faizul said, and un-paused the Sky box. "What kind of chief puts a marble in her mouth? Idiot. Bet you was bricking it."

"Oi, she saved your life," said Julie, the eldest child, whom Fatou generally liked the least. "Fatou saved your life. That's deep."

"I woulda just done this," Faizul said, and performed an especially dramatic Heimlich to his own skinny body. "And if that didn't work I woulda just start pounding myself karate style, bam bam bam bam bam—"

"Faizul!" Mr. Derawal shouted, and then turned stiffly to Fatou, and spoke not to her, exactly, but to a point somewhere between her elbow and the sunburst mirror behind her head. "Thank you, Fatou. It's lucky you were there."

Fatou nodded and moved to leave, but at the doorway to the den Mrs. Derawal asked her if the lamb had defrosted and Fatou had to confess that she had only just taken it out. Mrs. Derawal said something sharply in her language. Fatou waited for something further, but Mr. Derawal only smiled awkwardly at her, and nodded as a sign that she could go now. Fatou went upstairs to collect the clothes.

This section holds two scenes—scenes that contrast sharply with each other. Watch the way time slows and little details emerge as we enter the first scene. Fatou is upstairs. Three of the four rooms are empty. A television is "blaring" from downstairs. Fatou is carrying the laundry she has emptied from the "matching wicker baskets" in each room. Entering the scene, we have the sensory details. When Fatou enters Asma's room, we enter the moment-by-moment scene. "Entering Asma's room, hearing nothing, assuming it empty, Fatou headed straight for the laundry bin in the corner. As she opened the lid she felt a hand hit her hard on the back; she turned around." We know what Fatou hears and feels. We see her turn around. As the scene continues, we stay in the sensory moments, realizing as Fatou realizes that Asma is choking. The emotion comes moment-by-moment too. Fatou's anger and fear at her anger, then her realization.

Important moments in the story happen in this scene. We know from the rest of the story that Fatou worries about the Devil and wonders why God lets some people suffer more than the rest. We also know Fatou is a slave in this house. We know the children are cruel. Yet she saves this child's life. This is part of Fatou's character development. At the same time, Fatou's action here leads to the Derawal's throwing her out of the house without warning and without means. In this scene, we see a crucial moment in the narrative arc, and we understand more about Fatou's character.

In the scene immediately after Fatou saves the child's life, she takes the child downstairs where the Derawal family is watching their flat-screen television. Again, the scene moves moment by moment. Again, Smith describes sensory details and depicts the body movements of the characters. In this scene, though, there is no saving. The family receives the news of Asma choking and Fatou saving her life with annoyance, barely pausing the television.

The children tease. Mr. Derawal offers an awkward thank-you. Mrs. Derawal asks after the defrosting lamb. This scene serves almost as a foil to the chocking scene. What it reveals is completely different. Here the Derawals do not react the way we would expect a family to react when their housekeeper has just saved a child's life. They treat Fatou with indifference, even annoyance, even as the butt of a joke.

Notice the other sharp difference between the two scenes? The choking scene is written in near silence, except for the noise from the television downstairs. There are no words. In the living room scene, direct and indirect dialogue, mostly from the Derawals, conveys much of what happens, and the dialogue is punctuated with action to hold us in the scene and show us exactly what is happening for all of the characters in that living room.

Both scenes are important to the story. Both are worth slowing down and focusing in. Both are connected to Fatou's fate. And, as we've discussed, both happen in the same section. Indeed, this section is composed only of these two scenes.

Short, Long, and In-between: How Much Page Space Should a Scene Use?

As we can see from our discussion of scenes from "Grace," "Sea Urchin," and "The Embassy of Cambodia," writers dedicate varying amounts of page space to writing scenes. How much space a writer dedicates to scenes in any given piece, pretty much comes to these considerations:

- Length of the entire piece
- Writer's style/style of the piece
- Attention-holding for the reader

When reading a scene, think about the importance of that particular moment, what is at stake, and why this merits a scene. Next, consider the length of the entire piece, the writer's style, and how the scene holds your attention as a reader. Each of these considerations comes into play when a writer is deciding whether to include a scene and how long the scene should be.

For example, both "The Sea Urchin" and "The Embassy of Cambodia" are prose narratives, and both were first published in the *New Yorker*. "Sea Urchin" is a shorter piece Lee wrote for a brief series of short pieces exploring the theme of first tastes. I explain this to say that this story is intended to be a shorter read. "The Embassy of Cambodia" was first published as a lengthy stand-alone story, and later on its own as a novella-length book. Readers will approach these two stories with different sets of expectations, and the writers know that. "The Embassy of Cambodia" is long enough to sustain the page space Smith dedicates to scene. In these moments when so much is at stake, Zadie Smith writes scenes that hold the reader's attention. While Chang-rae Lee writes longer scenes that are compelling and attention-holding in his novels, "Sea Urchin" doesn't have room for long scenes. Instead, as we discussed earlier in the lesson, Lee packs much scenic rendering into two paragraphs.

Notice the differences in writing style between these narratives, too. While Smith writes "The Embassy of Cambodia" in an encompassing style that opens every aspect of Fatou's life, Lee's style in "Sea Urchin" is succinct. He explains the pertinent parts of his family's visit to Seoul using relatively few words. For example, to explain that they are there during the protests over the military's brutal response the Kwangju Uprising, Lee writes: "On the wide streets near the city center, there are student demonstrations; my cousin says they're a response to a massacre of citizens by the military down south in Kwangju." This succinct style carries into the scenes in the narrative as well.

Scenic Rendering without Full Scenes

Another part of reading for scene is noticing when scene is *not* there. In short works, writers might not include scene at all. Several short pieces in Lesson 3 use concrete, sensory details and explain what the characters are doing, feeling, and thinking, without ever opening the narrative into a full-fledged scene. When scene is not part of the writing, pay attention to which parts of scenic rendering come in.

Look, for example, at these two separate tweeted micro essays from Chris Galvin Nguyen.

Blackbird couple. A flurry of feathers, a flash of red and yellow epaulets. Sometimes fighting and flirting look the same.

Caregiving for a parent with dementia is trying at best, but also rewarding in unexpected ways, like the gift of poetry in what first seems like garbled words. "All ice today. Awful," he says, "cars falling down on slippery." I hide my smile and write it down.

We can study elements of scenic rendering without full scene in micro prose in the same way we read for elements of scenic rendering in poetry. We look for details of scene—however scant—that show up in very few words, and we read to see how these scenic details bring the piece to life on the page or screen.

In so few characters, writing a full scene is impossible, and full scenes don't always—or even often—lend themselves well to micro-narrative. In the blackbird micro essay, Galvin Nguyen uses vivid detail to evoke the senses. In the caregiving micro essay, she writes dialogue rich with sensory image. Then she explains her immediate reaction in terms of physical movement.

Reading the micro essays with an eye trained on scene, you can see we are noting many of the aspects that make up a well-rendered scene, even though no full scene develops. When you read to study scene, you will see how the techniques of scenic rendering can be used to add depth and anchor the reader in detail, even without a full scene.

Scene in Visual Hybrids

In graphic and photographic narrative, scene is something we actually (well) see.

In photo essay, where the photographs appear separately from the text, the photographs are scenes in themselves. The photos are the places where we slow down and see moments that are vital to the piece.

Study this excerpt from Randi Ward's "Hestur: A Photo Essay."

Ebbe in the Sheepfold
Sheep husbandry and agriculture have been an integral part of the Faroe Islands' culture and
economy for centuries. Flock management is, in some ways, still based on statutes outlined
in Seyðabrævið of 1298. In this photograph, Ebbe Rasmussen, one of the two parish clerks of
Hestur, is caught up in the excitement of driving sheep into the fold.

Here, we see Ebbe, standing in the sheep fold. Notice the close view we have of his face, his
worn coat with the broken—or unzipped—pocket zipper, his woolen sweater and hat. We see
the stone walls behind him and behind that, the windswept land. Notice his face, mouth open
as if breathing hard and almost grinning. Through the photograph, we stay suspended in the
moment. Through the caption beneath the photo, we understand the context. Here, Ward sets
the scene. Ebbe is engaged in a centuries-old practice of sheep husbandry. And he is more than
a farmer; he is also a parish clerk. One of the lovely parts of this caption is also that it sets the
scene for Ebbe. This is Ebbe, "caught up in the excitement." Through this photographic scene
and its caption, we get important character development for Ebbe, and we come to know him,
just a little.

Graphic narrative, with its panels including image and words, works a little differently. In
graphic narrative, the words do much of the same work they would in text-based narrative,
while the image shows whatever the words do not convey.

Study this page of Sophie Yanow's *The Contradictions*.

On this page, the panels work together to create a scene—a time when the narrative slows to depict the crucial moment of Sophie meeting the girl on the bike. This moment will change Sophie's trajectory, and it's the first time in the story that she connects with someone in a meaningful way. First, the words: As in many narrative scenes, dialogue is key. The dialogue bubbles show us what the characters are saying to each other. The words are sparse, but the way Yanow draws the dialogue ("Heyyyyyy") helps us "hear" the way the characters are speaking. The dialogue is also punctuated with Sophie's thoughts—she is thinking about the girl—"black bandanna," "black everything"—and her bike—"no brakes"—and what that might mean about her. Meanwhile, the girl is telling Sophie what she thought of Sophie and Sophie's messenger bag. Notice how bikes come in here, too. In this graphic narrative, Yanow accomplishes in speech bubbles and captions what any well-written scene between two people can do.

The rest comes to us through image. We see how hard Sophie is breathing. We see how tired she is from sprinting to catch the girl on the bike. We see the girl on the bike. We see how the moon is a crescent and how the characters are standing, how they are close, but not too close to each other. In this scene, Yanow literally shows us the details of the scene. Notice, too, how Yanow makes each moment in the scene distinguishable. She draws different moments of activity in separate panels. During the moments when the girl is telling Sophie what she thought of her at orientation, the panels change to black. There is no background image, just the girl on her bike, talking to Sophie. Though we know she is wearing dark clothes, the solid black behind her makes her look bright almost like Sophie is seeing her in a spotlight in these moments.

In any genre, savvy readers will notice scene. When you find one, pause to study it. Consider the reasons the writer is developing a scene. Pay attention to the page space the writer gives to the scene. Notice the details.

Lesson 9 Discussion Questions and Writing Prompts

Discussion Questions: Focus on Scene

1. Gwen E. Kirby uses scene in various places in "Jerry's Crab Shack: One Star" (found in the Readings section). Identify the scenes and explain why you think Kirby writes scenes in these places in the narrative. Why does she slow the piece down at these points? What does the slowing accomplish? What areas of conflict or character development do these scenes bring into focus?

2. Compare the use of scene in Randi Ward's "Hestur: A Photo Essay" and Erin Pushman's blog post "They Point at Her Face and Whisper" (both found in the Readings section). Both take nontraditional forms, and both use scene. Which elements of scene do both narratives use? Which elements are used only by one? What do you think might be the reasons for the differences? Consider form, style, and genre as you answer the question.

3. Read the poem "Sixteen Ways Old People Terrify the Young," by Alan Michael Parker (found in Lesson 2, page 31). Find the elements of scene Parker uses in the poem and explain how Parker uses scene—even in small ways, to engage the reader.

Writing Prompts: Focus on Scene

Generative Prompt

You know that idea you have for a new story or narrative poem? Try writing the beginning by opening the piece with a scene. Remember to write inside specific time. Include detail, physical movement, sensory descriptions, and dialog.

Revision Prompt

Get out that narrative or poem you have been drafting. Figure out what is the most important moment in the piece—a moment when much is at stake. Develop a scene or use the elements of scenic rendering to bring that moment to heightened clarity and attention for the reader. Remember to slow the piece down, write inside specific time, include detail, action or interaction, and dialogue.

LESSON 10
LANGUAGE

Whatever the form, whatever the genre, whatever the length, and wherever published, all creative writing has one important thing in common: It comes to us through words. Even hybrid forms that rely in part on image come to the reader through words too. You might say all writing, creative or otherwise, comes to the reader through words, which is true. But in creative writing, writers pay literary attention to the language.

Developing a Literary Ear: Structure, Shape, Length, and Sound

You could also say that we have already discussed language in most of the previous lessons. After all, the details about plot, character, setting, and scene (for example) come to us through language. In this lesson, though, we will focus on the language itself. When writers read, they pay careful attention to the language—or the way authors put words, phrases, and sentences together. Many writers develop a literary ear, or a way to almost hear the way language is working in a piece of writing.

To do this, you have to slow down as you read. Read each word. Read not only to find out what is happening but to see the way the words tell you what is happening. Try to "listen" the sound of the words. Try to "feel" the shape of the sentences. Reading for language means studying diction (the words writers choose) and syntax (the way writers structure sentences and phrases). Reading for language also means paying attention to the punctuation, both how it works inside the syntax and how it influences the way a sentence moves—a stop, a pause, an extension.

As we read for language in this lesson, we will read works form fiction, creative nonfiction, and poetry. Writers can develop a literary ear by reading for language in all genres. Writers in one genre can learn to approach language in nuanced ways by studying the way writers in another genre work the language.

Let's begin by reading this paragraph from section 0–14 of Zadie Smith's "The Embassy of Cambodia."

---

0 – 14

On Monday, Fatou went swimming. She paused to watch the badminton. She thought that the arm that delivered the smashes must make a movement similar to the one she made in the pool, with her clumsy yet effective front crawl. She entered the health center and gave a guest pass to the girl behind the desk. In the dimly lit changing room, she put on her sturdy black underwear. As she swam, she thought of Carib Beach. Her father serving snapper to the guests on the deck, his bow tie always a little askew, the ugly tourists, the whole scene there. Of course, it was not surprising in the least to see old white men from Germany with beautiful local girls on their laps, but she would never forget the two old white women from England—red women, really, thanks to the sun—each of them as big as two women put together, with Kweku and Osai lying by their sides, the boys hooking their scrawny black bird-arms round the women's massive red shoulders, dancing with them in the hotel "ballroom," answering to the names Michael and David, and disappearing into the women's cabins at night. She had known the boys' real girlfriends; they were chambermaids like Fatou. Sometimes they cleaned the rooms where Kweku and Osai spent the night with the English women. And the girls themselves had "boyfriends" among the guests. It was not a holy place, that hotel. And the pool was shaped like a kidney bean: nobody could really swim in it, or showed any sign of wanting to. Mostly, they stood in it and drank cocktails. Sometimes they even had their burgers delivered to the pool. Fatou hated to watch her father crouching to hand a burger to a man waist high in water.

Throughout this passage, Smith varies the sentence length and the syntax. In English, the most common way to construct sentences is a subject, verb, object pattern, like this: *I went to the store.* As regular people, when we write and speak in English, we use this sentence construction by default. *I went to the store. Maria came with me. We bought avocados and quinoa, and we went home.* Subject, verb, object, and subject, verb, object. But that's not what Smith does with the syntax. Some of the sentences follow the subject, verb, object structure, but others begin with prepositions, for example, the first sentence. A couple begin with conjunctions, for example, "And the girls themselves had boyfriends among the guests." Note, here, that varying sentence structure means *sometimes* writing in a structure other than subject, verb, object. Trying to do so all the time would lead to some pretty odd, awkward writing. When you read with an eye to syntax, notice how often writers diverge from the subject, verb, object structure, and how they accomplish it.

While varying the syntax does give Smith's readers some, well, variety, it is also an important part of the style of this narrative. In this section, as in the others with a close third narrator telling Fatou's story, the syntax flows around Fatou's thoughts and experiences.

Reread the two highlighted sentences. Read them out loud if you can. What do you notice about them? Yes, one of the sentences is short. One is long. One is not a complete sentence at all, but a fragment. Smith varies the lengths of the sentences for a style that keeps the reader's interest. She also uses punctuation to give the sentences shape. Read the punctuation in the long sentence. The punctuation makes the long sentence work, and it shows us how to read the sentence. The commas guide us through the phrases and clauses of the sentence. The em dashes (the long dashes) emphasize the "red women"—drawing attention to the way Fatou sees them.

Now consider the syntax this way: What happens as Fatou begins swimming? She begins remembering Carib Beach. What happens to the syntax? It ebbs and flows. It drifts through a long fragment. It buoys Fatou's thoughts in a long, winding sentence, flowing as Fatou's thoughts flow—through the water she is swimming in now, and to Carib Beach and what happened there. Here, Smith embodies what the character is doing—swimming—and what she is thinking—swimming through the hurtful memories of Carib Beach—in the syntax.

Writers also read (and write) with an ear to the way words sound. Many of the devices we think of as poetic work this way—alliteration, rhythm, and rhyme, for example. The importance of the sound of words also reaches beyond these poetic devices to hard and soft sounds and how these sounds matter in a piece of creative writing.

Look at number thirteen in Alan Michael Parker's hybrid poem "Sixteen Ways Old People Terrify the Young."

---

13. It's like grout or glue or maybe gum. Whatever holds those bones together.

In this line, we hear the alliteration in "grout or glue or maybe gum." We also hear the hard "g" sound. Notice, though, how the beginning of this line includes other hard consonant sounds— "t," "k." The later part of the line gets all gentle and flowing in its sound. Hear all the "o" sounds in "holds those bones." The other gentle sounds, the "w" in "Whatever" for example, add to the flow of the second part of the line. In this line, the differences in sound reflect the crucial aspects of the poem, the biting humor beside a poignant reflection on aging and death.

Reading sentences and lines in this way will help you develop a literary ear. An ear that listens for sound, length, structure, punctuation, and shape. An ear ready to help read for language in other ways, too—ways we will discuss in the rest of this lesson.

Sensory Language

Sensory language is often part of what makes a piece of creative writing sing. Another part of reading for language is discovering when a writer evokes the physical senses or emotional feelings. Writers do this by choosing active verbs and writing descriptions that prick the senses.

Read the prose poem "Cartography," by Poornima Laxmeshwar, looking for sensory language.

"Cartography"

Their eighth anniversary was on its way, just like a cheesy pizza. Just that it came every year on 26th Feb even if they didn't want it. This year they spoke about unexplored Europe.

She was excited about Amsterdam. The infamous Red light district, the coffee shops, she was already preparing her to-do list while he wanted Venice—a boatman singing, the flowing romance and her.

They slept with their own set of dreams and the map led them to places where they wanted to go.

The anniversary arrived and departed like a birdsong. The map supine on the study table next to the books appeared like a heart with spread arteries. It gained thin layers of dust, became an unfulfilled promise.

A map knows not to lie.

Writers know that different words evoke different meanings. I think of this as *meaning differently*. Choosing active verbs that mean differently helps writers create sensory experiences for their readers. One way to read for active verbs is to imagine replacing active verbs with being verbs or with active verbs that have similar but not quite the same meaning. In the second sentence of the second paragraph of "Cartography," for example, what if "she was already *making* her to-do list while he *needed* Venice—a boatman singing, the flowing romance and her." Changing those verbs to the ones I have inserted in italics or to any other verbs would give a different feel to the passage. The passage would mean differently than it means now. The lines work better Laxmeshwar's way, of course. She chose the verbs she did because of their precise meanings and the way they work inside the lines of this prose poem.

Also worth pointing out is the idea that using active verbs does not mean never using being verbs. Look again at the first sentence "was on its way." The being verb works here because "was" makes it possible for the anniversary to be "on its way," like pizzas often are. Here we see a being verb being needed to make the writing mean just what the writer wants it to mean.

Selecting specific words to create a specific meaning—to mean differently—does not only apply to verbs. It applies to all the words, including words used together to create descriptions or details.

Selecting specific words to create a nuanced meaning is part of the emotionally evocative and sensory language Laxmeshwar writes in "Cartography." Look at the first two sentences. Right away, taste and texture come into play and in surprising ways. Who thinks of an anniversary as coming like a pizza, a cheesy one at that? Giving readers a new way of envisioning something in language gives readers something they may not have experienced before. It also brings a specific meaning. A cheesy pizza is delicious and mundane. Its coming is predictable and convenient and sometimes in lieu of a meal that would take more time, money, planning, work, passion, and energy. So right away, reading this sentence, we have taste, texture, maybe even smell on our hands, and we have it in the context of a wedding anniversary being on its way. Here Laxmeshwar evokes the senses and an emotional feeling.

The next sentence brings the idea to an uncomfortable place—"weather they wanted it or not"—which evokes more emotional feelings. A less nuanced way of writing this might have been something like this: They were ambivalent about their approaching anniversary, as they were every year. But that sentence would not mean the way the first two sentences of "Cartography" do.

What else is significant in the language Laxmeshwar employs to evoke sensory and emotional feelings? Notice all the words and phrases that might evoke a (shall we say?) sensual romance? Here is a list of those words and phrases in the order in which they appear: came, unexplored, excited, infamous, red light district, wanted, boatman singing, flowing romance, slept, led, wanted, supine, heart, spread, arteries, layers, promise.

Wow. Read that list of words and phrases again. Laxmeshwar has turned up the heat with this language. That's one of the reasons this piece is so poignant, isn't it? The language is as hot as the relationship is cold.

It takes a careful reader, a reader who reads like a writer, to pick up on language and its importance to the overall piece this way. But once you start to notice the way language can *mean*, it will change the way you read.

Breaking the Formal Rules

We often think of poets as being free to eschew the formal rules of writing. No one blinks when a poet forgoes punctuation or capitalization. But notice two things. First, many poems—the poems included in this book, for example—follow the rules. Second, all creative writers are allowed to break the rules. The key is that when writers break the rules, the breaking has to be intentional and has to work inside the piece.

We cannot discuss every formal rule and why it might be broken inside of this lesson. That would take its own book. We can discuss a few of the most common rule-breakings and study examples of when writers make the rule-breaking work.

Always write in complete sentences. Never begin a sentence with "and," or "but," or any other conjunction word. Never use "you." Never end a sentence with a preposition. Always. Never. Blah. Blah. Rules like these are written to be broken. By creative writers. Who know what they are doing.

Part of reading for language means reading to see when writers break rules and why breaking those rules works. For example, never use "you." Since we have already had a lesson on POV, we already know "you" can work as a second-person point of view. The "you" perspective shows up in two of the short pieces from Lesson 3: Karen Donley-Hayes's "What You Learn in College" and Beth Uznis Johnson's "Negative Results."

As to the other formal rules, when writers break them, they do the breaking on purpose, not by accident. And they break formal rules only when the broken rules will serve the piece, keeping the reader's attention instead of causing the reader to become confused or distracted. Let's take a look.

Always write in complete sentences. Not all sentences need to be grammatically complete to present a complete idea. Look again at Zadie Smith's fragment sentence from "The Embassy of Cambodia," which we studied earlier in this lesson.

As she swam, she thought of Carib Beach. Her father serving snapper to the guests on the deck, his bow tie always a little askew, the ugly tourists, the whole scene there.

The first sentence is short but complete. The second sentence is a fragment. A fragment that resonates with the sentence before it. We expect fragments to be short. Sometimes they are. In this case, the sentence preceding the fragment is shorter than the fragment itself. The fragment builds on the idea from the first sentence, and it builds with a list. The fragment is nothing but list. It works here because, thanks to the sentence before, its meaning is clear.

The fragment also works because here the language breaks down. Just as the flowing, meandering sentence we discussed earlier embodies Fatou's thinking, the fragment mirror's Fatou's experience. The language becomes incomplete, un-whole as Fatou begins thinking of a place that is "unholy," a place where her father is belittled by the tourists, a place where she is raped. In other words, this fragment—this broken sentence—embodies for the reader a time when Fatou's life is broken. The fact that the fragment sentence is also long holds the reader in that broken place for longer; it shows us how Fatou is held there.

For the record, the fragment we are discussing here is the complicated kind, one that has a subject and a verb ("father" and "bending," respectively) but is still a fragment because to make sense, it depends on the sentence in front of it. (That, of course, is why it works inside the piece.) Reading writers who need more explanation about fragments can check out Grammar Girl, aka Mignon Fogarty. Just Google "Grammar Girl fragments," or look fragments up on the Quick and Dirty Tips website. The same goes for any other questions about formal writing rules.

Never begin a sentence with a conjunction word. Never end a sentence with a preposition. Sometimes writers break more than one formal rule in one paragraph. Read this excerpt from Beth Uznis Johnson's "Negative Results" looking for the broken rules.

So now, you've got yourself to worry about, one person who lies, one who probably doesn't but might. He's worried. All this leads to the need for confirmation, you have no choice as you owe it to yourself, the man who probably doesn't lie, and even the man who does. The test is tenfold and includes the window period. You hear the word negative. You see it on the page. Ten times. You're relieved, of course, but now that you know it's negative (you knew it would be), you're relieved because it means the liar is somewhat truthful, he wasn't that bad, even though you're done sleeping with him. You hate him for putting you through it even though you knew going in. Risks are risks, but being stupid is entirely different and, now that you know the new man is actually truthful, it makes you like him even more.

Uznis Johnson begins this paragraph with a conjunction—"so." She also ends a sentence with a preposition—"in." For that matter, she writes a fragment too—"Ten times." This may be a lot of formal rule-breaking for one paragraph, but it works with the style of the piece. "Negative Results" is a stream of conscious narrative. We roll through the narrator's troubled thoughts along with her. Formality does not come into it. In this narrative, too, we see language breaking down as the character is breaking down—or at least she recognizes the lies are threatening her health. She is also waiting for STD test results, ending an affair with one man, beginning an affair with another. Again, we see broken language embodying the broken parts of the character's life. In this passage, breaking the formal rules makes the piece feel authentic.

Minding the Writerly Rules

Writers have their own set of rules. Those taking creative writing workshop courses or working in independent writing groups have probably heard many of them. We can't discuss all of the writerly rules in this lesson either, but we will cover two that often come up in creative writing workshops: Use adverbs with extreme caution. Don't use clichés. Studying the ways writers mind—or break—these two writerly rules will provide context for considering the other rules and admonitions you might encounter as you read and write like a writer.

Underpinning the writerly rules is the idea that writers work the language. We work the language to make sure it reaches the reader in ways that will hold the reader on the page. We work the language to make sure it is nuanced and stunning. We work the language so it will stick to our readers, and they will remember what we had to say. Clichés, for example, are neither nuanced nor stunning nor memorable. We can usually (adverb) say the same thing about adverbs, which often do the opposite of holding us to the page.

Read Mary Oliver's "Lead." Look for the cliché and the adverb.

Lead

Here is a story
to break your heart.
Are you willing?
This winter
the loons came to our harbor
and died, one by one,
of nothing we could see.
A friend told me
of one on the shore
that lifted its head and opened
the elegant beak and cried out
in the long, sweet savoring of its life
which, if you have heard it,
you know is a sacred thing,
and for which, if you have not heard it,
you had better hurry to where
they still sing.
And, believe me, tell no one
just where that is.
The next morning
this loon, speckled
and iridescent and with a plan
to fly home
to some hidden lake,
was dead on the shore.
I tell you this
to break your heart,
by which I mean only
that it break open and never close again
to the rest of the world.

A broken heart is as clichéd as it is possible to get. But here the cliché is part of Oliver working the language. She does this by turning the cliché on its end to offer the reader something new. This is heartbreaking in a different way, a way that opens. If we let Oliver break our hearts like this, we become willing to see the dying loons and all the other casualties of environmental destruction.

Oliver uses one adverb in this poem—"only." Any more adverbs would feel like too much and would slow the poem down. Any more adverbs would mean Oliver was not using adverbs with caution. And pay attention to where the adverb comes: in the lines about what Oliver intends for a broken heart. The adverb comes in the right place in that it is not trying too hard to do the heart breaking. Adverbs that seem bent on pulling the reader's heartstrings tend to feel overdone or even icky. Imagine, for example, how adverbs used immoderately and in the wrong places could pull us out of the poem. Imagine if adverbs were attached to the verbs explaining how the loons move, sing, or die. As readers, we would feel like Oliver was trying too hard to yank our emotional strings. Adverbs there would have the opposite effect Oliver intends. Adverbs there would not break our hearts.

After reading this paragraph, some will be wondering about that one successful writer who seems to use adverbs incautiously. Many of us enjoy the occasional book whose writer really gets away with using adverbs frequently. All we can do here is be glad for those writers and read carefully enough to figure out why they get away with it. (We can also keep slogging through our own manuscripts, pulling out every adverb we cannot justify.)

Working the Language

Paying attention to language helps readers see how plot, narrative arc, character, development, setting, scene, and all the rest come through on the page. Reading for language reminds us that language is the medium writers use to create art. Language is the way we give readers our poetry, our fiction, our creative nonfiction.

When writers write, they work the language. They work the language by paying attention to the words they chose and the way they structure sentences, the rules they keep, and the rules they break. Part of what writers do when they revise is work to get the language right. An important part of reading the way writers read is reading to see how writers work the language.

Lesson 10 Discussion Questions and Writing Prompts

Discussion Questions: Focus on Language

1. Read Chang-rae Lee's "Sea Urchin" (found in the Readings section) or Alan Michael Parker's "Sixteen Ways Old People Terrify the Young" (found in Lesson 2, page 31). Read to study language. "Hear" the sentences or lines. "Walk" through them. Pay attention to the length, structure, and punctuation of each sentence/line. Explain which sentences/lines resonate the most for you and why. Discuss what the writer accomplishes with the language in these lines/sentences.

2. Mary Oliver's poem "Lead" (found on page 163) and Randi Ward's "Hestur: A Photo Essay" (found in the Readings section) both follow the formal rules. Gwen E. Kirby's "Jerry's Crab Shack: One Star" (found in the Readings section) sometimes does and sometimes does not. Why do you think the Oliver and Ward make the choice to follow the formal rules? Why do you think Kirby sometimes makes the choice to break them? What does following the rules bring to these pieces? What does Kirby's occasional rule-breaking do for her story?

3. Read Beth Uznis Johnson's "Negative Results" (found in Lesson 3, page 44). Now re-read the paragraph that begins with "So now ... " Count the number of words in each sentence in the paragraph. How varied are the lengths of these sentences? What does Uznis Johnson accomplish with this varied length? Why are the short sentences short and the long sentences long?

Writing Prompts: Focus on Language

Generative Prompt

Pick your favorite piece from the works in this book. Read through it paying close attention to the words. Then select a sentence (prose) or a line (poetry) you are drawn to because of the language. Study the sentence or line. Figure out how the language works. Then write a sentence or line of your own using language in ways similar to the way the writer does in the piece you read. (The trick here is to write your own sentence or line in a similar way, not to copy the writer, changing only a word or two.) After you complete one sentence or line, select another from the reading and do the same thing. Then another. Write until you run out of ideas.

Revision Prompt

Reread one of your manuscripts-in-progress. Find a page, paragraph, or stanza you'd like to revise. Write a revision specifically to work the language. Keep in mind that you are working on one small part here—a page, paragraph, or stanza. Take your time. Make changes that will matter to words and sentences. You can revise the rest of the manuscript later.

THE END (OR AFTERWORD)

As a writer reading this book, you will have noticed how often we've drifted from discussing reading like a writer to writing. If it's possible to explore reading the way writers must without concentrating on writing, I don't know how to do it. And I urge you not to try. When you read as a writer, you think about your own writing, often without meaning to. It is as natural a progression as can be. In essence, this progression is the very reason to read as a writer.

Thinking about your own writing and yourself as a writer as you read will help you hone your writing craft around the elements we've discussed in the lessons of this book. Maybe you will explore different genres or hybrids in your own work. Maybe you will heighten the conflict in your own plots or come up with more nuanced characters. Maybe you will experiment with scene and POV. Maybe you will work the language in ways you have not before.

Thinking about your own writing as you read will also help you think about publishing opportunities and platforms. Do you have a Tiny Truth to tweet? A blog post to write? Would the short story you are writing be a good fit for the literary magazine that published the short story you are reading? When you read the way writers read—and read thinking of your own work—you begin to see your own place in the world of creative writers.

Each time you read, ask yourself what you can learn from the piece. Make connections between what you are reading and what you are working on with your own writing. Read to explore how the creative writing you read changes the way you write.

On a final, but important, note, reading writers become stewards of the literary community. Without readers, writers cannot survive. As you read more and more and with an eye toward readying your own work for publication, read knowing that each literary magazine or book you buy means you are supporting the literary community. Reading creative writing online and sharing works you enjoy through your own social media accounts mean you are helping to promote digital platforms for creative writing. Participating in the literary community as a reader helps keep the literary community sustainable.

So keep reading. Read in your own genre. Read in other genres. Read outside of genres. Read on the page, and read on the screen. Read for pleasure, and read to learn. Read like the writer you are becoming.

READINGS

Additional Readings

The following additional readings may be found in their entity inside the lessons themselves.

"Lead" by Mary Oliver (poetry) Lesson 1, page 12; Lesson 4, page 60; Lesson 5, page 79; Lesson 7, page 120; Lesson 10, page 159.

"Lead" is from *New and Selected Poems* by Mary Oliver. Published by Beacon Press Boston Copyright © 2005 by Mary Oliver. Reprinted by permission of The Charlotte Sheedy Literary Agency Inc.

"Grace" by Joy Harjo (poetry, prose poem) Lesson 2, page 43; Lesson 5, page 80.

"Grace" from *In Mad Love and War* © 1990 by Joy Harjo. Published by Wesleyan University Press and reprinted with permission.

"Sixteen Ways Old People Terrify the Young" by Alan Michael Parker (poetry, list hybrid) Lesson 2, page 31.

Alan Michael Parker, "Sixteen Ways Old People Terrify the Young" from Long Division. Copyright © 2012 by Alan Michael Parker. Reprinted with the permission of The Permissions Company, LLC, on behalf of Tupelo Press, www.tupelopress.org.

"What You Learn in College" by Karen Donley-Hayes (creative nonfiction, flash) Lesson 3, page 39.

"What You Learn in College" was first published in *Creative Nonfiction*, Fall 2014, the "Mistakes" issue, and is reprinted here with permission of the author.

"Negative Results" by Beth Uznis Johnson (fiction, micro) Lesson 3, page 41.

"Negative Results" was first published by *The Rumpus* and is reprinted here with permission of the author.

"Cartography" by Poornima Laxmeshwar (fiction, micro, prose poem) Lesson 3, page 68.

"Cartography" was first published in *Hoot* issue 45 and is reprinted here with permission of the author.

Two Tweeted Micro Essays by Chris Galvin Nguyen (creative nonfiction, micro) Lesson 3, page 46; Lesson 9, page 151.

These two micro essays were first tweeted by Chris Galvin Nguyen (@ChrisGNguyen), re-tweeted by Creative Nonfiction (@cnfonline) as winners of the #cnftweet contest, later published as *Tiny Truths* in *Creative Nonfiction*, and reprinted here with permission of the author.

Sea Urchin

Chang-rae Lee

July, 1980. I'm about to turn fifteen and our family is in Seoul, the first time since we left, twelve years earlier. I don't know if it's different. My parents can't really say. They just repeat the equivalent of "How in the world?" whenever we venture into another part of the city, or meet one of their old friends. "Look at that–how in the world?" "This hot spell, yes, yes–how in the world?" My younger sister is very quiet in the astounding heat. We all are. It's the first time I notice how I stink. You can't help smelling like everything else. And in the heat everything smells of ferment and rot and rankness. In my grandfather's old neighborhood, where the two- and three-room houses stand barely head-high, the smell is staggering. "What's that?" I ask. My cousin says, "Shit."

"Shit? What shit?"

"Yours," he says, laughing. "Mine."

On the wide streets near the city center, there are student demonstrations; my cousin says they're a response to a massacre of citizens by the military down south in Kwangju. After the riot troops clear the avenues, the air is laden with tear gas–"spicy," in the idiom. Whenever we're in a taxi, moving through there, I open the window and stick out my tongue, trying to taste the poison, the human repellent. My mother wonders what's wrong with me.

I don't know what's wrong. Or maybe I do. I'm bored. Maybe I'm craving a girl. I can't help staring at them, the ones clearing dishes in their parents' eateries, the uniformed schoolgirls walking hand in hand, the slim young women who work in the Lotte department store, smelling of fried kimchi and L'Air du Temps. They're all stunning to me, even with their bad teeth. I let myself drift near them, hoping for the scantest touch.

But there's nothing. I'm too obviously desperate, utterly hopeless. Instead, it seems, I can eat. I've always liked food, but now I'm bent on trying everything. As it is, the days are made up of meals, formal and impromptu, meals between meals and within meals; the streets are a continuous outdoor buffet of braised crabs, cold buckwheat noodles, shaved ice with sweet red beans on top. In Itaewon, the district near the United States Army base, where you can get anything you want, culinary or otherwise, we stop at a seafood stand for dinner. Basically, it's a tent diner, a long bar with stools, a camp stove and fish tank behind the proprietor, an elderly woman with a low, hoarse voice. The roof is a stretch of blue poly-tarp. My father is excited; it's like the old days. He wants raw fish, but my mother shakes her head. I can see why: in plastic bins of speckled, bloody ice sit semi-alive cockles, abalones, eels, conchs, sea cucumbers, porgies, shrimps. "Get something fried," she tells him, not caring what the woman might think. "Get something cooked."

A young couple sitting at the end of the bar order live octopus. The old woman nods and hooks one in the tank. It's fairly small, the size of a hand. She lays it on a board and quickly slices off the head with her cleaver. She chops the tentacles and gathers them up onto a plate, dressing them with sesame oil and a spicy bean sauce. "You have to be careful," my father whispers, "or one of the suction cups can stick inside your throat. You could die." The lovers blithely feed each other the sectioned tentacles, taking sips of soju in between. My mother immediately orders a scallion-and-seafood pancake for us, then a spicy cod-head stew; my father murmurs that he still wants something live, fresh. I point to a bin and say that's what I want–those split spiny spheres, like cracked-open meteorites, their rusty centers layered with shiny crenellations. I bend down and smell them, and my eyes almost water from the intense ocean tang. "They're sea urchins," the woman says to my father. "He won't like them." My mother is telling my father he's crazy, that I'll get sick from food poisoning, but he nods to the woman, and she picks up a half and cuts out the soft flesh.

What does it taste like? I'm not sure, because I've never had anything like it. All I know is that it tastes alive, something alive at the undragged bottom of the sea; it tastes the way flesh would taste if flesh were a mineral. And I'm half gagging, though still chewing; it's as if I had another tongue in my mouth, this blind, self-satisfied creature. That night I throw up, my mother scolding us, my father chuckling through his concern. The next day, my uncles joke that they'll take me out for some more, and the suggestion is enough to make me retch again.

But a week later I'm better, and I go back by myself. The woman is there, and so are the sea urchins, glistening in the hot sun. "I know what you want," she says. I sit, my mouth slick with anticipation and revulsion, not yet knowing why.

"Sea Urchin" was first published in *The New Yorker,* August 2002, and is reprinted here with permission of the author.

The Embassy of Cambodia
Zadie Smith

0 – 1

Who would expect the Embassy of Cambodia? Nobody. Nobody could have expected it, or be expecting it. It's a surprise, to us all. The Embassy of Cambodia!

Next door to the embassy is a health center. On the other side, a row of private residences, most of them belonging to wealthy Arabs (or so we, the people of Willesden, contend). They have Corinthian pillars on either side of their front doors, and—it's widely believed— swimming pools out back. The embassy, by contrast, is not very grand. It is only a four- or five-bedroom North London suburban villa, built at some point in the thirties, surrounded by a red brick wall, about eight feet high. And back and forth, cresting this wall horizontally, flies a shuttlecock. They are playing badminton in the Embassy of Cambodia. Pock, smash. Pock, smash.

The only real sign that the embassy is an embassy at all is the little brass plaque on the door (which reads, "*the embassy of cambodia*") and the national flag of Cambodia (we assume that's what it is—what else could it be?) flying from the red tiled roof. Some say, "Oh, but it has a high wall around it, and this is what signifies that it is not a private residence, like the other houses on the street but, rather, an embassy." The people who say so are foolish. Many of the private houses have high walls, quite as high as the Embassy of Cambodia's—but they are not embassies.

0 – 2

On the sixth of August, Fatou walked past the embassy for the first time, on her way to a swimming pool. It is a large pool, although not quite Olympic size. To swim a mile you must complete eighty-two lengths, which, in its very tedium, often feels as much a mental exercise as a physical one. The water is kept unusually warm, to please the majority of people who patronize the health center, the kind who come not so much to swim as to lounge poolside or rest their bodies in the sauna. Fatou has swum here five or six times now, and she is often the youngest person in the pool by several decades. Generally, the clientele are white, or else South Asian or from the Middle East, but now and then Fatou finds herself in the water with fellow-Africans. When she spots these big men, paddling frantically like babies, struggling simply to stay afloat, she prides herself on her own abilities, having taught herself to swim, several years earlier, at the Carib Beach Resort, in Accra. Not in the hotel pool—no employees were allowed in the pool. No, she learned by struggling through the rough gray sea, on the other side of the resort walls. Rising and sinking, rising and sinking, on the dirty foam. No tourist ever stepped onto the beach (it was covered with trash), much less into the cold and treacherous sea. Nor did any of the other chambermaids. Only some reckless teen-age boys, late at night, and Fatou, early in the morning. There is almost no way to compare swimming at Carib Beach and swimming in the health center, warm as it is, tranquil as a bath. And, as Fatou passes the Embassy of Cambodia, on her way to the pool, over the high wall she sees a shuttlecock, passed back and forth between two unseen players. The shuttlecock floats in a wide arc softly rightward, and is smashed back, and this happens again and again, the first player always somehow able to retrieve the smash and transform it, once more, into a gentle, floating arc. High above, the sun tries to force its way through a cloud ceiling, gray and filled with water. Pock, smash. Pock, smash.

0 – 3

When the Embassy of Cambodia first appeared in our midst, a few years ago, some of us said, "Well, if we were poets perhaps we could have written some sort of an ode about this surprising appearance of the embassy." (For embassies are usually to be found in the center of the city. This was the first one we had seen in the suburbs.) But we are not really a poetic people. We are from Willesden. Our minds tend toward the prosaic. I doubt there is a man or woman among us, for example, who—upon passing the Embassy of Cambodia for the first time—did not immediately think: "genocide."

0 – 4

Pock, smash. Pock, smash. This summer we watched the Olympics, becoming well attuned to grunting, and to the many other human sounds associated with effort and the triumph of the will. But the players in the garden of the Embassy of Cambodia are silent. (We can't say for sure that it is a garden—we have a limited view over the wall. It may well be a paved area, reserved for badminton.) The only sign that a game of badminton is under way at all is the motion of the shuttlecock itself, alternately being lobbed and smashed, lobbed and smashed, and always at the hour that Fatou passes on her way to the health center to swim (just after ten in the morning on Mondays). It should be explained that it is Fatou's employers—and not Fatou—who are the true members of this health club; they have no idea that she uses their guest passes in this way. (Mr. and Mrs. Derawal and their three children—aged seventeen, fifteen, and ten—live on the same street as the embassy, but the road is almost a mile long, with the embassy at one end and the Derawals at the other.) Fatou's deception is possible only because on Mondays Mr. Derawal drives to Eltham to visit his mini-market there, and Mrs. Derawal works the counter in the family's second mini-mart, in Kensal Rise. In the slim drawer of a faux-Louis XVI console, in the entrance hall of the Derawals' primary residence, one can find a stockpile of guest passes. Nobody besides Fatou seems to remember that they are there.

Since August 6th (the first occasion on which she noticed the badminton), Fatou has made a point of pausing by the bus stop opposite the embassy for five or ten minutes before she goes in to swim, idle minutes she can hardly afford (Mrs. Derawal returns to the house at lunchtime) and yet seems unable to forgo. Such is the strangely compelling aura of the embassy. Usually, Fatou gains nothing from this waiting and observing, but on a few occasions she has seen people arrive at the embassy and watched as they are buzzed through the gate. Young white people carrying rucksacks. Often they are scruffy, and wearing sandals, despite the cool weather. None of the visitors so far have been visibly Cambodian. These young people are likely looking for visas. They are buzzed in and then pass through the gate, although Fatou would really have to stand on top of the bus stop to get a view of whoever it is that lets them in. What she can say with certainty is that these occasional arrivals have absolutely no effect on the badminton, which continues in its steady pattern, first gentle, then fast, first soft and high, then hard and low.

0 – 5

On the twentieth of August, long after the Olympians had returned to their respective countries, Fatou noticed that a basketball hoop had appeared in the far corner of the garden, its net of synthetic white rope rising high enough to be seen over the wall. But no basketball was ever played—at least not when Fatou was passing. The following week it had been moved closer to

Fatou's side of the wall. (It must be a mobile hoop, on casters.) Fatou waited a week, two weeks, but still no basketball game replaced the badminton, which carried on as before.

0 – 6

When I say that we were surprised by the appearance of the Embassy of Cambodia, I don't mean to suggest that the embassy is in any way unique in its peculiarity. In fact, this long, wide street is notable for a number of curious buildings, in the context of which the Embassy of Cambodia does not seem especially strange. There is a mansion called *garyland*, with something else in Arabic engraved below *garyland*, and both the English and the Arabic text are inlaid in pink-and-green marble pillars that bookend a gigantic fence, far higher than the embassy's, better suited to a fortress. Dramatic golden gates open automatically to let vehicles in and out. At any one time, *garyland* has five to seven cars parked in its driveway.

There is a house with a huge pink elephant on the doorstep, apparently made of mosaic tiles.

There is a Catholic nunnery with a single red Ford Focus parked in front. There is a Sikh institute. There is a faux-Tudor house with a pool that Mickey Rooney rented for a season, while he was performing in the West End fifteen summers ago. That house sits opposite a dingy retirement home, where one sometimes sees distressed souls, barely covered by their dressing gowns, standing on their tiny balconies, staring into the tops of the chestnut trees.

So we are hardly strangers to curious buildings, here in Willesden & Brondesbury. And yet still we find the Embassy of Cambodia a little surprising. It is not the right sort of surprise, somehow.

0 – 7

In a discarded *Metro* found on the floor of the Derawal kitchen, Fatou read with interest a story about a Sudanese "slave" living in a rich man's house in London. It was not the first time that Fatou had wondered if she herself was a slave, but this story, brief as it was, confirmed in her own mind that she was not. After all, it was her father, and not a kidnapper, who had taken her from Ivory Coast to Ghana, and when they reached Accra they had both found employment in the same hotel. Two years later, when she was eighteen, it was her father again who had organized her difficult passage to Libya and then on to Italy—a not insignificant financial sacrifice on his part. Also, Fatou could read English—and speak a little Italian—and this girl in the paper could not read or speak anything except the language of her tribe. And nobody beat Fatou, although Mrs. Derawal had twice slapped her in the face, and the two older children spoke to her with no respect at all and thanked her for nothing. (Sometimes she heard her name used as a term of abuse between them. "You're as black as Fatou." Or "You're as stupid as Fatou.") On the other hand, just like the girl in the newspaper, she had not seen her passport with her own eyes since she arrived at the Derawals', and she had been told from the start that her wages were to be retained by the Derawals to pay for the food and water and heat she would require during her stay, as well as to cover the rent for the room she slept in. In the final analysis, however, Fatou was not confined to the house. She had an Oyster Card, given to her by the Derawals, and was trusted to do the food shopping and other outside tasks for which she was given cash and told to return with change and receipts for everything. If she did not go out in the evenings that was only because she had no money with which to go out, and anyway knew very few people in London. Whereas the girl in the paper was not allowed to leave her employers' premises, not ever—she was a prisoner.

On Sunday mornings, for example, Fatou regularly left the house to meet her church friend Andrew Okonkwo at the 98 bus stop and go with him to worship at the Sacred Heart of Jesus, just off the Kilburn High Road. Afterward Andrew always took her to a Tunisian café, where they had coffee and cake, which Andrew, who worked as a night guard in the City, always paid for. And on Mondays Fatou swam. In very warm water, and thankful for the semi-darkness in which the health club, for some reason, kept its clientele, as if the place were a night club, or a midnight Mass. The darkness helped disguise the fact that her swimming costume was in fact a sturdy black bra and a pair of plain black cotton knickers. No, on balance she did not think she was a slave.

0 – 8

The woman exiting the Embassy of Cambodia did not look especially like a New Person or an Old Person—neither clearly of the city nor of the country—and of course it is a long time since this division meant anything in Cambodia. Nor did these terms mean anything to Fatou, who was curious only to catch her first sighting of a possible Cambodian anywhere near the Embassy of Cambodia. She was particularly interested in the woman's clothes, which were precise and utilitarian—a gray shirt tucked tightly into a pair of tan slacks, a blue mackintosh, a droopy rain hat—just as if she were a man, or no different from a man. Her straight black hair was cut short. She had in her hands many bags from Sainsbury's, and this Fatou found a little mysterious: where was she taking all that shopping? It also surprised her that the woman from the Embassy of Cambodia should shop in the same Willesden branch of Sainsbury's where Fatou shopped for the Derawals. She had an idea that Oriental people had their own, secret establishments. (She believed the Jews did, too.) She both admired and slightly resented this self-reliance, but had no doubt that it was the secret to holding great power, as a people. For example, when the Chinese had come to Fatou's village to take over the mine, an abiding local mystery had been: what did they eat and where did they eat it? They certainly did not buy food in the market, or from the Lebanese traders along the main road. They made their own arrangements. (Whether back home or here, the key to surviving as a people, in Fatou's opinion, was to make your own arrangements.)

But, looking again at the bags the Cambodian woman carried, Fatou wondered whether they weren't in fact very old bags—hadn't their design changed? The more she looked at them the more convinced she became that they contained not food but clothes or something else again, the outline of each bag being a little too rounded and smooth. Maybe she was simply taking out the rubbish. Fatou stood at the bus stop and watched until the Cambodian woman reached the corner, crossed, and turned left toward the high road. Meanwhile, back at the embassy the badminton continued to be played, though with a little more effort now because of a wayward wind. At one point it seemed to Fatou that the next lob would blow southward, sending the shuttlecock over the wall to land lightly in her own hands. Instead the other player, with his vicious reliability (Fatou had long ago decided that both players were men), caught the shuttlecock as it began to drift and sent it back to his opponent—another deathly, downward smash.

0 – 9

No doubt there are those who will be critical of the narrow, essentially local scope of Fatou's interest in the Cambodian woman from the Embassy of Cambodia, but we, the people of

Willesden, have some sympathy with her attitude. The fact is if we followed the history of every little country in this world—in its dramatic as well as its quiet times—we would have no space left in which to live our own lives or to apply ourselves to our necessary tasks, never mind indulge in occasional pleasures, like swimming. Surely there is something to be said for drawing a circle around our attention and remaining within that circle. But how large should this circle be?

0 – 10

It was the Sunday after Fatou saw the Cambodian that she decided to put a version of this question to Andrew, as they sat in the Tunisian café eating two large fingers of dough stuffed with cream and custard and topped with a strip of chocolate icing. Specifically, she began a conversation with Andrew about the Holocaust, as Andrew was the only person she had found in London with whom she could have these deep conversations, partly because he was patient and sympathetic to her, but also because he was an educated person, currently studying for a part-time business degree at the College of North West London. With his student card he had been given free, twenty-four-hour access to the Internet.

"But more people died in Rwanda," Fatou argued. "And nobody speaks about that! Nobody!"

"Yes, I think that's true," Andrew conceded, and put the first of four sugars in his coffee.

"I have to check. But, yes, millions and millions. They hide the true numbers, but you can see them online. There's always a lot of hiding; it's the same all over. It's like this bureaucratic Nigerian government—they are the greatest at numerology, hiding figures, changing them to suit their purposes. I have a name for it: I call it "demonology." Not 'numerology'— 'demonology.'"

"Yes, but what I am saying is like this," Fatou pressed, wary of the conversation's drifting back, as it usually did, to the financial corruption of the Nigerian government. "Are we born to suffer? Sometimes I think we were born to suffer more than all the rest."

Andrew pushed his professorial glasses up his nose. "But, Fatou, you're forgetting the most important thing. Who cried most for Jesus? His mother. Who cries most for you? Your father. It's very logical, when you break it down. The Jews cry for the Jews. The Russians cry for the Russians. We cry for Africa, because we are Africans, and, even then, I'm sorry, Fatou"— Andrew's chubby face creased up in a smile—"if Nigeria plays Ivory Coast and we beat you into the ground, I'm laughing, man! I can't lie. I'm celebrating. Stomp! Stomp!" He did a little dance with his upper body, and Fatou tried, not for the first time, to imagine what he might be like as a husband, but could see only herself as the wife, and Andrew as a teen-age son of hers, bright and helpful, to be sure, but a son all the same—though in reality he was three years older than she. Surely it was wrong to find his baby fat and struggling mustache so off-putting. Here was a good man! She knew that he cared for her, was clean, and had given his life to Christ. Still, some part of her rebelled against him, some unholy part.

"Hush your mouth," she said, trying to sound more playful than disgusted, and was relieved when he stopped jiggling and laid both his hands on the table, his face suddenly quite solemn.

"Believe me, that's a natural law, Fatou, pure and simple. Only God cries for us all, because we are *all* his children. It's very, very logical. You just have to think about it for a moment."

Fatou sighed, and spooned some coffee foam into her mouth. "But I still think we have more pain. I've seen it myself. Chinese people have never been slaves. They are always protected from the worst."

Andrew took off his glasses and rubbed them on the end of his shirt. Fatou could tell that he was preparing to lay knowledge upon her.

"Fatou, think about it for a moment, please: what about Hiroshima?"

It was a name Fatou had heard before, but sometimes Andrew's superior knowledge made her nervous. She would find herself struggling to remember even the things she had believed she already knew.

"The big wave …" she began, uncertainly—it was the wrong answer. He laughed mightily and shook his head at her.

"No, man! Big bomb. Biggest bomb in the world, made by the U.S.A., of course. They killed five million people in *one second*. Can you imagine that? You think just because your eyes are like this"—he tugged the skin at both temples—"you're always protected? Think again. This bomb, even if it didn't blow you up, a week later it melted the skin off your bones."

Fatou realized that she had heard this story before, or some version of it. But she felt the same vague impatience with it as she did with all accounts of suffering in the distant past. For what could be done about the suffering of the past?

"O.K.," she said. "Maybe all people have their hard times, in the past of history, but I still say—"

"Here is a counterpoint," Andrew said, reaching out and gripping her shoulder. "Let me ask you, Fatou, seriously, think about this. I'm sorry to interrupt you, but I have thought a lot about this and I want to pass it on to you, because I know you care about things seriously, not like these people." He waved a hand at the assortment of cake eaters at other tables. "You're not like the other girls I know, just thinking about the club and their hair. You're a person who thinks. I told you before, anything you want to know about, ask me—I'll look it up, I'll do the research. I have access. Then I'll bring it to you."

"You're a very good friend to me, Andrew, I know that."

"Listen, we are friends to each other. In this world you need friends. But, Fatou, listen to my question. It's a counterpoint to what you have been saying. Tell me, why would God choose us especially for suffering when we, above all others, praise his name? Africa is the fastest-growing Christian continent! Just think about it for a minute! It doesn't even make sense!"

"But it's not him," Fatou said quietly, looking over Andrew's shoulder at the rain beating on the window. "It's the Devil."

0 – 11

Andrew and Fatou sat in the Tunisian coffee shop, waiting for it to stop raining, but it did not stop raining, and at 3 *p.m.* Fatou said she would just have to get wet. She shared Andrew's umbrella as far as the Overground, letting him pull her into his clammy, high-smelling body as they walked. At Brondesbury station Andrew had to get the train, and so they said goodbye. Several times he tried to press his umbrella on her, but Fatou knew the walk from Acton Central to Andrew's bed-sit was long and she refused to let him suffer on her account.

"Big woman. Won't let anybody protect you."

"Rain doesn't scare me."

Fatou took from her pocket a swimming cap she had found on the floor of the health-club changing room. She wound her plaits into a bun and pulled the cap over her head.

"That's a very original idea," Andrew said, laughing. "You should market that! Make your first million!"

"Peace be with you," Fatou said, and kissed him chastely on the cheek. Andrew did the same, lingering a little longer with his kiss than was necessary.

0 – 12

By the time Fatou reached the Derawals', only her hair was dry, but before going to get changed she rushed to the kitchen to take the lamb out of the freezer, though it was pointless—there were not enough hours before dinner—and then upstairs to collect the dirty clothes from the matching wicker baskets in four different bedrooms. There was no one in the master bedroom, or in Faizul's, or Julie's. Downstairs a television was blaring. Entering Asma's room, hearing nothing, assuming it empty, Fatou headed straight for the laundry bin in the corner. As she opened the lid she felt a hand hit her hard on the back; she turned around.

There was the youngest, Asma, in front of her, her mouth open like a trout fish. Before Fatou could understand, Asma punched the huge pile of clothes out of her hands. Fatou stooped to retrieve them. While she was kneeling on the floor, another strike came, a kick to her arm. She left the clothes where they were and got up, frightened by her own anger. But when she looked at Asma now she saw the girl gesturing frantically at her own throat, then putting her hands together in prayer, and then back to her throat once more. Her eyes were bulging. She veered suddenly to the right; she threw herself over the back of a chair. When she turned back to Fatou her face was gray and Fatou understood finally and ran to her, grabbed her round her waist, and pulled upward as she had been taught in the hotel. A marble—with an iridescent ribbon of blue at its center, like a wave—flew from the child's mouth and landed wetly in the carpet's plush.

Asma wept and drew in frantic gulps of air. Fatou gave her a hug, and worried when the clothes would get done. Together they went down to the den, where the rest of the family was watching "Britain's Got Talent" on a flat-screen TV attached to the wall. Everybody stood at the sight of Asma's wild weeping. Mr. Derawal paused the Sky box. Fatou explained about the marble.

"How many times I tell you not to put things in your mouth?" Mr. Derawal asked, and Mrs. Derawal said something in their language—Fatou heard the name of their God—and pulled Asma onto the sofa and stroked her daughter's silky black hair.

"I couldn't breathe, man! I couldn't call nobody," Asma cried. "I was gonna die!"

"What you putting marbles in your mouth for anyway, you idiot," Faizul said, and un-paused the Sky box. "What kind of chief puts a marble in her mouth? Idiot. Bet you was bricking it."

"Oi, she saved your life," said Julie, the eldest child, whom Fatou generally liked the least. "Fatou saved your life. That's deep."

"I woulda just done this," Faizul said, and performed an especially dramatic Heimlich to his own skinny body. "And if that didn't work I woulda just start pounding myself karate style, bam bam bam bam bam—"

"Faizul!" Mr. Derawal shouted, and then turned stiffly to Fatou, and spoke not to her, exactly, but to a point somewhere between her elbow and the sunburst mirror behind her head. "Thank you, Fatou. It's lucky you were there."

Fatou nodded and moved to leave, but at the doorway to the den Mrs. Derawal asked her if the lamb had defrosted and Fatou had to confess that she had only just taken it out. Mrs. Derawal said something sharply in her language. Fatou waited for something further, but

Mr. Derawal only smiled awkwardly at her, and nodded as a sign that she could go now. Fatou went upstairs to collect the clothes.

0 – 13

"To keep you is no benefit. To destroy you is no loss" was one of the mottoes of the Khmer Rouge. It referred to the New People, those city dwellers who could not be made to give up city life and work on a farm. By returning everybody to the land, the regime hoped to create a society of Old People—that is to say, of agrarian peasants. When a New Person was relocated from the city to the country, it was vital not to show weakness in the fields. Vulnerability was punishable by death.

In Willesden, we are almost all New People, though some of us, like Fatou, were, until quite recently, Old People, working the land in our various countries of origin. Of the Old and New People of Willesden I speak; I have been chosen to speak for them, though they did not choose me and must wonder what gives me the right. I could say, "Because I was born at the crossroads of Willesden, Kilburn, and Queen's Park!" But the reply would be swift and damning: "Oh, don't be foolish, many people were born right there; it doesn't mean anything at all. We are not one people and no one can speak for us. It's all a lot of nonsense. We see you standing on the balcony, overlooking the Embassy of Cambodia, in your dressing gown, staring into the chestnut trees, looking gormless. The real reason you speak in this way is because you can't think of anything better to do."

0 – 14

On Monday, Fatou went swimming. She paused to watch the badminton. She thought that the arm that delivered the smashes must make a movement similar to the one she made in the pool, with her clumsy yet effective front crawl. She entered the health center and gave a guest pass to the girl behind the desk. In the dimly lit changing room, she put on her sturdy black underwear. As she swam, she thought of Carib Beach. Her father serving snapper to the guests on the deck, his bow tie always a little askew, the ugly tourists, the whole scene there. Of course, it was not surprising in the least to see old white men from Germany with beautiful local girls on their laps, but she would never forget the two old white women from England—red women, really, thanks to the sun—each of them as big as two women put together, with Kweku and Osai lying by their sides, the boys hooking their scrawny black bird-arms round the women's massive red shoulders, dancing with them in the hotel "ballroom," answering to the names Michael and David, and disappearing into the women's cabins at night. She had known the boys' real girlfriends; they were chambermaids like Fatou. Sometimes they cleaned the rooms where Kweku and Osai spent the night with the English women. And the girls themselves had "boyfriends" among the guests. It was not a holy place, that hotel. And the pool was shaped like a kidney bean: nobody could really swim in it, or showed any sign of wanting to. Mostly, they stood in it and drank cocktails. Sometimes they even had their burgers delivered to the pool. Fatou hated to watch her father crouching to hand a burger to a man waist high in water.

The only good thing that happened in Carib Beach was this: once a month, on a Sunday, the congregation of a local church poured out of a coach at the front gates, lined up fully dressed in the courtyard, and then walked into the pool for a mass baptism. The tourists were never warned, and Fatou never understood why the congregants were allowed to do it. But she loved to watch their white shirts bloat and spread across the surface of the water, and to hear the weeping and singing. At the time—though she was not then a member of that church, or of any church except the one in her heart—she had felt that this baptism was for her, too, and that it kept her safe, and that this was somehow the reason she did not become one of the "girls" at the Carib Beach Resort. For almost two years—between her father's efforts and the grace of an unseen and unacknowledged God—she did her work, and swam Sunday mornings at the crack of dawn, and got along all right. But the Devil was waiting.

She had only a month left in Accra when she entered a bedroom to clean it one morning and heard the door shut softly behind her before she could put a hand to it. He came, this time, in Russian form. Afterward, he cried and begged her not to tell anyone: his wife had gone to see the Cape Coast Castle and they were leaving the following morning. Fatou listened to his blubbering and realized that he thought the hotel would punish him for his action, or that the police would be called. That was when she knew that the Devil was stupid as well as evil. She spat in his face and left. Thinking about the Devil now made her swimming fast and angry, and for a while she easily lapped the young white man in the lane next to hers, the faster lane.

Cuttings
Vivian I. Bikulege

1. Bits

A.

There is a snapshot in the archives of the *New York Daily News* of Leiby Kletzky waiting on the street for Levi Aron to pay his dental bill. The Brooklyn boy got lost walking home from camp and the moment was captured by a surveillance camera on July 11, 2011. Leiby waited seven minutes before getting into Aron's 1990 Honda Accord trusting the next stop would be home.

B.

I walk my beagle Toby on a path beside the Coosaw River. A tidal creek splits from the river cutting into the marsh forest. We play a running game to the top of a sandy ridge in the South Carolina lowcountry. As I wait for my chubby friend, I catch sight of a white heron wading on stilt legs in the pluff mud, quiet and focused.

C.

Mary Oliver, the poet, hears a voice in the weeds. She is heading toward blueberry fields and wonders if the voice is from a beetle or a toad. Her imagination gives life to an image of elves bearing a deceased elf away in a casket made of a flower petal.

D.

Videos of Islamic State beheadings are available on-line. I consider watching because seeing may help me process what I do not understand. As the brutality becomes part of the global topography in 2014, I remember Leiby. I ask myself, "Why do we cut one another into bits?"

2. Grids

A.

Borough Park is a neighborhood inside greater Brooklyn Borough and home to one of the largest Jewish populations in the United States. The heart of the community is inside a grid between 11th and 18th avenues, and 40th and 60th streets. Leiby met Aron on 18th Avenue. The boy was supposed to meet his mother at the corner of 13th Avenue and 50th Street.

B.

On July 12, I drive south on Interstate 95 to the Savannah/Hilton Head International Airport. I will fly to Newark and take a train into Manhattan for business the following day. The one o'clock news reports the murder and dismemberment of an eight-year-old boy in Brooklyn. The newscaster is exact and remote in his delivery of the story. My breath catches in my throat and I turn off the radio.

C.

In *The Journey,* Oliver delivers a prophesy. She predicts coming days, wisdom-filled, when I will know what I have to do. In spite of bad advice, and the clamor of naysayers, she gives me permission to begin, encourages me through the finality of days.

D.

Hervé Gourdel, a French mountaineering guide, was kidnapped shortly after his fifty-fifth birthday while hiking the mountains in Djurdjura National Park in Algeria. Gourdel is beheaded by ISIS in retaliation for French government air strikes against them. The name Djurdjura comes from the word *Jjerjer* which means "great cold" or "elevation". Confronting cold-blooded murder with art, with pencil, or pen and paper, I can elevate beauty over brutality. Disconnected people and places find common ground in poetry.

3. Pieces

A.

Who opened the refrigerator freezer and found Leiby's feet? Where do you turn when you are lost? Why is it I can save no one?

B.

After my meeting on Park Avenue, I attend Mass at St. Patrick's Cathedral. I am late and miss the homily but join the community in the Prayers of the Faithful. Father Tyrrell ends the prayers by remembering "the boy in Brooklyn," and asks us to pray for him. I am aware, and I remember when I first learned about Leiby on the radio, in my car, driving in South Carolina, and I marvel at being on New York soil, only a subway ride away from Brooklyn and the Kletzky family, and I pray for them. I believe God hears all of us as he watches his theater of fools.

C.

A Carolina wren lifts in short flight from a palmetto to my bird feeder and announces her presence in a sweet warble of notes. A painted bunting, dressed in a feather jacket of red, purple and green, joins the wren. From my chaise lounge I read *Evidence*, a poetry collection, and search for solace and sanity in Mary Oliver's verses. My melancholy rises and disperses through the leaves of water oaks as the distant drone of a lawn mower sings bass in summer's chorus.

From the page, I hear Mary whisper about wolves and broken worlds, heaven puddles for golden finches, and my right to understand that my words were mine all along. The poet does not ask the same questions she asked when she was younger, and she leaves hope behind to wander into a pasture to sleep.

Unlike Oliver, it is too soon for me to leave hope behind. I cannot abandon faith or refrain from seeking love. If I touch pain, I hear better. When I cry over cruelty, I sit shiva with the world.

D.

Beheadings continue, and Japanese nationals Yakawa and Goto are on their knees, in the sand, on the nightly news. I recall illustrations of David hoisting the head of Goliath in my religion class workbook of Old Testament lessons. In the New Testament, after dancing for King Herod, Salome requests the head of John the Baptist, and receives it on a platter. I do not remember that picture in my workbook.

Today, ISIS and the media deliver digital images of headless bodies. Somewhere, a child is a real-time witness, or the executioner, or the child is the act. Innocence is the victim of violence, dying every second, and imaginary elves do not soften death in woodland processions.

What is left of my life needs to read like gentle poetry, days when I blend pain and ink on a blank sheet of paper, revise, and leave behind word cuttings for a white resurrection.

4. Fragments

A.

A year after Leiby's murder, the Kletzky's have a baby girl, their sixth. Were they hoping for a son? Are they happy, disappointed, or numb? Sometimes, we make love to fill the gaps. We procreate to mock death. We move on.

B.

I get my news in fragments - evening television after dinner, drive time radio, in hotels and airports, local and national newspapers, and texts. It is rarely poetic. I am amazed by the capacity of my heart and psyche to process the shock and sorrow of murder, to acknowledge dismemberment, and contemplate the value of another person as barter in the illegal trade of human organs.

C.

Oliver writes to break my heart, to break it open. Do not shy away from truth or agony, she teaches. Stay open - to the world, to elves, to the long tremolo of a wailing loon, to cries from the womb, to the soft touch of communion on the tip of your tongue. Never close. *Lead.*

D.

For now, experience terror as metaphoric heart surgery but respond as a healer. Open your chest cavity to release warmth, stretch the rib cage to welcome beauty, and allow every vessel to fill with love and resilience in response to terror, evil, and to hate.

"Cuttings" was first published in *The Petigru Review* as the winner of the 2018 Carrie McCray Memorial Literary Award in Creative Nonfiction and is reprinted here in slight revision with permission of the author.

Jerry's Crab Shack: One Star
Gwen E. Kirby

Jerry's Crab Shack: One Star
Gary F.
Baltimore, MD
Yelp member since July 14, 2015
Review: Jerry's Crab Shack
Review posted: July 15, 2015, 2:08am
1/5 stars

After perusing the restaurant's website and reading the positive reviews on Yelp, my wife and I went to Jerry's Crab Shack this evening. We did not have a good experience. It was not "a home run," as another reviewer suggested. I don't know where these reviewers usually go to dinner, and I won't post the speculations I typed and then deleted because they were unflattering and, dare I say, so accurate as to be hurtful and it is not my intention to be hurtful. I simply want to correct the record.

I'm going to review Jerry's Crab Shack in a methodical, fair-minded way so that other people who use this site, people like my wife and I who are new to Baltimore and rely on this site to make informed dinner plans, can know what they are getting into and make their own decisions. If you are going to take the time to do something, as my dear wife says, take the time to do it right or don't bother with it and let her do it like she does everything else (ha ha).

*Location

Jerry's Crab Shack is near Fell's Point (not in historic Fell's Point, as their website leads one to think). In fact, the "shack," which is not a shack but a regular storefront wedged between a hair salon and a mattress store, is several blocks to the east, in a less-than-savory bit of neighborhood. If after reading this, you, future Yelp user, still plan to go to Jerry's Crab Shack, I would suggest that you do not park your car near Jerry's. Park it in Fell's Point proper and walk. Even if you are mugged, the criminals will only take your wallet and not, as happened to us, your front right window (shattered), your Garman navigation system, and five CDs, including a Smithsonian Folkways 2-CD set, Rhythms of Rapture: Musics of Haitian Vodou, that you were looking forward to listening to on your commute.

*Décor

When you first walk in, Jerry's seems all right. I said this review would be fair, and I meant it. Some people don't know how to separate their feelings about a thing from the thing itself, but I do. That is why I am willing to admit that even if I did not enjoy the 3D sensation Avatar and even if I do not understand the appeal of jogging, they have value independent of me. Just because hard-boiled eggs make everything in the refrigerator smell like hard-boiled eggs and that smell triggers my sensitive gag reflex, I understand why some people would feel differently and want to eat them for breakfast every day. Different strokes, etc.

Jerry's commits to its nautical theme. The bar has a charming fishing net draped above it, and caught in the net are plastic starfish and a cardboard mermaid. On the walls are pictures of sailboats, not framed but tacked to the plaster, the edges curled and yellowing as they might do in a more briny environment. At the end of the bar is a rubber crab, lovingly cuddled up to a Bud Light. A sign next to it says: No One Feels Crabby with a Bud Light! (You can feel crabby with a Bud Light. I would say, considering all the better beers out there in the world, that you should feel crabby with a Bud Light. I would also say that since the staff of Jerry's Crab Shack seems so invested in their status as "native" Baltimoreans, they might consider supporting Maryland businesses and serving only local beers.)

There are eight tables, each covered with a laminated red-and-white-check tablecloth, the kind that has holes through which you can feel the soft white polyester fuzz. We were expecting more of a "restaurant restaurant" (my wife's words), and less of a "bar with some tables" (also my wife). The pictures on the website do not accurately reflect the interior, so this was not my fault. I was lead to expect more of a nautical bistro atmosphere, which my wife later suggested was "not a thing." The point is, I promised my wife a special dinner. I told her this place would be quintessentially "Baltimore." I hoped that we would finally be able to unwind and enjoy an evening out of the house, away from the half unpacked boxes and nearly empty rooms.

*Cleanliness

Not the cleanest.

While waiting to be seated (before we realized it was more of a seat-yourself establishment), I watched my wife lift her heel, up and down, again and again, testing the fly-strip stickiness of the floor. Her face got that set look I recognize. It's so authentic, I said, hoping to cut any potential negativity off at the pass. (I was noticing and appreciating the already-mentioned netting as well as the bathroom doors labeled Pirate and Lady Pirate, which I thought very egalitarian.) Janet, her name is Janet, can get it in her head to not a like a thing and then there is no changing her mind. The woman could be unhappy at her own birthday party (which she has been, multiple times). So the place wasn't the cleanest! I think with the word shack in the title, you have been forewarned.

The floor could use a mop. They could stand to "swab the decks." But our table was wiped down, and we did not see any cockroaches. My wife would feel that that is a low bar to set for cleanliness, so I will also add that I saw a sign saying they had passed their health inspection and that that sign was placed prominently in the window, where it is legally required to be.

*Service

Service was, at first, fine. A woman too old to be wearing a pirate wench costume welcomed us and took our order—two softshell crab sandwiches (according to Yelp, their "star" dish) and a side of slaw. Her wench bodice (though maybe I should say Lady Pirate bodice) was black faux leather and her breasts overfilled it, not the way young breasts do, pushing plumply up and over, but like balloons that have begun to lose some helium, balloons three days after the birthday party is over.

(I want to pause here a moment and say that I do not normally complain about restaurant service. As the child of a father who complained, loudly and ad nauseam, about slow waitresses, unfriendly waitresses, slutty waitresses, indeed, as a boy too often embarrassed by the impatience and insensitivity of an authority figure, I usually take a bit of bad service on the chin. Waitresses are people, too, and not every meal I eat has to be the best of my life. I've choked down a few dinners in my life and kept my mouth shut about it. My wife is perhaps a little less forgiving, a little prone to complain when food comes out cold or I forget to buy milk at the store even when I promised I would remember, but she really only complains when it is warranted. She does not let people "walk all over her," and I "shouldn't either." What happened tonight was not the waitress's fault. I don't know what my father expects. Waitresses are not wizards. All I expect from them is the transportation of food from one point to a different point, and they don't even need to smile because what in the hell is there to smile about when you are working as a waitress at Jerry's Crab Shack and your manager has you stuffed into a corset two sizes too small and you have three kids at home and corns on your feet and two people in their DC-black suits sit down in your section and one of them asks whether the crabs are locally sourced, which of course they are which is why that woman looked at us like we were morons and clearly not from around here even though we are now local homeowners.)

Food took forty-five minutes. Or I should say: after forty-five minutes, things at the table had become tense. We were both tired and hungry. Moving is a lot of work. There have been more than a few nights spent eating leftover pizza on the floor because the new table we ordered online is stuck in a warehouse in St. Louis and even when my wife called the company and used her most terrifying voice they told her that we would have to wait, that they were working on it. We had both been looking forward to this dinner.

Are they sending someone out to catch the crabs first, Janet said, and I knew she was about to stand up and ask where our food was. So I got up first, to avoid making a scene. I hate drama in restaurants. I hate it a lot. I may have snapped at Janet before going over to the bar, but that was kind of on her, since she knows how much I hate when people bother waitresses who are just doing their jobs.

(You know, Janet has a lot of good qualities. I want to say that right now. This is not a review of my wife.)

If this were a review of my wife, I might review her based on:

1. Supportiveness
2. Empathy
3. Stability
4. Sense of humor
5. Physical appearance
6. Tolerance for me

Janet is supportive. When I wanted to go to graduate school for a masters in musicology, she said I should do it, and then she paid for it even though we weren't married yet. (Janet is a lawyer.) I think supporting her then–long term boyfriend's masters in musicology also speaks to her empathy, because when you tell people you are a musicologist they mostly look at you like you are insane or made your job up. She did not do that. She loves that I love music and that I work for Smithsonian Folkways, which is my dream job, and so what if I now live an hour-and-a-half commute away from that dream job and can't go out with coworkers after work because she wants to own a house, which we can't afford to do in DC, and have children.

Obviously, I want those things too.

Janet is very stable. You could call her a boulder. A flat-bottomed boulder. Not that she has a flat bottom. (Rating her on attractiveness I give her a 10++.) What I mean is, you couldn't roll her down a hill or something because she isn't that type of boulder. When she says she is going to do something, she does it. If she had said we were going to a nice restaurant, we would have shown up at Jerry's to discover a bodega with white linen and locally sourced cocktail bitters. Sometimes I think she simply wills things and people into line with the force of her mind.

She also has a wonderful sense of humor. When we walked into Jerry's Crab Shack and she saw the rubber crab, she smiled.

The only item about which I might have anything at all negative to say would be number 6) Tolerance for me, and really only tolerance for me lately. She is "all in" about our move to Baltimore. If I "had doubts," I should have "said something before we bought the goddamn house and moved all our shit up here." I don't disagree with that. She just doesn't see that I am both all in, in the sense that I am sure she knows what's best, and not all in, in the sense that I am not sure what will happen next or that I'll like it.

*Service (bar)

And here we get to the crux of the issue. I don't know where Jerry hires his bar staff, but they are the rudest, most unpleasant people on the face of the earth.

I walked over to the bar and asked the bartender, politely, when our food might be ready. And this bartender, someone obviously on work release from a local prison or recently kicked out of his biker gang for being too obnoxious even for them, tells me It'll be ready when it's ready. Then, he rather grudgingly looked over at the order-up window and said, soon probably. I realize that doesn't sound so bad. In retrospect, it seems pretty reasonable. But I could not go back to the table and tell Janet that the food would be out "soon probably." I needed a timetable. Or a reason the food was being so slow. A kitchen fire, a death in the chef's family, a sudden crab shortage sweeping the Chesapeake. I had already screwed up dinner. I was going to be assertive. This was the one thing I could do right for her. So I said, Can you go back and check? Or find our waitress? And he said, I've got a bar to tend, dude. Unless you want a drink, I got other customers to worry about. The other men at the bar were starting to look at me. I could see them judging me, for my suit and the way I hold myself, which I know is a little awkward. I have unusually long arms. I said, This is simply unacceptable, again, not because I felt that it was that unacceptable but because I wanted to make Janet happy. I think I asked to speak to Jerry. My voice may have gone up in volume. That was when the bartender said that I should sit the fuck down in my faggy DC suit and wait like everyone else. The other men sitting at the bar laughed that rumbling masculine chuckle, as if something funny had happened, and they laughed again when the bartender accused me of "blushing." I did not say anything back because there isn't anything to say to that kind of behavior. I absolutely do not regret not saying anything at that moment and simply walking back to my table.

I don't know what people in this city have against DC. Not everyone from DC is an asshole. And I'm not even from DC. I'm from Ohio.

It feels good to have gotten that off my chest. I don't want to lie to you, future Yelp reader. I feel like we are connecting, unburdening ourselves. I'll tell you a few more things. I am drinking a beer right now, my third, and it is only beginning to help. My wife went to sleep hours ago. I am sitting with my computer, the empty bottles, and a little lamp on the wooden floor of what will be the living room because I don't have a desk yet and I don't want to go upstairs. This isn't where I hoped I would be. I was hoping to have "an extra special" night. And by extra special, I mean I was hoping I would be having sex. There, I said it. I don't have a problem talking about natural acts between a man and his wife. Unlike the bartender, I am not so insecure about my sexuality that I have to resort to homophobic, inappropriate name-calling. It did not make me feel good to be called "faggy" in front of my wife. In fact, it made me feel shitty. I do not like that bartender's comment repeating in my head, or testing out ways I might have responded, things I might have said. Because again, I'm absolutely not sorry that I walked away.

I actually do have a problem talking about sex sometimes. I could say that I used a euphemism for sex because I didn't want to shock more conservative Yelp users by talking about the birds and bees and the beast with two backs, but the truth is, there are moments like right now when being a person in a body seems impossible. All the parts working in chorus, repetitive involuntary rhythms, a near miracle of coordination. Bodies are strange, so fleshy and pierceable. Sometimes when I am on my endless commute I think about the parts of my car which, in an accident, would be most likely to run me through. The steering column. The parking brake. A shard from the other car. I don't like to think about how thin a membrane my skin actually is, but once I get it in my head, it's hard to get it out. This is why I am upset about the loss of my CDs.

Have you ever listened to Haitian Vodou music? It's not what you would expect. A low patter of rain beat out on the drum. The song a chant, one woman leading, the village following. Call and response. They invite the spirits to come and ride them. But in the end, it's the music that rides you.

I don't know how I got here.

Janet has an outie bellybutton. It's cute, like a little pigtail on her stomach. She hates it. Like it's an inefficiency she wants to eliminate. And she doesn't like when I touch it. She says it "feels weird," as if I am poking a sensitive cord that sends shocks to a place in her body she can't name, a secret nestling between her uterus and stomach. It is hard to fuck someone and not rub up against their outie bellybutton. Also, because I know I can't touch it, sometimes touching it is the only thing I can think about.

Janet doesn't use sites like Yelp. She isn't like me and you. She doesn't trust "random" people's opinions. She reads food critics, peruses "Best of" lists. Since we moved here, she has started to read the Baltimore Sun. I like this about her. She does her research and she has high standards.

If Janet were reviewing me, I wonder what criteria she would use. I think she would say that I make her laugh. I think she would say she finds me handsome instead of saying that I am handsome. I think she would use the word frustrated and point to the small things: taking out the trash, removing expired food from the refrigerator, planning dates. I hope she would say that I am loyal and that she would rank that quality above all others, because I think it's the best one I have. I think if she understood that, she'd see why I didn't raise a fuss about moving here, why I go along when maybe I should speak up. I worry that perhaps she likes this quality in me least of all.

*Food

We left after the incident at the bar. When I sat back down, neither of us said anything. We waited five minutes. I hoped she would make a scene, which I have never hoped for before in a restaurant, but she just twisted her napkin in silence. I said I thought we should call it a night and we picked up Wendy's on the way home and ate it in the car. So I cannot speak to the quality of the food at Jerry's Crab Shack. If it is truly the best softshell crab in the city, then we will never eat the best softshell crab. We will settle for second best, and probably not know the difference.

"Jerry's Crab Shack: One Star" was originally published in *The Mississippi Review*, Summer 2016, and is reprinted here with permission of the author.

Hestur: A Photo Essay
Randi Ward

Anxious to disembark, I went about gathering my luggage into a manageable pile on the rumbling car deck of Teistin. The ferry's hydraulics made a shrill yelp when the hull opened and the ramp began to lower, jouncingly, toward Hestur's deserted quay. The final crash of the heavy ramp striking rain-soaked concrete made me flinch, and then it hit me: I was the only person going ashore that afternoon. The rest of the passengers were waiting for the ferry to resume its course across Skopunarfjørð to the more populated island of Sandur.

Hestur, which literally means "Horse," is one of 18 storm-swept islands situated north-northwest of Scotland, approximately halfway between Iceland and Norway, in the North Atlantic Ocean. As a self-governing territory of the Danish Kingdom, the have their distinct language, culture, parliament, and flag. The capital city of Tórshavn, along with the surrounding villages incorporated into its municipality, is home to nearly 20,000 of the archipelago's 52,000 inhabitants. Hestur's 20 residents joined Tórshavn's municipality in 2005, but the population of the village itself continues to decrease. Those who remain, most of whom are at or well-beyond retirement age, divide their days between farming/fishing and part-time jobs in the public sector providing services that keep the island habitable.

Though many people have labeled Hestur a "dying village," I witnessed firsthand the traditions and various acts of kindness and reserved devotion that sustain the community's infrastructure and morale. These touching deeds seem even more remarkable in the face of the subtle tensions between families or individuals, resentments that have simmered for generations and occasionally threaten to disturb the village's delicate balance.

It was rather inevitable that I too would become subject to the roiling social currents of the village of Hestur. As a newcomer to the island, its youngest resident, an independently employed, single female and a foreigner to boot, my life was ripe for interpretation; it wasn't long before my daily routines and social interactions came under all kinds of scrutiny. Yet it was this complex configuration of intense proximity and solitude that made my time in Hestur, where I spent my last 6 months in the Faroe Islands, exquisitely vivid. I experienced an incredible spectrum of life and humanity and often participated in it to near-overwhelming extremes. Whether I was assisting at the sheepfold, raking freshly mown hay, enjoying a colorful conversation with Hjørleiv, teaching Jørmund how to use email, or borrowing Ebbe's clothesline for an afternoon, perhaps my most tender act of solidarity was simply turning on my kitchen light of an evening so people could see I was still there.

Drying Hay on Trestles

The Faroe Islands' maritime climate at 62°00'N means that consecutive days of dry weather are relatively rare. Precipitation falls an average of 260 days per year. This makes it difficult, and labor intensive, for farmers to dry enough hay for their livestock's supplemental winter fodder. Some farmers use trestles to take advantage of stiff ocean winds for drying the grass they've mown.

Ebbe in the Sheepfold

Sheep husbandry and agriculture have been an integral part of the Faroe Islands' culture and economy for centuries. Flock management is, in some ways, still based on statutes outlined in Seyðabrævið of 1298. In this photograph, Ebbe Rasmussen, one of the two parish clerks of Hestur, is caught up in the excitement of driving sheep into the fold.

Ull er Føroya Gull

There are approximately 580 sheep grazing the island of Hestur. Long before the fishing industry emerged, woolen goods were one of the main staples of the Faroe Islands' economy. Wool, however, is no longer considered "Faroese gold"; its market value is so low that people often burn it rather than selling or processing it into yarn.

The Flock

Today there are an estimated 70,000 sheep grazing the archipelago's 18 islands. The Faroese breed is a hardy variant of the Northern European short-tailed sheep. Most rams have horns and approximately 67% of ewes are polled. Farmers and other landowners slaughter their sheep themselves each autumn.

Hjørleiv & Jørmund

Hjørleiv Poulsen and Jørmund Zachariassen grew up together in the village of Hestur and have remained friends and neighbors. Hjørleiv was the village postman for 37 years. Jørmund assumed the position shortly after Hjørleiv's retirement, and he also serves as organist in Hestur's church.

Tea for Two

Hjørleiv Poulsen is photographed in the kitchen of his home where he lives alone on Hestur. Fewer than 20 people live on the island year-round, and no more children attend school in the village.

The People's Church
Around 80% of the Faroese population belongs to the state's Evangelical Lutheran Church, Fólkakirkjan. The village church in Hestur celebrated its centennial in 2011.

The Gatekeeper
In April, during the lambing season, members of each Faroese village participate in driving flocks from the outfields into the fold. Here the sheep are medicated against various parasites and diseases. Ebbe Rasmussen is helping to keep the sheep moving forward in the fold while also preventing them from escaping over the stone walls.

"Hestur: A Photo Essay" was first published in *Cold Mountain Review*, Fall 2012, and is reprinted here with permission of the author.

191

They Point at Her Face and Whisper

Erin Pushman

Lucille stood in her room, surrounded by a pile of discarded uniform options, her frustration welling into tears.

"I have to wear a skirt," she said, kicking a pair of uniform shorts across the wood floor.

"But you love shorts," I said, trying to hand her a pair with pretty pleats. This was only the second week of school, early September in North Carolina, where we were still broiling in summer heat.

"No," she said batting my hand away. I dropped the pleated shorts and put my hand to my chin, something I've tried not to do in front of Lucille but end up doing anyway. "My outfit needs to look pretty," Lucille said. I pulled my hand away from my face.

By now, I was frustrated too. The minutes were ticking down toward eight o'clock, and she still had to eat breakfast, brush her teeth, and find her shoes. We aren't a family known for punctuality, but we make an effort to get the kids to school on time. Anyway, good parents probably don't let their children earn tardy marks during the second week of second grade.

"We just bought you all these new shorts to wear to school," I said, my frustration rising. Here the new shorts were, all in the prescribed khaki and navy, piled up on the floor. Lucille attends a public school with a uniform policy, and buying enough pairs of uniform shorts to get through these last weeks of heat had been an end-of-summer-break priority, one I'd tended to between Lucille's medical appointments.

"I need a skirt," Lucille insisted, her enlarged chin jutting out, reminding me to be gentle.

"Why?"

"They say I look like a boy."

So there it was.

"Tell me about it," I said, pulling my oldest child close, cupping her face in my hand, holding the bone that holds the tumor.

Lucille began to explain about the older kids who were pointing at her face and whisper-talking.

We should have expected this. Hearing people's comments about Lucille's face was nothing new. Well-intentioned, ill-intentioned, or innocent, the comments came. A chiropractor asked if Lucille had Lion's disease and suggested we watch the movie Mask. Two smirking kids at the pool pointed to Lucille's head, called her "bigmouth," and asked what she had swallowed. A tiny child in a public restroom simply asked "What happened to your face?" And on. So, too, many, many people, who know and love us have said, "She's still pretty."

Still. Right.

Lucille has a tumor, specifically a central giant cell granuloma, a CGCG in the medical literature. This tumor is lodged in the middle of her mandible, her lower jaw bone. It is rare. It is aggressive. It is benign. It is not cancer, but it behaves like a cancer in many ways.

Often, this type of tumor is treatable with surgery or steroid injections, or both. Not so for Lucille. When the standard treatment failed, she became a rare case of an already rare disease.

What does the tumor look like? Lucille's surgeon and her oncologist measure in centimeters and speak of facial disfigurement. I think the tumor looks like a ripe apple, wrapped in skin, right at the place where, a year ago, Lucille had a normal chin.

So here Lucille and I were, facing each other in her room on a busy fall morning. Her tumor stood between us and the rest of the day. If she didn't get dressed now, she'd be late for school, and I'd be late for work. She turned her head to stare out the window. In profile, I could see so clearly how she looked to the rest of the world. Her pretty, disfigured face. Her elongated apple-chin. She looked like a caricature of herself.

Tardy-shmardy. Oh well.

I put my arms around my daughter and walked with her to the bed. We sat down on her purple comforter and talked about the fact that she doesn't look like everyone else. This was not a new conversation. We'd had it, in various forms, with the hospital social workers and child life specialists, with the teachers and counselors at Lucille's school, with each other. It is a conversation we would continue to have—the kind that picks up where it left off, but not when you expect it to, the kind that nuances itself to the occasion.

I wasn't expecting the conversation today because the school counselor and the hospital social worker had visited Lucille's classroom to explain why her face looks the way it does. But they could not visit every classroom.

"Do you know the phrase, 'body diversity'?" I asked, trying to keep my hands off my own chin and on my daughter.

"I don't think so," Lucille said. We talked about all the different body shapes Lucille sees at school. We talked about other ways of being different. We talked about wheel chairs. We talked about skin color. We talked about braces and glasses. We talked about freckles and birthmarks. We talked about acne. We talked about hair.

We all have to deal with a lack of acceptance sometimes. We all face naysayers, about the way we look, the choices we make, the clothing we wear. And the list goes on. We feel the impact of harsh or ridiculing words, but we cannot let those words overpower us.

I had hoped my daughter would not have to learn this lesson at seven. And I had simply not imagined she would have to learn it while battling a disfiguring disease. But what I needed to help my daughter understand this morning was not so different from what other parents help their children understand in the face of teasing and bullying.

I held my daughter and let her cry in the safety of my arms. When the tears passed, I explained that she is beautiful and that we each have our own kind of beauty. I told her there will always be people who don't look like everyone else, and there will often be people who have something mean to say about it.

"Lucille, not looking like everyone else will always be okay," I said. "Sometimes, not looking like everyone else will even be a good thing." I also told her that there are times when we all have to hear meanly-spoken words, but we do not have to listen to them. I told her that living with this tumor in her jaw was going to help her learn how to ignore bullies and meanies and be a good friend to other people who look different.

It was a tidy end to an honest conversation and not a bad pep talk. Even as I squeezed her shoulders and stood up, though, I did not want to send her off to school—or any place I would not be to defend her or whisper love into her ear.

Another parenting moment when the only way forward was to go on as normally as possible. And this:

"You know what else," I said. "You are strong. And I have your back." Lucille smiled and hugged me—hard.

Then I helped my daughter pick out a pretty uniform skirt and a pretty purple necklace and a pretty headband. She went to school, late but present, and willing to face the day.

Originally published as a post on my blog *The Face of Bravery* and in slightly revised form in *Mutha Magazine*.

The Contradictions
Sophie Yanow

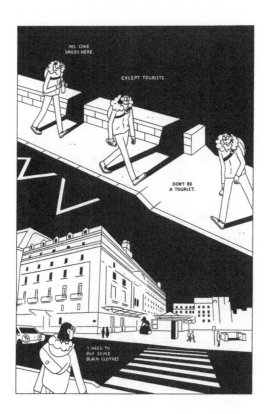

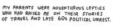

My parents were adventurous lefties who had raised me on their stories of travel and late 60s political unrest.

Here I was, age twenty, and so far I felt I had few stories worth telling.

I'd always been too nervous for risky behavior — with the exception of some thoroughly researched drug use — and too wishy-washy to stick it to the man.

But now I was abroad. If something was going to change, surely this was the place for it.

Hey, mom.

Can you call me back so I can save minutes?

BZZ

BZZZ

I wish I'd brought my bike...

No, I do like the metro.

Except nobody smiles...

When I get home, I literally have, like, a layer of dirt on my skin...

Just from walking around.

It's kinda gross.

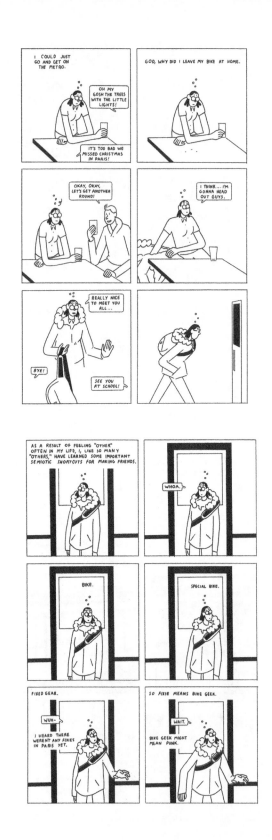

Sophie Yanow's *The Contradictions* was published by Drawn & Quarterly and is excerpted here with permission of the publisher.

INDEX